SOCIOLOGICAL

Classical and Contemporary Social Theory

Series Editor: Stjepan G. Mestrovic, Texas A&M University, USA

Classical and Contemporary Social Theory publishes rigorous scholarly work that re-discovers the relevance of social theory for contemporary times, demonstrating the enduring importance of theory for modern social issues. The series covers social theory in a broad sense, inviting contributions on both 'classical' and modern theory, thus encompassing sociology, without being confined to a single discipline. As such, work from across the social sciences is welcome, provided that volumes address the social context of particular issues, subjects, or figures and offer new understandings of social reality and the contribution of a theorist or school to our understanding of it. The series considers significant new appraisals of established thinkers or schools, comparative works or contributions that discuss a particular social issue or phenomenon in relation to the work of specific theorists or theoretical approaches. Contributions are welcome that assess broad strands of thought within certain schools or across the work of a number of thinkers, but always with an eye toward contributing to contemporary understandings of social issues and contexts.

Also in the series

A Sociology of the Total Organization
Atomistic Unity in the French Foreign Legion
Mikaela Sundberg
ISBN 978-1-4724-5560-4

Arendt Contra Sociology
Theory, Society and its Science
Philip Walsh
ISBN 978-1-4094-3863-2

Being Human in a Consumer Society
Edited by Alejandro Néstor García Martínez
ISBN 978-1-4724-4317-5

Hegel's Phenomenology and Foucault's Genealogy
Evangelia Sembou
ISBN 978-1-4094-4308-7

Sociological Amnesia

Cross-currents in Disciplinary History

Edited by

ALEX LAW
Abertay University, UK

ERIC ROYAL LYBECK
University of Cambridge, UK

Routledge
Taylor & Francis Group

LONDON AND NEW YORK

First published 2015 by Ashgate Publishing

2 Park Square, Milton Park, Abingdon, Oxfordshire OX14 4RN
52 Vanderbilt Avenue, New York, NY 10017

Routledge is an imprint of the Taylor & Francis Group, an informa business

First issued in paperback 2019

British Library Cataloguing in Publication Data
A catalogue record for this book is available from the British Library

The Library of Congress has cataloged the printed edition as follows:
Sociological amnesia : cross-currents in disciplinary history / [edited] by Alex Law and Eric Royal Lybeck.
        pages cm. -- (Classical and contemporary social theory)
    Includes bibliographical references and index.
    ISBN 978-1-4724-4234-5 (hardback : alk. paper)

    1. Sociology--History. I. Law, Alex. II. Lybeck, Eric Royal.

HM435.S635 2015
301--dc23

                                                                                        2015004238

ISBN 978-1-4724-4234-5 (hbk)
ISBN 978-0-367-87978-5 (pbk)

Contents

Notes on Contributors

Peter Baehr is Professor of Social Theory at Lingnan University, Hong Kong. His books include *Caesar and the Fading of the Roman World* (1997), *Hannah Arendt, Totalitarianism and the Social Sciences* (2010) and *Founders, Classics, Canons: Modern Disputes over the Origins and Appraisal of Sociology's Heritage* (2nd edn 2015). Current interests centre on the political writings of Rebecca West, and the history of exposure practices (denunciation, informing, unmasking, whistleblowing) since the French Revolution.

Matteo Bortolini is Assistant Professor of Sociology at the University of Padova, Italy, where he teaches undergraduate classes on the logic of the social sciences. His research covers the fields of intellectual and artistic success, post-secularized societies, and Foucauldian technologies of the self from the standpoint of a strongly culturalist sociology. He is currently writing a sociological biography of Robert N. Bellah from the standpoint of the sociology of the intellectuals, and a book on secularization together with the Italian philosopher, Paolo Costa.

Andrea Cossu teaches Cultural Sociology at the University of Trento and the University of Bologna. He has been a Visiting and Faculty Fellow of the Center for Cultural Sociology at Yale University. He works mainly in the fields of cultural and political sociology, with a particular focus on the relationship between memory and the formation of identities and reputations. He is also the author of *It Ain't Me Babe: Bob Dylan and the Performance of Authenticity*, and his work has appeared – among other journals – in *Memory Studies, Journal of Classical Sociology, Modern Italy*.

Neil Davidson lectures in Sociology at the University of Glasgow. He is the author of *The Origins of Scottish Nationhood* (2000), the Deutscher-Prize winning *Discovering the Scottish Revolution* (2003), *How Revolutionary Were the Bourgeois Revolutions?* (2012) and, most recently, *Holding Fast to an Image of the Past* (2014). Davidson has also co-edited and contributed to *Alasdair MacIntyre's Engagement with Marxism* (2008), *Neoliberal Scotland* (2010) and *The Longue Durée of the Far-Right* (2014). His work has appeared in a number of journals including *Cambridge Review of International Affairs, Capital and Class, Historical Materialism, New Left Review* and *Science and Society*.

Matt Dawson is Lecturer in Sociology at the University of Glasgow. He has research interests in social theory, political sociology, normativity, the history of sociology and asexuality. Matt is the author of *Late Modernity, Individualization and Socialism: An Associational Critique of Neoliberalism* (Palgrave Macmillan, 2013) and is currently writing a book outlining visions of alternative societies offered throughout the history of the discipline. He has also published articles on the work of theorists such as Bauman and Durkheim in a variety of journals.

Kieran Durkin is Graduate Teaching Assistant at the University of Glasgow. His research interests are in Social Theory, and in Humanist Marxism, Critical Theory, and the thought of Erich Fromm in particular. He is the author of *The Radical Humanism of Erich Fromm* (Palgrave Macmillan, 2014).

Bridget Fowler is Professor Emerita of Sociology at the University of Glasgow. Her main research interests are in social theory, Marxist-feminism, and the sociology of culture. She remains greatly indebted to the thought of Pierre Bourdieu, on whom or around whom her own work has been published, including two books *Pierre Bourdieu and Cultural Theory: Critical Investigations* (Sage, 1997) and *The Obituary as Collective Memory* (Routledge, 2007). Her most recent work has been an article on the significance of welfare state support to British drama and how this affects Bourdieu's arguments about cultural production ('Pierre Bourdieu, Social Transformation and 1960s British Drama', *Theory, Culture and Society*, May 2012), a chapter on the relationship of Bourdieu to Marx ('Bourdieu: Unorthodox Marxist?' in S. Susen and B.S. Turner [eds], *The Legacy of Pierre Bourdieu*, Anthem, 2011), and an evaluation of Bourdieu's former collaborator, and founder of the Pragmatic Sociology of Critique: Boltanski ('Figures of Descent from Classical Sociological Theory: Luc Boltanski', in S. Susen and B.S.Turner [eds], *The Spirit of Luc Boltanski*, Anthem, 2014).

Alex Law is Professor of Sociology at Abertay University. His most recent book, *Social Theory for Today* (Sage, 2015), examines the historical relationship between crisis and social theory. He is interested in developing a reflexive history of sociology as a means of orientation for sociology in the present. His work develops a relational sociology to account for, amongst other things, the disciplinary 'failure' of Patrick Geddes' sociology, changing power-balances in Scotland, and international sport and the national habitus.

Eric Royal Lybeck is an historical sociologist of education at the University of Cambridge. His dissertation research focuses on the 'academization process' and the institutionalization of the modern research university in Germany and the United States since 1800. He has also published research in the fields of general social theory and the history of the social sciences.

Charles Masquelier is Lecturer in Sociology at the University of Surrey. His research assumes an interdisciplinary outlook, crossing over the fields of social theory, political theory and political philosophy, with particular interests in critical theory, social movements, the libertarian socialism of G.D.H. Cole and the cooperative movement. He has published articles in international journals and a book entitled *Critical Theory and Libertarian Socialism* (Bloomsbury).

E. Stina Lyon is Professor Emerita in the Faculty of Arts and Human Sciences, London South Bank University. Her recent research interests lie in the areas of the history of sociology and social research, inequality and the welfare state. Her most recent work has been on the contribution to sociology of Viola Klein and the Swedish social scientists and reformers Alva and Gunnar Myrdal. She is a Fellow of the Academy of Social Sciences in Britain.

Christos Memos is a Lecturer in Sociology at the Department of Sociology, University of Abertay, UK. He has previously taught at the Department of Politics, University of York. His research interests include Critical Social and Political Theory, the Thought of Cornelius Castoriadis, Marx and Marxism, Council Communism and Anarchism, Social Movements and Anti-capitalism. He is the author of *Castoriadis and Critical Theory: Crisis, Critique and Radical Alternatives* (Palgrave, 2014).

Stephen Mennell is Professor Emeritus of Sociology at University College Dublin. His books include *All Manners of Food: Eating and Taste in England and France from the Middle Ages to the Present* (1985), *Norbert Elias: Civilization and the Human Self-Image* (1989), and *The American Civilizing Process* (2007). He holds the degrees of Doctor in de Sociale Wetenschappen (Amsterdam) and Doctor of Letters (Cambridge). He is a member of the board of the Norbert Elias Foundation, Amsterdam, of the Royal Netherlands Academy of Arts and Sciences, the Royal Irish Academy and Academia Europaea.

Álvaro Santana-Acuña is College Fellow in the Department of Sociology at Harvard University. His research focuses on the intersection between material culture and processes of valuation. His dissertation, 'The Making of a National Cadastre', studies cadastral mapping and its contribution to the nationalization of the French territory between 1763 and 1807. He is currently finishing a book manuscript on the process by which some literary books attain 'classic' value.

Liz Stanley is a feminist sociologist and ESRC Professorial Research Fellow at the University of Edinburgh, where she also holds the established chair in Sociology. Her interests include all aspects of sociological theorizing and questions of methodology, while much of her research has involved historical topics. Recent books include *Mourning Becomes: Post/Memory and the Concentration Camps of the South African War* (2006), *Documents of Life Revisited* (2013) and *The World's Great Question: Olive Schreiner's South African Letters* (2014), with a book on archive methodology and another on 'race' and social change hovering in the wings.

Acknowledgements

Alex Law wishes to thank his co-editor Eric for helping to sustain the project from the start, all the contributors for their cooperation, patience and efforts, and John Scott and Ray Bromley for their insights into and support for a historical sociology of sociology. Last but no means least, he would like to acknowledge Jan for tolerating his constant state of distraction over many years.

Eric Lybeck would likewise wish to thank his co-editor Alex and all the contributors for their endurance and efforts. Members of the RASTA group at Cambridge, including Martin Fuller, Nicolas Fleet and Marjan Ivkovic, provided essential feedback during the conceptualization of this book. And for their untiring support, unending gratitude goes to Ellie and my parents.

The editors would also like to thank Neil Jordan, assisted by Lianne Sherlock, for much needed editorial support and guidance at each stage in the development of the book, and Carolyn Court and Jacqui Cornish for steering the book safely through the production process.

Chapter 1

Sociological Amnesia: An Introduction

Alex Law and Eric Royal Lybeck

Trajectories: Success and Failure

In the late nineteenth century, a group of around twenty members of the American Economic Association (AEA) met in a private dining-room of a hotel for an informal talk about the subject of 'sociology'. Albion Small, who was present at the AEA meeting, recalled a pent-up desire among those in attendance to determine once and for all a roadmap for the establishment of sociology as a traditional social science. During the meeting a theologian, president of a prominent New England seminary, declared that a starting place should be a radical reordering of the classification of the sciences. Many in the room, including Lester F. Ward, leaned forward in anticipation until the seminarian suggested, 'in my judgment there never will be any reliable sociology until it has its place in a system of sciences founded on theology' (Small 1924: 344). Ward, who was at the time the most well-known American sociologist, let out an exasperated gasp as he threw himself back in his chair in disgust and despair. Small noted that this was 'last appearance of that particular Doctor of Divinity as a constructor of sociology' (Small 1924: 344).

This would not be the last time that possible trajectories were excised from a discipline as it became increasingly conscious of itself as a discourse requiring a clear and stable basis for demarcation. During the so-called era of Classical sociology in the nineteenth and early twentieth century, intellectuals struggled within competitive discursive fields as academic disciplinary boundaries were established via the setting up of institutional positions and university departments, the framing of course syllabi, scientific conferences, introductory textbooks, and practical applications of sociology. During this period, in France, Émile Durkheim institutionalized sociology as a science of 'social facts', and, in Germany, Max Weber took up his chair in sociology at Munich (Lukes 1972; Mommsen and Osterhammel 1989).

Sociology was marked deeply by the uneven national contexts within which it struggled to establish itself. Its early development in France stamped the sociology envisioned by Auguste Comte with an overweening ambition to crown it 'Queen of the Sciences' based on a flimsy or non-existent empirical kingdom. As Claude Lévi-Strauss (1945: 503) put it in his mid-twentieth century review of French sociology: 'French sociology was born early, and it still suffers from the gap which existed, at the time of its birth, between the boldness of theoretical premonitions and the lack, or insufficiency, of concrete data'. A century beforehand, Karl Marx had argued that the closed philosophical systems formed by the eternal principles of nineteenth-century Germany were theoretical idealizations of the country's socio-political under-development. Later, at a time of rapid social and economic development in Germany, Weber entered his critical dialogue with the ghost of Marx by developing a substantive form of sociology that famously allowed rationality considerable autonomy in the making of capitalism. In his lecture on 'Science as a Vocation', Weber (2013: 341) expected that the sociology of his and each generation would be superseded by the discoveries and developments of future generations. It is the fate of all science that it faces imminent obsolescence. Supersession is the *meaning* of 'progress' in science, Weber argued, the 'inner attitude' that sociologists are driven to adopt towards their own profession. All that can be done is to accept this daemonic fate and work towards it as the forced choice that needs to be made between the 'warring gods' of ultimate values. As only one alternative between warring cultural values, sociology is best pursued without edifying illusions about itself, Weber warned.

In America, dramatic material development amidst cultural and political spectacles appeared to give rise to sociology as the newest, most advanced science of modernity. The first department of sociology in the US, at Chicago, was established by 1892. Yet, like the discipline more widely, the cooperative efforts of determined individuals who constructed sociology contributed a rather eclectic and disparate undertaking, mixing European influences, notably the sociology of Georg Simmel, with emerging national concerns, such as urbanism. Around the same time, the weak and halting development of sociology in Britain was put down to the relative stability of social and political conditions since the eighteenth century unlike the rapid transition and crises experienced elsewhere in Europe and America (Rumney 1945). Gradual change without bouts of social upheaval and crises, it was argued, relieved British intellectuals from the need to study social processes, structures and relations too closely or systematically and to adopt piecemeal analyses and local surveys. At most, social stability and slow, incremental reform in Britain supported the dominant evolutionary schemas of Herbert Spencer and L.T. Hobhouse. However, such accounts omit the pioneering momentum of British sociology during the Edwardian period, before it subsided into passivity, allowing an alternative national sociological tradition to be forgotten or dismissed (Renwick 2012; Scott and Bromley 2014).

Once securely established, the history of sociology overwhelmingly focuses on 'the winners'. During the 1930s, in America, Talcott Parsons aimed to resolve a perceived theoretical crisis by selectively consolidating the 'classics' (minus Marx) in *The Structure of Social Action* as a 'canon' of sociological thought (Camic 1989; Parsons 1937). Parsons believed that a general theory could be woven from the conceptual fragmentation bequeathed by the founders of sociology in order to provide empirical study with more solid foundations. General theoretical systems of the kind constructed by Parsons and, more recently Habermas, tend to reproduce the problem of fragmentation that they were devised to overcome (Holmwood 1996). Any purely formal arrangement of premises and concepts like 'structure' and 'action' seems bound to succumb to repeated crises of fragmentation and theory reconstruction.

Sociologists from the past most routinely recognized today belong to the Trinitarian 'canon' of classical sociologists, Marx, Durkheim, and Weber, sometimes supported by other bit players like Comte or Simmel. More contemporary additions to the canon emerge typically out of a dialogue with 'the classics', either to synthesize, revise or challenge that legacy. This process of successively restricting sociology to the winners impoverishes sociology's claim to be a form of historically reflexive knowledge. In this sense sociology can be considered a collective form of 'amnesia' insofar as the discipline's self-knowledge avoids reconstruction of its own history and modes of thought, past and present. The overall field of the history of sociology results in an eternal dialogue with these most famous precursors, these heroes. In so doing, the uneven processes and struggles of sociology's own making as a form of disciplinary knowledge is obscured and largely forgotten.

This book presses in the opposite direction. It focuses on sociologists who are largely forgotten today, as well as sociologists whose fortunes were revived after languishing in obscurity. By looking at now forgotten figures who were significant in their own time and previously obscure but now revived figures, new insights are opened up into not only individual sociologists themselves, but, more pointedly, our understanding of the discipline of sociology itself – its trajectories, forgotten promises and dead ends.

A Reflexive Sociology of Sociology

This distinctive approach is not intended as a compendium or history of sociology and sociologists. Its aim is to contribute towards the development of a historical sociology of sociology formed within and, at the same time, producing particular institutional and interpersonal fields. What did 'sociology' mean to those scholars present at the birth of the discipline? How has the discipline been shaped, organized, and institutionalized since? One cannot address these questions adequately guided solely by the light of our canonical ancestors. Rather, it becomes most important to understand who, when, where, and why sociologists became excluded from the canon, how they became 'failures'. How does a figure as prominent as Lester Ward, the first president of the American Sociological Society (ASA), by all accounts the 'father of American sociology', become forgotten within a decade? What were the political, economic, and ideological conditions that led to Raymond Aron's prominence during the post-war era, and how have those conditions changed, such that he is almost erased from sociological discourse today?

We are therefore interested in 'failures', that is, sociologists whose projects did not 'catch on'. These figures might have been minor academics throughout their career, but many had considerable success within the discipline during their lifetimes, only to find themselves left behind. Others, like Norbert Elias, as Stephen Mennell shows in his chapter, were neglected for much of their career, headed toward obscurity, when suddenly his oeuvre and reputation was resurrected, not least through the collective efforts of strategically-situated individuals, as well as the physical and intellectual energies of the ageing Elias himself. How does such a comeback occur late in life? What were the conditions and chances that occurred to draw such attention to an obscure, often misunderstood figure disinclined toward self-promotion? Who were his allies? What was the role of publications, journals, and other resources mobilized on his behalf?

Indeed, in all cases, the institutional resources, materials, and practices of scholarly labour are essential objects of interest in establishing any sociology of sociologists. This approach, in line with the emerging 'new sociology of ideas' (Camic and Gross 2004; Camic, Gross, and Lamont 2011), focuses on the local interactions of academics 'in the wild' so to speak. Authors' texts are placed within the context in which they were written. The current turn toward academic practice, however, has the potential to neglect broader, macro-sociological factors that condition the development of ideas. Theoretically, we therefore adopt a 'processual' or 'relational' approach informed by the social theories of Pierre Bourdieu, Norbert Elias, and Michel Foucault (Bourdieu 2004; Elias 1987; Foucault 2002). The concepts of 'field', 'capital', and '*habitus*' are familiar to contemporary sociologists, and have been applied within the academic context in Bourdieu's *Homo Academicus* (1988) and *The State Nobility* (1996). Elias' process theory highlights the interaction between social habitus and individual habitus, while also alerting us to the 'social fund of knowledge' which pre-exists knowledge production (Elias 1987). Though not a figurational theorist, Foucault's archaeological method provides one means of analysing discourses as structures composed of internal relations that develop across epistemological 'thresholds' (Foucault 2002).

Our approach is equal parts *archaeological, figurational* and *reflexive* in so far as it draws upon the sociologies of knowledge presented by Foucault, Elias and Bourdieu (Elias 1987; Foucault 2002, Bourdieu 2004). In the *Archaeology of Knowledge*, Foucault laid out his program for understanding what a discourse *is*, and what considerations must be taken into account should one attempt to grasp where, when, and how they emerge and evolve (Foucault 2002). The first task in this regard is a radical deconstruction of the signifier itself – in this case, 'sociology'. Foucault wrote, 'These pre-existing forms of continuity, all these syntheses that are accepted without question, must remain in suspense' (Foucault 2002: 29). What was meant by the term 'sociology' in the nineteenth century was very different from our contemporary conception. It circulated within a context of interrelated institutions, economic and social processes, behavioral patterns, norms, and epistemic virtues that were substantially different from the relations and institutions of later phases. For Foucault (1989) an *épistème* can be identified retrospectively as the apparatus that establishes the conditions of possibility for statements that are acceptable to and verified by a field of scientific expertise from all the possible statements and delimits what statements might be classified as 'scientific'. Such *épistèmes* are, therefore, conditional on relations that are both internal and external to the discourse itself. Their norms, procedures and signifying content exist as constellations and as processes which bear some resemblances to other discursive forms, but are also highly particular and unique.

In order to sift through the 'wheat of relevant information', we should try to locate possible *points of diffraction* of the discourse, characterized by either incompatibility or equivalence between two objects, types of enunciation, or concepts (Foucault 2002: 58, 73). For example, the periods before and after the formations of the American and British sociological associations were such moments of possible diffraction. However, we must also study the *economy* of the discursive constellation; that is, the intellectual space available within the emergent positivity. We must consider the discourse of sociology in relation to the *function* (or lack thereof) that the discourse served for a field of *non-discursive practices*.

Thus, we have three formal levels of discursive analysis: points of diffraction, the economy of the field, and the external function; all of which are co-dependent yet irreducible to the others. Foucault proceeded to outline four potential emergences within a discursive formation's evolution:

1. *Threshold of positivity* – the moment in which a discursive practice achieves individuality and autonomy; as a single system that enables the formation of statements to be put in operation.
2. *Threshold of epistemologization* – when a group of statements are articulated that claim to validate coherent norms over a realm of knowledge.
3. *Threshold of scientificity* – when the above epistemological figure obeys a number of formal criteria and certain laws for the construction of propositions.
4. *Threshold of formalization* – when this scientific discourse, in turn, defines axioms, legitimate propositional structures, and mechanisms for tolerating transformations (Foucault 2002: 205–6).

These thresholds are points of reference within multi-directional evolutions across all dimensions of the discourse. As historical emergences, they do not exist independently of, or fully replace, pre-existing forms of discourse. Rather, different thresholds represent identifiable moments in which rules, patterns of behavior, and inter-relationships, both internal and external, are made more concrete, predictable, and determining.

Along broadly similar lines, Norbert Elias' figurational sociology suggested an analysis of the 'sociogenesis' and 'psychogenesis' of processes of structural formations (Elias 2000). Elias' sociology opens the possibility for biographical consideration of particular figures while maintaining recognition of the structural, disciplinary field within which they were constituted. Like Foucault, Elias conceived of knowledge not as the unfolding accumulation of inherently accurate or true knowledge as perceived by a transcendental subject. Rather, Elias considered individual contributions to knowledge as always premised upon the historical accumulation and context of knowledge that exist at particular points of time. Despite its many ruptures and 'breaks' knowledge is always constituted *in media res*.

> Sociological theories of knowledge have to break with the firmly entrenched tradition according to which every person in terms of her or his own knowledge is a beginning. No person ever is. Every person, from the word go, enters a pre-existing knowledge stream. He or she may later improve and augment it. But it is always an already existing social fund of knowledge which is advanced in this manner, or perhaps made to decline (Elias 1987: xvii).

The development of knowledge is a process, not a static system that is settled at any moment. The modern detached scientific perspective on nature, emerged from prototypical versions of this way of thinking as it became increasingly defined by rules and habitualized practices (Elias 1987: xx). As such, one can always extend one's analysis farther and farther back in time *ad infinitum*. Particular ways of knowing are preceded by other ways of not-knowing, and may later regress back into relative ignorance, providing the conditions for a novel emergence within the creative process of discovery. Which direction these movements take cannot be imputed *a priori*, but must be understood within the theoretical frame of figurations formed by dynamic processes.

At the same time, the construction of disciplines takes place within a field of competitive intellectual actors (Bourdieu 1988; Collins 1998). Thus, sociologists at the turn of the twentieth century engaged in what Thomas Gieryn called 'boundary-work': the concerted effort to distinguish real science from amateur and non-scientific versions of sociology (Gieryn 1983). The task that lies before us, then, is to position the figures of interest in the broadest context of what might be called their sociopolitical 'worldview', as well as within a specific spatio-temporal field of forces struggling for individual and disciplinary recognition within and outside of the university.

Since the sociologist is necessarily situated in the world that they seek to analyse, a degree of reflexivity must be brought to bear on sociology's implicit assumptions and misrecognitions of itself and the problems of complicity with the spontaneous immediacy of everyday forms of knowledge. As Bourdieu argued, the 'sociology of sociology is a fundamental dimension of sociological epistemology' (Bourdieu and Wacquant 1992: 68). It is not merely a question therefore of focussing on the biographical trajectory of individual sociologists. This would excessively individualize what Elias (1991) usefully called the 'social habitus'. Within the complex chains of interdependency that ensnare individual sociologists, one – the sociological – acquires a special significance. Such a 'sociological habitus' always emerges as a break with the general social habitus formed by everyday routines and the implicit assumptions of national societies.

The 'sociological habitus' begins to re-model the seemingly unmediated, spontaneous nature and implicit national habitus of everyday life. Acquiring a sociological habitus opens up a process of specialization and separation from the practical immediacy of everyday life. As the discipline comes to appear too remote from urgent problems, calls are made for a re-engaged 'public sociology'. Yet the sociological habitus is far from a serene calling unto itself. It involves choices and struggles between alternative, competing perspectives, research problems, methodologies, and professional and political networks. It demands a display of scholarly competence appropriate to the field and sub-field, demonstrating an ease and familiarity with its approved knowledge set and modes of self-presentation. Professional habit and self-images, as well as the profits of ritualistic transgression, only became possible once sociology has acquired institutional recognition as a basic university subject.

Without the collective effort of reflexive self-understanding, sociologists run the risk of projecting their individual habitus onto the object of study in which 'scientific discourse' is mobilized to express unconscious sentiments like resentment, ambition, disdain, a whole range of unanalysed experiences and feelings about the social world (Bourdieu and Wacquant 1992). The theoretical approach adopted here, therefore, focuses historical attention on disciplinary fields and formations, including:

a) the overall trajectory of discipline(s),
b) the internal elements and relations between theories and statements, and
c) canonization projects during or after a scholar's career.

This represents the first or 'sociological' dimension of the study, establishing the 'context' in its wider sense. The second level of analysis examines the individual biography of one or more agents within this context. Here we are interested in the entry of individuals into the disciplinary field at a certain stage in its institutional development. Specific dates and geographical locations are established in relation to the epistemological structure of the discipline at that time and place. We must further evaluate the relationship of individual 'habitus' to the content of theories and the trajectory of the disciplinary field, past, present, and future. Finally, institutional support, including material resources, student acolytes, and peer recognition, are significant factors for plotting the direction of the sociologist's trajectory.

How to be Forgotten

In this volume, we have sought a wide range of contributions to address the question of why certain sociologists and schools of thought become forgotten. The issue of who can be deemed 'forgotten' or 'failed' is a complicated definitional issue, and, indeed, we do not imply the sociologists as individuals have 'failed' in a purely epistemological sense. Rather the discipline of sociology has *itself* failed in two senses: first, by restricting its historical self-conception to canonical figures it neglects the actual history of its discursive developments. The second failure follows from the first insofar as sociology's claim to be a form of reflexive knowledge is limited by the arrest or misrecognition of sociological thought past and present. This book represents a move towards recovering this forgotten legacy and attempts to begin the process of reflexive reconstruction.

As Elias would chide us, the sociology of sociology does not begin from a zero-point in the present. It builds on previous work in the field of the 'sociology of sociology'. From its earliest origins, sociology has concerned itself with the emergence of sociological thought. August Comte's three stage model moving from the Theological to Metaphysical to Positivist phases of human history and thought sought to connect changes in the infrastructure of social order to changes in the orientation of social thought (Comte 1975). Regardless of the merits of the Positivist legacy, subsequent generations of sociologists have concerned themselves with the organization of their own disciplinary knowledge, seeking to root the development of social understanding (or, perhaps, lack thereof) in relation to changes in the structure of the social environment.

Karl Mannheim, for example, isolated the shift from epistemological to psychological to sociological interpretations of knowledge during the rapid transformation of social mobility since the Enlightenment (Mannheim 1985). His colleague in Frankfurt, Herbert Marcuse, similarly sought explanation for the shift from Hegelian 'Reason' to Marxist 'Revolution' in the changing structure of industrial capitalist society (Marcuse 1941). Subsequent analyses, drawn from the New Left critique of monopoly capitalism and the neglected standpoints of the working class, women and ethnic minorities, critically reassessed the hegemonic discourse of structural functionalism and quantitative social research (Gouldner 1970; Schwendinger and Schwendinger 1974; Therborn 1976). While much of this sociology of sociology provided insights into the relationship between social scientific ideology and the broader class structure of late capitalism, rarely did these works penetrate to the level of academic practice.

Under the influence of Thomas Kuhn, a number of scholars and historians began consideration of sociology as a shared 'paradigm' established by a scholarly community (Haskell 2000; Kuhn 1962; Ross 1992). Among the most promising of these agendas was the 'schools' approach recommended by Edward Tiryakian (1979). Since sociology rarely accumulates 'knowledge' in the manner of scientific communities described by Kuhn, the sociology of sociology should dedicate attention to study of various 'schools' of sociology. Charismatic founders of schools like structural-functionalism promoted methodological approaches that were subsequently 'depersonalized' and diffused by students. The institutional dynamics which extend the reputation of the school also foreshadows its inevitable downfall as success leads to attempts by rivals to overthrow the newly dominant paradigm. One need think only of the unchallenged dominance of Parsonian structural functionalism and its rapid wholesale overhaul during the last third of the twentieth century.

Similar studies focus on the institutional dynamics, particularly the patronage networks and resource bases of sociological research, as in Turner and Turner (1990). In covering the history of American sociology in relation to the base of economic support, the authors note shifts during the pre-World War I, interwar and post-war periods, which corresponded with changes in the institutional support for academic sociological research. More recently, the so-called 'new sociology of ideas' has rooted such developments in relation to interdisciplinary struggles for position. Charles Camic, for example, explains the success of Parsons' *Structure of Social Action*, with reference to the disciplinary battles between sociology, economics and biology raging at Harvard at the time of Parsons' writing (Camic 1989). This struggle to exercise command over interdisciplinary turf explains the success of Parsons' charter for a yet to be institutionally established discipline.

Other research, such as that of Andrew Abbott (1999, 2001), shares with the new sociologists of ideas and the institutionalists, an interest in the disciplinary and resource struggles amongst academics, and retains the insight of the Tiryakian 'schools' approach that sociology does not tend to accumulate knowledge in the traditional scientific sense. Rather, sociologists recycle broadly similar concerns while constantly revolutionizing the categorical terms used to describe them, such as the cyclical repetition of the supposed opposition between 'realism' and 'constructionism'. These patterns of cultural recycling tend to occur in generational waves as young scholars engage in an Oedipal struggle against the gerontocracy of elders who monopolize the reward structures of the academic profession. Abbott admitted that this patterned generational change, or 'slip-clutch', does embody a form of dynamism, 'even if that change is organized in a regular succession whereby the young build their careers on forgetting and rediscovery, while the middle-aged are doomed to see the common sense of their graduate school years refurbished and republished as brilliant new insight' (Abbott 2001: 148).

Various approaches have the potential to address the concerns of the present book. Most commentaries are dedicated to canonical or 'successful' sociologists who receive funding, establish a paradigm and contribute to the hegemonic stabilization of sociological knowledge in a given period. But, what about those scholars who do not extend into the history books and drop out of the conservation of sociological networks? Are the dynamics which lead to the success of a paradigm the same as that which leads to 'failure'? Such is the question addressed by Neil McLaughlin in 'How to become a Forgotten Intellectual', a study of Erich Fromm, in contrast to the new sociologist of ideas, Michele Lamont's analysis of Derrida's success (Lamont 1987; McLaughlin 1998). McLaughlin demonstrates that the rise and fall of Fromm's reputation had much to do with the success of his ideas in the broader public sphere. The popularity of his research in public discourse, and the broadness of his humanistic concerns, in fact, contributed to the decline of his reputation within specialized academic disciplines. This example points to a dynamic of considerable interest for the present volume, namely the limiting role of academic disciplinarity as contributing to the 'failure' of given sociologists and sociological traditions. As we will see time and again, those scholars whose work transcends the boundaries of sociology as institutionally defined tend to be isolated from the canonical lineage.

It is not only sociology that engages in intellectual fratricide. Randall Collins (1998) traces how intellectual networks in the oldest discipline, philosophy, have been beset by disagreement and rivalry in ways that structure the creative possibilities of the field. Such a social constructivist theory of intellectual field does not fatally undermine epistemological judgements about the reality of the object of study. Truth cannot be 'true' in itself, the pre-social outpouring of a disembodied mind. All the criteria mobilized for establishing the truth of statements about reality emerge as a process over generations through social networks. Truth, including the truth of the network itself, is communicated through verbal symbols formed by shared rituals of interaction. As Collins (1998: 860) argues, echoing Elias, 'we are always in media res, in the middle of things'. Individuals only form ideas as part of the conversation and problems of wider social networks. This is why sociological reflexivity often appears as such an affront to the established truths of science and philosophy.

Sociological Amnesia

We have sought original contributions from a range of scholars interested in developing a reflexive historical sociology of sociology. We have asked the authors to study their 'cases' in relation to the concern with disciplinary 'amnesia'. This includes the trajectory of scholars who were once famous, but later fell into relative obscurity. Peter Baehr's study of Raymond Aron's reputation in British sociology is the first of subsequent chapters. Baehr highlights the considerable reputation that Aron enjoyed within postwar British sociology, as well as his popularity among intellectual journals and public opinion more broadly. However Baehr's research into the syllabi of British undergraduate sociology reveals his near absence from teaching. This reflects the importance of synthetic texts consolidating a thinker's point of view, as well as the role of teaching as a necessary condition for retention of a sociologist's oeuvre.

The next chapter, by Bortolini and Cossu, focuses, not on the neglect of scholars themselves, but rather on two similar books written by Clifford Geertz and Robert Bellah. The study charts the course and migration of the books due to the nature of the disciplines in relation to the authors' performative contribution. Bortolini and Cossu's conceptual innovation of considering the works and the authors themselves as cultural objects effectively demonstrates the interaction between what might be called the 'variation and selection process' bearing on the disciplinary field. The chapter also gives insight in the context of other disciplines at the time – e.g., religious studies, anthropology and history – and why certain opportunities for cross fertilization were available for Geertz and not Bellah.

The role of disciplinary interfaces is also important in Kieran Durkin's chapter on Erich Fromm. Following a biographical review that builds to the period analysed by McLaughlin, Durkin returns to consider what else is lost when a sociologist drops off the map: namely the content of the research. Summaries of two cases of empirical research put to rest assumptions that Fromm was an armchair psychoanalyst, while demonstrating the promise of recovering Fromm's insights into character and social psychology.

Similar issues relating to the role of content and ideas emerge in the chapters by E. Stina Lyon on Viola Klein and Liz Stanley on Olive Schreiner. Stina Lyon assesses the merits of Klein's forgotten dissertation on the French novelist, Celine. There are many instances of 'amnesia' within the chapter, including Klein's own neglect of this work in her later achievements. It is interesting to see the way in which Klein's analysis connect to changes in Celine's career as they occurred in real time. This draws attention to the potential pitfalls of direct application of the sociology of knowledge to single authors. In Stina Lyon's retrieval of Klein's dissertation, the reader encounters the way Klein's analysis of Celine's 'detached' literary style contributed to her later work on patriarchy in language. Her concluding assessment of Klein's rejection of Mannheim's advice demonstrates that it was the literary and linguistic side of her analytic style that was retained, while the sociology of knowledge was sidelined. One can see from earlier reflection on her dissertation that Klein had already experienced the 'failure' of the Mannheimian approach.

In her study of Schreiner, Stanley opens up a productive contrast between networks and figurations that contribute to exploration of long-term relationships as significant factors within social outcomes. Here, figurational analysis is used to show how Schreiner's work and fate was shaped by the confluence of international connections, at once political, sociological and cultural, at the interstices of 'race', nation, class and gender in the context of imperialism and militarism. The analysis effectively demonstrates the way in which political-ethical concerns seemed to drive intellectual interaction as much as the content of the ideas. Similarly, these interests contribute to different patterns of integration with academic disciplines, and eventually to patterns of 'forgetting' within these disciplines.

In her chapter, Bridget Fowler provides a powerful restatement of Lucien Goldmann's relevance (and some limitations) for present-day sociology. The structure of the chapter allows a careful unpicking of the 'tragic vision' and social structure leading to more programmatic statements for a sociology of literature and class. These observations strengthen the comparison with Bourdieu that Fowler develops across the chapter. As she reminds us, Bourdieu adopted Goldmann's concept of 'genetic structuralism' as part of a response to the now largely forgotten 'structuralist controversy' that engulfed the human sciences in France in the 1960s as a way to by-pass the false opposition posed between existentialism and structuralism.

In their chapter, Dawson and Masquelier's distillation of G.D.H. Cole's associational sociology reminds us that one need not be called a 'sociologist' to be a sociologist. While recognizing the work going on in the supposedly empty period in British sociology prior to 1950, the authors' comparison with Durkheim and a kind of Rousseauean sociology is especially striking. Through this lens, we observe the way that Cole's political and normative commitment to guild socialism was shaped by his now neglected social theory.

More recently, the rise of actor-network-theory has revived interest in the work of Gabriel Tarde. Álvaro Santana-Acuña's study considers Tarde's monadology in light of the uncanonized field. The resulting chapter becomes a study of one 'path not taken', for sociology as a whole. Santana-Acuña's summarization of monadology, including the prehistory and Tarde's innovation of making monads 'social' introduces the reader to the significance of his work, while attending to potential reasons why Tarde's sociology has begun making a comeback in the contemporary context of poststucturalism, the rehabilitation of agency and the crisis of the 'social'.

Not all of our contributors adopt an explicitly figurational or relational approach to the dynamics of the sociological field. Indeed, not all of the figures discussed can be considered 'sociologists' in a strict sense. As the chapters by Davidson and Memos illustrate, some like Castoriadis and MacIntyre would have categorized themselves as philosophers and it is only with elastic semantic tension that the label of sociology can be appended to their work. Philosophers have generally been content to establish the epistemological, ethical and political preconditions for sociology as an empirical science. Even here, however, philosophers grappling with social and political problems cannot help but stray into territory that sociology would like to reserve for itself. A politically-committed philosopher like Louis Althusser, for instance, was inspired by certain 'striking turns of phrase' to read very closely a limited number of texts and from this to elaborate contrasts, oppositions and connections as the basic procedure for constructing theory: 'I constructed a whole philosophical system as if it had no object (in the sense that science has an object), but was rather a practical and polemical affair, and I began to develop a practical and polemical view of philosophy, based on a model of political thought I was working out at the same time' (Althusser 1993: 169). Polemical intent, of course, did not prevent philosophers from pronouncing on matters of sociological enquiry. Radical political philosophy was defined for much of the twentieth century by the crisis of Marxism and the class nature of Soviet society. Too often, as Memos reminds us, solutions were proclaimed polemically by stale political categories like 'totalitarianism', dictatorship or socialist state in the absence of a comparative historical sociology of social structure, relations and dynamics.

As important as the analysis of 'failed' or 'forgotten' sociologists or sociological texts are, we are equally interested in the rare occasions in which a sociologist moves from obscurity to renown. The most dramatic instance of this shift is the case of Norbert Elias. In his chapter Stephen Mennell situates Elias in the intellectual and political context of his time in post-war Britain. Then, the intellectual field was shaped by a number of forces, including the anti-Marxism of the Cold War years, advanced not least by the ideological pronouncements of the philosopher of science Karl Popper; a stifling intellectual culture induced by empiricism, social administration, and hegemonic American sociology; and the post-imperial reaction of anthropologists (who exercised a neglected element of hegemony over sociologists). Against the self-evidence of national figurations, Elias (2014: 53–134) posed the problem of what Rodney Needham (1972) called 'the question of the logical unity of mankind', something that both Elias and Needham argue cannot be resolved by a priori epistemological fiat but must be determined by empirical study.

As Mennell reminds us, sociological amnesia is aided and abetted by the disciplinary schism between empiricism and theoreticism. A form of sociology concerned with supposedly pre-theoretical forms of data is subject to the effects of heterogeneous influences over the construction of sociological problems. These come to be defined by the immediate concerns of research agencies, governmental policy or media agendas. Constrained by the short-term horizons of the present, empiricist amnesia surrenders the disciplinary autonomy required as a means of orientation for understanding the longer-term trajectory of human society, its possibilities and probabilities. Social theory, meanwhile, wriggles free from its necessary moorings in sustained empirical inquiry. At best, a few examples culled from newspapers often suffices to illustrate intricately constructed conceptual edifices about the latest new beginning in social theory. By calling for a more reflexive approach to sociology's 'failures', this volume begins to offer a corrective to the double trap set for sociology by epistemological and methodological reification.

References

Abbott, Andrew. 1999. *Department and Discipline: Chicago Sociology at One Hundred*. 1st edn. Chicago: University of Chicago Press.

Abbott, Andrew. 2001. *Chaos of Disciplines*. Chicago: University of Chicago Press.

Althusser, Louis. 1993. *The Future Lasts a Long Time*. London: Chatto & Windus.

Bourdieu, Pierre. 1988. *Homo Academicus*. Stanford, CA: Stanford University Press.

Bourdieu, Pierre. 1996. *The State Nobility: Elite Schools in the Field of Power*. Cambridge: Polity Press.

Bourdieu, Pierre. 2004. *Science of Science and Reflexivity*. 1st edn. Chicago: University of Chicago Press.

Bourdieu, Pierre and Loïc J.D. Wacquant. 1992. *An Invitation to Reflexive Sociology*. Chicago: University of Chicago Press.

Camic, Charles. 1989. 'Structure After 50 Years: The Anatomy of a Charter'. *The American Journal of Sociology* 95(1): 38–107.

Camic, Charles and Neil Gross. 2004. 'The New Sociology of Ideas', in *The Blackwell Companion to Sociology*, edited by Judith R. Blau. Oxford: Blackwell Publishing Ltd, pp. 236–49.

Camic, Charles, Neil Gross, and Michèle Lamont. 2011. *Social Knowledge in the Making*. Chicago: University of Chicago Press.

Collins, Randall. 1998. *The Sociology of Philosophies: A Global Theory of Intellectual Change*. Cambridge, MA: Belknap Press of Harvard University Press.

Comte, Auguste. 1975. *Auguste Comte and Positivism: The Essential Writings*, edited by Gertrud Lenzer. New York: Harper & Row.

Elias, Norbert. 1987. *Involvement and Detachment*. Oxford; New York: Blackwell Publishing.

Elias, Norbert. 1991. *The Society of Individuals*. 1st English language edn. Oxford; Cambridge, MA: Wiley-Blackwell.

Elias, Norbert. 2000. *The Civilizing Process: Sociogenetic and Psychogenetic Investigations*, edited by Eric Dunning, Johan Goudsblom, and Stephen Mennell. Oxford and Malden, MA: Blackwell Publishers.

Elias, Norbert. 2014. *Supplements and Index to the Collected Works of Norbert Elias, Volume 18*. Dublin: UCD Press.

Foucault, Michel. 1989. *The Order of Things: Archaeology of the Human Sciences*. London: Routledge.

Foucault, Michel. 2002. *Archaeology of Knowledge*. London; New York: Routledge.

Gieryn, Thomas F. 1983. 'Boundary-Work and the Demarcation of Science from Non-Science: Strains and Interests in Professional Ideologies of Scientists', *American Sociological Review* 48(6): 781–95.

Gouldner, Alvin W. 1970. *The Coming Crisis of Western Sociology*. New York: Basic Books.

Haskell, Thomas L. 2000. *The Emergence of Professional Social Science: The American Social Science Association and the Nineteenth-Century Crisis of Authority*. Baltimore: The Johns Hopkins University Press.

Holmwood, John. 1996. *Founding Sociology? Talcott Parsons and the Idea of General Theory*. London: Routledge.

Kuhn, Thomas S. 1962. *The Structure of Scientific Revolutions*. Chicago: University of Chicago Press.

Lamont, Michele. 1987. 'How to Become a Dominant French Philosopher: The Case of Jacques Derrida', *American Journal of Sociology* 93(3): 584.

Lévi-Strauss, Claude. 1945. 'French Sociology', in *Twentieth Century Sociology*, edited by Georges Gurvitch and Wilbert E. Moore. New York: Philosophical Library.

Lukes, Steven. 1972. *Émile Durkheim; His Life and Work, a Historical and Critical Study*. New York: Harper & Row.

Mannheim, Karl. 1985. *Ideology and Utopia: An Introduction to the Sociology of Knowledge*. San Diego: Harcourt Brace Jovanovich.

Marcuse, Herbert. 1941. *Reason and Revolution: Hegel and the Rise of Social Theory*. London; New York: Oxford University Press.

McLaughlin, Neil. 1998. 'How to Become a Forgotten Intellectual: Intellectual Movements and the Rise and Fall of Erich Fromm', *Sociological Forum* 13(2): 215–46.

Mommsen, Wolfgang J. and Jürgen Osterhammel. 1989. *Max Weber and His Contemporaries*. London: Unwin Hyman.

Needham, Rodney. 1972. *Belief, Language and Experience*. Oxford: Basil Blackwell.

Parsons, Talcott. 1937. *The Structure of Social Action*. New York: The Free Press.

Renwick, Chris. 2012. *British Sociology's Lost Biological Roots: A History of Futures Past*. Basingstoke: Palgrave Macmillan.

Ross, Dorothy. 1992. *The Origins of American Social Science*. Cambridge: Cambridge University Press.

Rumney, J. 1945. 'British Sociology', in *Twentieth Century Sociology*, edited by Georges Gurvitch and Wilbert E. Moore. New York: Philosophical Library.

Schwendinger, Herman and Julia R. Schwendinger. 1974. *The Sociologists of the Chair: A Radical Analysis of the Formative Years of North American Sociology (1883–1922)*. New York: Basic Books.

Scott, John and Ray Bromley. 2014. *Envisioning Sociology: Victor Branford, Patrick Geddes, and the Quest for Social Reconstruction*. Albany, NY: State University of New York Press.

Small, Albion W. 1924. *Origins of Sociology*. Chicago: The University of Chicago Press.

Therborn, Göran. 1976. *Science, Class, and Society: On the Formation of Sociology and Historical Materialism*. London: NLB.

Tiryakian, Edward. 1979. 'The Significance of Schools in the Development of Sociology', in *Contemporary Issues in Theory and Research: A Metasociological Perspective*, edited by William E. Snizek, Ellsworth R. Fuhrman, and Michael K. Miller. London: Aldwych Press, pp. 211–34.

Turner, Stephen and Jonathan H. Turner. 1990. *The Impossible Science: An Institutional Analysis of American Sociology*. Illustrated edn. Newbury Park: Sage Publications, Inc.

Weber, Max. 2013. *Max Weber: Collected Methodological Writings*, edited by Hans Henrik Bruun and Sam Whimster. London: Routledge.

Chapter 2

British Sociology and Raymond Aron

Peter Baehr

Introduction

Some thinkers, Nietzsche observed, are born posthumously. Slighted or ignored by their contemporaries, they are vindicated by later generations. Far more common, however, is the reverse path: writers celebrated in their own time do not survive its passing. The career of Raymond Aron in Anglophone sociology attests to just this fate.

In the 1960s and 1970s, Aron achieved international fame as a journalist, scholar, and an interlocutor of the powerful; Henry Kissinger and Maurice Schumann were among his more regular discussants. While the French *marxisant* Left condemned Aron as a reactionary and a cold war apologist (he was neither), intellectuals across the Channel took a more sensible view. Aron's combative liberalism was understood, if not always admired. But British sociologists recognized a thinker of rare quality, engaging with issues of real importance, whose work deserved serious attention.

British recognition came early. During the war, Aron was based in London editing and writing a column for *France Libre*, the official organ of the Free French forces under General de Gaulle. 'Karl Mannheim, who was teaching at the London School of Economics, was my host on several occasions', Aron (1990: 133) recalled. Towards war's end, Morris Ginsberg urged Aron to take up a permanent position at the LSE. Impatient to return to France, he declined: 'I would be French or have no country.'[1] Still, when the LSE-based *British Journal of Sociology* began publication in March 1950, the editors saw fit to give Aron (1950a; and 1950b) its opening article.

More LSE tributes followed, among them the Auguste Comte Memorial Trust Lecture (1957), an Honorary Fellowship (1973), the Millennium Lecture on International Studies (1978), and the Government and Opposition Lecture (1981). Robert Colquhoun's (1986a; 1986b) magisterial intellectual biography of Aron was originally an LSE doctoral thesis pursued under the supervision of Donald MacRae. Three Directors of the School, albeit sometimes in pre-LSE incarnations, also took notice of Aron's work. Introducing Aron's Millennium Lecture on

---

1   Aron 1990: 133. Aron's daughter, Dominique Schnapper (Halsey and Runciman 2005: 117), says that, in 1944, Lionel Robbins asked Aron to 'become the chair of sociology' at the School. The recollections of father and daughter are not mutually exclusive.

'War and Industrial Society: A Reappraisal', Ralf Dahrendorf declared 'There cannot be a more sophisticated analyst of the socio-economics, the politics and the philosophy of war in the world today' (Aron 1978: 195). Anthony Giddens's (1973: 59–63, 76–8) judgement was cooler; advancing his own account of class structure required Giddens to challenge the 'industrial society' thesis of his older French rival. Similarly, Craig Calhoun (2012 [1989]) dissented, albeit mildly, both from Aron's characterization of the French revolution of 1848 and from his interpretation of witnesses (Marx, Comte, Tocqueville) who took its measure.[2]

Sociologists today show little interest in Aron's legacy. Why is that? This article examines Aron's British reception in his own day to help account for his eclipse as a sociologist in ours. An archive of British university teaching materials housed at the LSE, and assessments of Aron's books, are my main reference points. The next two sections are devoted to the assessments; in them, I include both British and American appraisals because they point in the same direction. The third section, examining the archive materials, draws on purely British sources. Given the descriptive and explanatory objectives of this article I seek here neither to defend Aron nor urge a reconsideration of his oeuvre. Nor, in the confines of a single paper, can I provide a full analysis of Aron's major commentators: in order of importance, John A. Hall, Ernest Gellner, Tom Bottomore and Anthony Giddens. A point worth bearing in mind as we proceed, however, is that the evaluation of Aron among British sociologists is also a window onto the discipline itself. It shows what sociologists consider distinctly sociological methods and arguments to be. It shows how difficult it is for specific kinds of thinkers to be read as vital sociologists and social theorists. It shows, in short, both the demands and the limits of the sociological imagination as currently construed.

Sociologist Without a System

The 1960s to the mid-1970s witnessed the high-water mark of Aron's global sociological reception. Especially respected was the first volume of *Main Currents in Sociological Thought* (Aron 1965) on Montesquieu, Tocqueville, Comte, Marx and the uprisings of 1848. Hailed as a triumph of civilized exposition, adjectives such as 'lucid', 'graceful', 'wise', 'judicious', 'urbane', 'elegant', 'insightful', 'perspicacious' and 'fair-minded' abound in the commentaries.[3]

---

2   Other British universities sought out the 'committed observer' (Aron 1983). He delivered the Montague Burton Lecture on 'Imperialism and Colonialism' in Leeds, and the1965 Gifford Lectures in Aberdeen on the topic of 'Historical Consciousness in Thought and Action'. But London was his British base. Perhaps his greatest work on the philosophy of history was delivered there in 1960 (Aron 2002a).

3   Emblematic of this praise are Feuer (1965: 331) and Poggi (1966: 209–11). Volume II (Aron 1967a) was far less appreciated, even by writers who admired Aron. MacRae (1968) called it 'tired', its bibliography 'ludicrously inadequate', and its discussion of

Yet from the beginning of the 1960s, reviewers express reservations that spell trouble for Aron's sociological appropriation. The most common complaint is that his writings are insufficiently systematic. Describing the French scholar to readers of the AJS as 'a kind of French Walter Lippmann', Benjamin Barber (1962: 592–3)[4] noted the fertile 'overlap' between 'the problems of sociology and philosophy' that Aron's work embraced. A downside was that 'Aron's essays are less systematic in theory and less rigorous in method and data than most sociologists would now like to be in their professional writing.' Writing in the BJS, Charles Madge (1962: 78–9) struck a similar note. Aron's breadth of vision was remarkable – 'Philosophy, history, sociology; around these three conceptions the agile mind of M. Aron never tires of playing' – yet this 'diversity of guises' loses 'something in theoretical rigor'.

A related set of criticisms concerned Aron's failure to articulate a rigorous, precise and systematic concept of the 'social'. The indictment was by no means arbitrary; Aron himself emphasized that sociology only emerges when thinkers self-consciously seek to grasp 'the social *as such*' and to theorize its distinctiveness from politics, regime or state (Aron, 1965: 8–9; cf. Aron, 1967a: vi). Roland Robertson (1966: 191–8) leveled a number of objections. One is that Aron's delineation of 'the boundaries of sociological analysis [is] not easy to follow'. Those boundaries are either too porous (Montesquieu and Tocqueville are evidently political writers and it is their political contribution that Aron so evidently values) or too impervious: can politics really be separated from the social? Whether 'political phenomena should be seen as a sub-category of a wider class of *social* phenomena is an issue about which Aron says very little' (192).

Another oddity for Robertson is that 'having stressed the aim of grasping the *social as such* as a defining attribute of sociology, [Aron] then proceeds to castigate those sociologists who have concentrated on doing just this'. The obvious case is Durkheim towards whom Aron exhibits a frank distaste. 'In a similarly ambiguous fashion, Aron,

> although at pains to point up the limitations in Marx's infrastructure-superstructure model, nevertheless states that modern societies can often best be understood in terms of their economic infrastructure.[5] Most of his difficulties

Durkheim unjust. Indeed, Aron 'stresses what has been ephemeral [in Durkheim] – the ethical aspiration, the pedagogy and the concern about the social solidarity of the French at the expense of the actual sociological achievement'. Coser (1965: 948–9) and Torrance (1969: 255) also found the Durkheim chapter tendentious. Not everyone agreed. Barbu (1968: 771) claimed that from 'an expository viewpoint, Durkheim gets by far the fairest deal', while Runciman's review (1968: 308–9) registers no protest at Aron's handling of Durkheim.

4 Barber (and Madge) were reviewing a collection of Aron's essays written mostly in the late 1950s, entitled *Dimensions de la conscience historique* (1961).

5 'Personally, if I want to analyse a society, whether it be Soviet or American, I often begin with the state of the economy, and even with the state of the forces of production, and then proceed to the relations of production and finally to social relations' (Aron 1965: 155).

stem from the assumption that one must either be a sociological reductionist *or* claim that non-social factors determine or heavily influence social factors. It is true that this dichotomy has relevance to any critique of Marx and Comte; but Aron seems to have allowed these two men to set the problem for him, instead of explicating it himself and *then* discussing their work ... Thus, although Aron is keen to discuss the boundaries between the sciences of man, he is never completely successful in this respect (1966: 194–5).

The problem is compounded, Robertson continues, by the fact that Aron chooses figures for his sociological gallery who themselves did not advance 'a clear formulation of the theoretical basis' of social analysis. It is doubtless true that Tocqueville's emphasis on social and cultural constraints contains an implicit sociological theory. It is also evident that he remains an influential thinker, especially for students of American society. But Aron employs neither Tocqueville nor Montesquieu 'to elaborate systematically a precise conception of social phenomena'.[6] Even when writing on Marx, Aron misses the opportunity to engage with contemporary sociological discussions of class structure. Hence despite Aron's 'ability to spot intriguing nuances' in the work of the classic writers, we are left with a writer more literary than scientific and 'the conclusion ... that his program of analysis has not been consistently carried out' (ibid.: 198).

The weakness of Aron's articulation of the social also perplexed Martin Albrow (1969: 112–14) when he reviewed the second volume of *Main Currents*. Albrow acknowledges Aron's gifts of erudite and controlled exegesis – the chapter on Pareto is especially commended for being *sine ira et studio* – but taxes him for matters that bear directly on theory itself and for 'critical comments' that 'seem so puny in relation to their targets'. John Torrance (1969: 255–6) concurred. While the condensation of Durkheim, Pareto and Weber is 'elegant' and 'judicious', as a '*critical* exposition, however, it is distinctly disappointing'. Yet, for Albrow more than for Torrance, a much greater problem is Aron's 'facile' ontology. Aron criticizes Durkheim's social realism by insisting that only human groups, rather than a society, actually exist. But to invoke a human group is already to take up a common ground with Durkheim for it gives the collectivity a sui generis existence, albeit on a lower level of generality than a society. 'Ontological arguments either rule out the existence of both groups and societies [as in methodological individualism] or accept both.' More generally, Aron is an example of a writer who appears to admire wistfully the great classical syntheses but seems unable to replicate them. Thus he contents himself with 'broad interpretations of industrial society' without 'systematizing' the 'conceptual framework' of the theoretical giants he depicts. Reinforcing these points, Anthony Giddens (1970: 134) observed that Aron's *Main Currents* fails to offer a 'systematic critique of the many difficulties and ambiguities inherent in the writings of the various social theorists whose work

---

6   Aron's doctoral sudent, Jon Elster (2009), later supplied the deficiency.

is portrayed'. Instead, and despite many penetrating observations, one receives mostly 'ad hoc' criticisms that 'are rarely developed at any length'.

These initial verdicts on Aron's work show the degree to which his writings engaged sociologists at an especially deep level of analysis. By clarifying what modern sociologists expect sociology to look like, they are also presentiments of his later reception failure. An inability to be systematic, to delineate the contours of the social, to develop core concepts, and to use exposition of the classics to launch a major theoretical restatement of his own – all detracted from Aron's credibility as a sociological theorist. As for Aron's more 'empirical' work on industrial society, this also provoked near ubiquitous theoretical and methodological complaint. The *Economist*'s reviewer (Anon 1967: 1664–5) was obviously puzzled at what Aron was up to in *Eighteen Lectures on Industrial Society* (1967b). The Frenchman's claim to be using an analytical framework amounts to little more than two juxtaposed concepts: a 'model of growth' and 'a type of industrial society'. But what exactly is a model on Aron's reckoning? And is it a model at all without formalization? Alas, the 'general impression is one of common sense discourse interspersed with fairly unrelated methodological pronouncements. Thus the notion that economic growth depends on economic attitudes – interest in science, the habit of economic calculation, the desire for progress – is perfectly acceptable, but superficial.'

Equally unimpressed were Aron's sociological colleagues. W.G. Runciman (1967: 23–4) declared the arguments of *Eighteen Lectures* to be 'unexceptionable' and 'a little disappointing'. The 'level of generality of the argument is throughout just a little too high' and too tentative: 'the provisos seem to swamp the hypotheses.' Steven Lukes (1967: 928–9) who, like Runciman, admired *Main Currents* wished that *Eighteen Lectures* were 'a little more analytical and systematic'. To be sure, Aron offers a welcome corrective to ideologically driven positions, and by reviving and reshaping Comte's idea of industrial society furnishes a 'valuable reorientation of perspective'. Yet what Aron says about modes of social inequality and the preconditions of industrialism is no longer fresh; it appears 'to be rather obvious, not to say banal'. Likewise, Wilhelm Baldamus (1967: 455–6), reviewing *Eighteen Lectures* and a related volume (Aron 1967c), considered the first to be old hat: 'Aron's contribution to the study of industrial development is already so well known in this country that a detailed report on these books is unnecessary.' Baldamus concedes Aron's 'versatility' but expresses a lack of sympathy with both his politics (while Aron confesses to a form of 'conservatism', Baldamus's 'own value commitments are roughly the opposite of Professor Aron's) and with his method. Aron tells us that disciplined sociological analysis must attend to objective economic facts and restrain ideological predilection. Fine. The problem is that the facts that Aron cites, the indices he employs to make sense of them, and the conclusions he adduces are crudely assembled. The abundant use of measurement, in the two books under review, is 'puzzling as no attempt is made to connect interdependent economic variables with each other; there is not a single reference to the vast literature on post-Keynesian growth theory in mathematical economics. It seems to me therefore that the emphasis which Aron puts upon measurable statistical "facts" is somewhat misplaced'. And if Aron's research relies chiefly on 'crude, non-correlational statistics, how are we ever to discover what kind of facts are sociologically relevant?'[7]

Even Jon Elster (1983/4: 6) who reckons *Eighteen Lectures* and *La lutte de classes* to be Aron's most durable texts, characterizes them as masterpieces of haute vulgarization and 'relentless common sense'. One should read these books, Elster adds delphically, 'not so much in order to learn about society, as in order to learn how to think about society'. Yet Elster also believes that while, as a political writer, Aron 'conveys above all the austere demand for intellectual honesty', and is a shrewd observer of telling details and spurious analogies, sociologically he is a weak thinker with little 'creative imagination'. He has 'no eye for hidden similarities', lacks the ability to generalize, and would have benefited from a more analytical philosophical training. Conversely, for Anthony Giddens (1973: 59–63, 76–8), it is precisely Aron's penchant to over-generalize that constitutes the main problem. It leads Aron to incorporate capitalism too readily into the master category of 'industrial society', to reduce 'class' (an explanatory realist concept in Marxian terms) to 'stratification' (a descriptive, nominalist or heuristic one in standard sociological renderings) and to treat 'stratum' and 'class' as if they were the same things. All considered, Aron's theory 'makes little contribution towards reconceptualizing the notion of class' (Giddens 1973: 77).

The publication of Aron's (1968a) *Progress and Disillusion: The Dialectics of Modern Society* prompted similarly negative reviews.[8] True, John Rex (1968a: 313–14) found its sweeping vistas 'exhilarating', a welcome respite from the dry as dust quantitative analysis for which sociology is notorious. Aron's analysis of the tensions among the three ideals of Western civilization – equality, personality and universality – is also stimulating. Yet Rex is unconvinced by Aron's explanations

---

7   The American reviews were even more damning. *Eighteen Lectures* was frivolous and lacked 'hard data' according to Remi Clignet (1967: 207), while *The Industrial Society* reminded Kim Rodner (1968: 302–3) of a 'speechwriter for a state college president' advertising his moderation. Aron's work, Rodner continued, came across as dated, poorly informed of relevant literature, laboured in its critiques, and tone deaf to 'cultural ecology' – Aron fails to recognize that growth means very different things in different societies, especially to the poor. Out of his depth in this domain, readers are better advised to consult *Main Currents*, a work with 'no equal in the historiography of these matters'.

The only strongly positive review of *The Industrial Society* I have found by a sociologist is MacRae's (1967: 234). He calls the first essay in the collection 'informed, skeptical, pluralist and politically wise' and, more generally, warms to Aron's critique of radical ideology and social engineering. More the pity, MacRae laments, that both are recrudescent among a new generation.

8   Among sociologists, at least, unless the anonymous *TLS* reviewer (Anon. 1969: 651) was one. *Progress and Disillusion* was 'a stimulating *tour de force* which presents with admirable clarity some of the major issues of modern social controversy'. Even so, some of Aron's 'judgements seem … to have been overtaken by events'.

and by the narrow range of alternatives he stakes out. Alasdair MacIntyre (1968: 203–4) was more severe. 'Time after time one is led along a path of argument marked by insight and originality to be confronted finally with an unveiled platitude.' Aron is trapped by generalizations of his own devising that issue in 'facile and empty' statements.[9]

Political Sociology

If Aron's writings on industrial society underwhelmed reviewers, his political sociology polarized them. On one side ranged critical enthusiasts – fallibilist big-tent thinkers such as Ernest Gellner and John Hall – for whom sociology was one identity among others; as if marking their own distance from the sociological mainstream, they wrote often in politics or literary journals. Gellner (1961) initially offered a heavily qualified endorsement. Reviewing a botched translation of Aron's 1938 doctoral thesis on the philosophy of history, Gellner pronounced it conceptually elliptical and linguistically clumsy, the 'early work of a man who has acquired, rightly, a quite outstanding reputation as a social thinker and an incisive writer'.

But if the early work was serpentine and vertiginous, the mature political writing was lucid and clear-headed. Aron's (1970) *Essai sur les libertés* deserved to 'stand beside' J.S. Mill's *On Liberty*, Gellner (1966: 258) enthused. He particularly warmed to Aron's sociological 'probabilism', the notion, adapted from Tocqueville, that while history advances along no single path, 'not all possibilities are open'. Similarly, Aron's critique of technological determinism, and his unflinching analysis of the forces that undermine liberal democracy, especially in France, could hardly be bettered as a framework 'to understand the alternatives and choices that face us' (ibid.: 260). Not that Gellner and Aron saw eye to eye on every issue. They disagreed, notably, in their appraisal of the prospects of liberalization in Central and Eastern Europe, Gellner being the more positive and, as it turned out, perspicacious party (Aron 1979a; Gellner 1979a, 1979b; also Hall 1986: 156–7, 206–9).[10]

---

9   The American appraisal was no better. For Harvard's Martin Peretz (1969: 437), Aron's book was a 'meandering, unfocused romp … [indeed] intellectual rigor mortis would not be too unfair a characterization of this synoptic and synthetic view'. Reinhard Bendix (1969: 481), a sympathetic reader who applauded a 'superb antidote to the anarchic utopianism so rampant in our time', was also less than fully satisfied. The book was too abstract and rigid. Where are the history makers in its canvass?

10   Gellner served with Aron on the editorial board of the *Archives européennes de sociologie* and, as a commissioning editor of Weidenfeld and Nicolson, procured the British rights of *Main Currents*. Aron's influence on Gellner's theory of industrial society is described in Hall 2010: 134–5. Gellner also appreciated, Hall points out, Aron's openness to complexity and his ability to 'understand French left-wing thought from the inside'.

Shortly after Aron's death, John Hall added his own encomium. Aron's greatest contributions, Hall averred, lay in his understanding of industrial society and in his geopolitical analysis. But a weakness haunted the Frenchman's greatest strength:

> His general model is Montesquieu, and the mention of one of his masters demonstrates that Aron's 'sociology' is to be understood in the largest sense, that is, not as the study of the social but of the full workings, economic, political and ideological, of society as a whole. It is the greatest pity that Aron did not systematize the three [Sorbonne] courses, on economy, class structure and polity of East and West Europe, into a single book: and it is further to be regretted that only two of these [*Eighteen Lectures on Industrial Society* and *Democracy and Totalitarianism*] were translated into English, and then without a full appreciation of the project as a whole (Hall 1984: 425).[11]

On the other side of the Aronian divide stood more perplexed or hostile critics. Reviewing *Peace and War* (1966) for the BJS, Robert Bierstedt (1967: 454–5) clearly wished Aron were an entirely different kind of political thinker, more utopian, less Machiavellian. While graced with a mind of unrivalled 'lucidity' and penetration, Aron 'offers us no vision of a new society'. On the contrary, he furnishes an 'entirely orthodox' view of the world, vouchsafing thereby 'comprehensive pessimism'. Aron's treatise 'is a sociology of international relations as they unfortunately are rather than a sociology of war and peace that would give us some perception, however dim, of a world that would war no more'. Roland Robertson (1968: 356–7), reviewing the same book for *Sociology* conceded its 'vast array of insights, perspectives and data on vitally important subjects'. When it comes to observation on 'concrete features' of the international order, Aron is unfailingly perceptive. But Robertson declared himself dissatisfied with a work that offers no evident means 'to tackle problems of analysis in the international field'. The problem, as Robertson saw it, was precisely Aron's inability to develop a sociology of international relations, notwithstanding his claim to do so. Aron's analysis was too traditional and hidebound, cleaving to a model of 'diplomatic-strategic action, *as opposed to social action'*. Socio-cultural factors, illuminated by writers such as Etzioni, Deutsch, Galtung, and Haas, are given 'virtually no attention'. Nor does Aron integrate into his analysis 'sociological concepts' such as conflict, power, structural balance and sociometric choice.

---

11 *La lutte de classes* (1964) remains untranslated. Hall planned to write an intellectual biography of Aron for the publisher Longmans. It never appeared. Still, an expressly sympathetic appraisal of Aron is Hall 1981: 156–96, a book framed largely as a contribution to the philosophy of history rather than to sociology proper. Hall's (1981; 1984a; 1984b; 2011) prolific work on Aron is too large a topic for me to examine properly here. Suffice it to say that, over three decades, no sociologist has done more, and done it more cogently, to keep Aron's ideas in play.

A more caustic opinion of Aron's political sociology was expressed by Bierstedt's compatriot Thomas Lough (1970: 559–60), who declared *Democracy and Totalitarianism* (1968b), 'dated, biased, and unsystematic' notwithstanding its 'interesting' analyses of violence, terror and political parties. The book is dated because it is a translation of lectures delivered at the Sorbonne in the later 1950s. It is biased because of its evident partiality towards the Western side of the cold war. And it is unsystematic because, lacking methodically gathered empirical data, its arguments are supported only by 'ad hoc historical facts'. John Rex (1968b: 612) likewise bemoaned a 'dreary wandering argument marked by a rather mean lack of objectivity in its discussion of matters relating to Marxism'. The book's pivot – a contrast between monopolistic and multi-party regimes – cannot disguise the fact that it has too little sociological analysis; the argument 'settles somewhere between that of Seymour Lipset's *Political Man* and the journalism of Peregrine Worsthorne'. It is all very well for Aron to be a multi-faceted, cross-discipline Simenon. The result is 'ultimately to base himself on no discipline at all'. We need sociology, Rex implores, not 'the better form of journalism'. *Democracy and Totalitarianism* simply fails to be what it sets out to be: 'a political sociology for our times.'[12]

Lough, in the previously mentioned assessment, offers another criticism that is especially telling of how Aron bucked the expectations of sociologists interested in politics. Political sociologists, Lough stipulates, are scholars 'concerned with poverty, pollution, militarism, racism, and weapons of mass destruction'. Yet precisely on these problems *Democracy and Totalitarianism* is silent, and this dates it and limits its usefulness. Evident in such an opinion is the marked difference in meaning of 'political sociology' as Lough and Aron conceived it. For Lough, political sociology is concerned with 'world problems', with the interface of social ills and political behaviors. Political sociology and the sociology of politics shade into one another. Aron, conversely, separates them analytically and substantively. As he sees it, political sociology is focally concerned to examine the impact of politics *on* society, not the other way round. Its task is to show how politics is an independent force with independent dynamics – without a monopolistic party system, for instance, the Soviet Union would never have been able to collectivize agriculture or set industrial prices and quotas. Equally, because such a system prohibits civil society it is also far less amenable to social pressure than constitutionally pluralist societies are. Here, then, it is not only Aron's particular arguments that are problematic or 'reactionary' (Starr 1971: 159) to sociologists; the approach itself is utterly alien to their way of thinking.

---

12 Similarly, the TLS reviewer (Anon. 1969: 651) who commented favorably on *Progress and Disillusion*, found *Democracy and Totalitarianism* 'somewhat disappointing'. Many of the 'phenomena with which it deals are by now so familiar that it is difficult to say anything new about them'. Moreover, 'it seems to suffer more than the others books in the [Sorbonne trinity] series from its origin in lectures and to give only a superficial survey of the question which it raises, often in the style of daily journalism'.

Yet, from a quite different vantage point, Aron's political theory was objectionable not because it was orthogonal but because it was conventional: a species of elite theory first articulated by Mosca, Pareto and Michels. For Tom Bottomore (1966), Aron was a political cousin of Schumpeter; both were theorists who considered democracy to be integrally a competition among elites. Yet Aron went further than Schumpeter by claiming that the plurality of elites – in government, trade unions, and in civil society – caused their division and lack of synchronization. This contrasted fatefully with the unified elite structure of the Soviet Union, orchestrated by the Communist Party. According to Bottomore, however, the Aronian approach is deeply conservative and tendentious. For one thing, Aron, like Schumpeter, appears to believe that Western democracy is somehow a completed project, whereas for democratic socialists such as Bottomore it is still in its infancy. Much more needs to be done to enable people to participate in decisions that affect their lives. For another, Bottomore disputes Aron's postulate that democracy in modern states is representative or it is nothing. Direct democracy is not the anachronism that many claim it to be, and if it is not a panacea it is at least a potential medium of involvement in the spheres of work and community. Indeed, Aron seems to concede as much in his remarks about the role played by professional and voluntary associations in modern life. Such organizations diffuse power by providing 'so many occasions and opportunities for ordinary men and women to learn and practice the business of self-government. They are the means through which government *by* the people is made more real and practical in a large, complex society' (ibid.: 126).[13]

What Gets Taught?

Until recently one could only speculate on how Aron's work, and that of numerous other writers, was communicated to students by British sociologists. Now we have a better sense, thanks to a cache of Sociology Teaching Materials collected by Jennifer Platt and archived in the LSE.[14] Platt is frank that the teaching materials – synoptic degree syllabi outlines; individual course reading lists; university Calendar digests – are not a 'representative sample of anything'; the cache represents all that she was able to gather, without any deliberate selection of topic areas. On one side of the spectrum, we have large collections of material: notably, from the universities of Edinburgh (1954–2003; nineteen folders), Hull (1957–2006; fourteen folders) and Leicester (1952–2004; eleven folders). On the other side, we have tiny deposits: for instance, from Brunel (c. 1969; ten sheets), Aberdeen (1972–1982; one folder), Kent (1969–2003; two folders), Durham

---

13   Bottomore's wide ranging critique also taxes Aron for failing to articulate his elite theory of democracy to a theory of social classes.

14   http://archives.lse.ac.uk/TreeBrowse.aspx?src=CalmView.Catalog&field=RefNo&key=STM

(1965–1998; three folders). Collections occupying the middle range include Sussex (1966–2002; nine folders) and Bristol (1970s–2003; seven folders). Other discrepancies are obvious. Some syllabi are more detailed than others; gap years, both of short and long duration, are evident where syllabi are missing and the trail goes cold; not all universities and polytechnics are represented; and so forth. Even so, the Platt archive is the richest documentation yet assembled on British teaching recommendations in sociology.

In regard to Aron, these materials tell us several things. They will tell us more, and with greater accuracy, if the archive is ever digitized. This would correct for human error (mine) by enabling accurate counts of Aron citations. Digitization would also enable the didactic usage of Aron to be compared with that of other sociologists. For instance, it would reveal precisely what I can only state impressionistically from a perusal, conducted over ten days in the spring of 2012, of all the folders and CDs: that, despite extensive translation, Aron is far less present in the syllabi that cover his topics (theory, stratification, political sociology) than contemporaries such as Frank Parkin, Ralf Dahrendorf, John Rex, Tom Bottomore, Reinhard Bendix, Robert Nisbet, W.G. Runciman and Anthony Giddens. I venture tentative explanations for this asymmetry as the story proceeds. For the moment, let some bald observations suffice. They should be treated as indicative of broad trends rather than rigorously systematic accounting. Many nuances are obliterated, much colour bleached, in the generalizations that follow.

First, the materials show which teachers cited Aron.[15] They include Peter Lasssman (Birmingham), Ian Hamnett (Bristol), David Marsland (Brunel), Robert Moore (Durham), Frank Bechhofer, John Holmwood and John Orr (Edinburgh), Colin Creighton and Martin Shaw (Hull), Frank Parkin, Ray Pahl and Richard Scase (Kent), Zygmunt Bauman and Paul Bagguley (Leeds), Steven Hill, Angus Stewart, Leslie Sklair and Elizabeth Weinberg (LSE), David ['Norman'] Ashton, Clive Ashworth, Eric Dunning, Nick Jewson and John Scott (Leicester), Peter Worsley and D.T.H. Weir (Manchester), Ken Plummer (Polytechnic of the South Bank), Tom Bottomore, Luke Martell, William Outhwaite and Jennifer Platt (Sussex), Steve Fuller and Charles Turner (Warwick), Philip Stanworth and Andrew Tudor (York). Note that to cite authors is not necessarily to teach them. In fact, no one, so far as I can see, now teaches or has taught Aron in the way they have taught Parsons, Dahrendorf, Parkin or Bourdieu – as a debate-shaping theorist who spins off concepts or distinctions that require, and are worthy of, narrative explication.

Second, the Platt archive confirms that of all Aron's cited works, the two volumes of *Main Currents* predominate by a large margin. My practice was to count each course syllabus in which an Aron text was cited; if in a particular syllabus the

---

15   In courses taught by more than one individual, it is unclear who initiated Aron's inclusion. Some courses show clear signs of inheritance as teachers adapt only slightly a course they have taken over. And many courses, including those that cite Aron, do not specify a lecturer at all.

same Aron text was cited more than once, I still counted the text only once. Using that method, Aron's work appears in at least 123 course syllabi.[16] Of that number, 79 references or sixty four per cent of the total refer to *Main Currents*, volume 1 being cited more often than volume 2. A more revealing number, however, is one that contrasts these 79 citations to the next most cited work – *German Sociology* (Aron 1964a) – which receives only ten hits. Most of the other books mentioned in sociology syllabi – for instance, *Opium of the Intellectuals* (1985 [1955]), *La Lutte de classes* (1964b), *Progress and Disillusion* (1968a) – garner four or fewer citations.

Suppose we divide Aron's texts into two broad categories: those principally of commentary or creative exegesis, and those that seek strategically to make a theoretical contribution in their own right. *Main Currents, German Sociology* and the books on the philosophy of history are salient examples of the former type;[17] the articles on class structure (Aron 1950, 1969a), *Democracy and Totalitarianism* (1968b), *Eighteen Lectures on Industrial Society* (1967b) are instances of the latter. On that basis, 91 counts or almost seventy four per cent of the total, refer to books of commentary, and 32 or only twenty six per cent refer to texts of theoretical contribution. The most cited theoretical article, at 8 counts, is the BJS two-parter (Aron 1950a and b), while its later elaboration (Aron 1967d) receives 3. Texts one would expect to be cited many times rarely receive a mention: the stunning example is *Eighteen Lectures* which picks up only eight mentions; the companion book *The Industrial Society* collects another four.

A third fact to emerge from the archive is doubtless related to the second. Because Aron was construed to be principally a commentator on the classical tradition rather than as an innovative theorist in his own right, Modern Theory courses tend to pass him by unless they have a prefatory section with a quasi-classics overview. Hence Aron is absent from Bryan Heading's (East Anglia, c. 1980) 18 page syllabus for *Sociological Theory*, a 'modern theory' course, dense with reading recommendations, whereas Giddens, Rex, Percy Cohen, Lenski, Runciman, Gouldner, Merton, Peter Blau, Ossowski and Dahrendorf all appear there. The same is true for John Holmwood's (Edinburgh, 1981–1982) course *Contemporary Sociological Theory*, Andrew Tudor's *Contemporary Sociological Theory* (York, 1981) and, further back, Terry Johnson's and Clive Ashworth's (Leicester, 1974/5) *Theoretical Sociology* and Christopher Dandeker's Leicester iteration of the following year. To this a few exceptions can be mentioned, among them Essex's *Theoretical Sociology* (1973/4) taught by H. Newby and

---

16   The majority of these courses are run-ons and adaptations: repeats of courses with either the same or similar titles. Sometimes the same instructor or instructors teach them, at other times new teachers take them over.

17   This is a simplification. As I show elsewhere, *Main Currents* does include a viable vision of sociology encrypted within its exegetical frame (Baehr 2013). Even so, this and *German Sociology* are not works where Aron stakes out deliberately and explicitly his theory of modern society.

G. Kolankiewicz, John Scott's (Leicester, 1991–92) *Sociological Analysis* and the Warwick courses *Sociological Imagination and Investigation* and *Forms of Sociological Investigation* (2000–2004) – but, in all cases the citations are to *Main Currents*. The conclusion to draw from the above is that Aron, sequestered in classical sociology, rarely makes the leap in to its modern equivalents. Teachers who deemed him a great guide to a past era left him there.

Worse, and this is the fourth observation, by the mid-seventies Aron's commentary on the classics had come to play second fiddle to Giddens's *Capitalism and Modern Social Theory* (1971). That book had several distinct advantages over Aron's *Main Currents*: it simplified the canon into the magic number 3, rather than dispersing it across seven individuals; it distilled those three authors into one volume, rather than Aron's two; and it set the classics in the frame of 'capitalism', a concept congenial to the Marxist tide in British sociology, instead of 'industrial society'.

More surprising is a fifth fact: that Aron often fails to appear in course syllabi that fall squarely in his major topic areas, as if he really were of no consequence to them. The most obvious example is courses or sections of courses that concern Industrial Society. Examples are *Industrial Society* (Durham, 1966–1967); *Sociological Theory and Industrial Society* (Aberdeen, 1972–1974, taught by Ellis Thorpe, Adrian Adams, Chris Wright, Bryan Turner and Peter McCaffery); *The Class Structure of the Industrial Societies* (Manchester, 1974, taught by Peter Martin). Instead, texts by Goldthorpe (1971), Giddens (1973), Scott (1979) and Kumar (1976, 1978) quickly supplant the earlier writings of people like Clark Kerr, Daniel Bell and Aron.[18] This process of author-text displacement is common: faculty read new books, write new ones, many of these are synoptic and good to teach with and, accordingly, reference to older authorities declines. In time, the secondary sources become the primary ones and the cycle then repeats itself.

Was the growing criticism of *Industrial Society* the main cause of Aron's being sidelined? Possibly. Yet it bears emphasis that the critique of concepts such as Industrial Society – or Culture, Citizenship and Nation – in no way necessitates their eclipse. Critique can burnish, rather than tarnish, the significance of its targets. Disputes keep works alive, totemic. The more individuals are criticized, the more entrenched their reputations become. The bigger problem for Aron, I suspect, was that the concept of Industrial Society was trumped by new labels that painted our social condition as 'post-industrial', post-modern', 'late modern', 'post-fordist' 'liquid' or 'risk' centred. Industrial Society, for all the sophistication Aron brought to it, looked antiquated.

If I am right that Aron was swept away by a tide of new terms and debates, why, then, is Dahrendorf ubiquitous in the Platt archive and still a fixture in sociology textbooks today? Was his book not about *Class and Class Structure in Industrial*

---

18   Goldthorpe (1971) defends Aron, Giddens (1973) and Scott (1979) critically appraise him, and Kumar (1976, 1978) largely ignores him. The best overall treatment of Industrial Society as a concept and theory, in which Aron figures prominently, is Badham 1986.

Society (1959)? Dahrendorf's sociological longevity is explained by the fact that his work, aside from enunciating a provocative theory of class as authority, was readily slotted into 'conflict theory' – a key category of the discipline. Much like power and class, conflict is a feature of all societies not just one type of them. It is constitutive rather than time bound. As a concept it can be continually finessed but it cannot, unlike Industrial Society, be deemed outdated. Accordingly Dahrendorf, like Rex,[19] became emblematic of the conflict 'school' or 'approach' or 'tradition' enshrined in sociological textbooks and surveys both pedestrian and refined (see Alexander 1987; Collins 1994, Joas and Knöbl 2009). The mercurial Aron is not so easily identified – unless it is under Industrial Society, a category most sociologists now consider shop soiled.

Before closing this brutally abbreviated section, shorn of many possible illustrations, I must address one area in which Aron (1966, 1974, 1985b, 1985c) is generally recognized a pioneer: the sociology of war and global conflict.[20] What presence does this aspect of his work have in the Platt archive? Practically none. As is well known, war and global conflict were not of pressing interest to most post-war British sociologists until the early eighties. But even then Aron is not conspicuously on the radar of those who taught these topics.

The paucity of Aron reference in this area may well be an artifact of the archive itself. It contains no syllabi on war and civil military relations of sociologists with a keen interest in these topics: Christopher Dandeker, John Hall, Anthony King, Lynn Jamieson and Donald MacKenzie. Michael Mann left Britain in 1987 to join the UCLA faculty; the previous decade he spent at the LSE has left no trace in the Platt archive. In any event, he tells me that 'Raymond Aron is one of the many distinguished social scientists whom I have barely ever read – in fact only *Main Currents* for teaching purposes' (email of July 3, 2012).[21] Clive Ashworth's Leicester syllabus on *European Societies* (Leicester 1986) emphasizes the neo-Machiavellian tradition of which Aron is a modern exemplar (Ashworth and Dandeker 1987: 7; also 1986); yet students are referred to Hall (1984b; cf. 1985) on Aron rather than any article or book by Aron himself.

Nor do Martin Shaw's syllabi at Hull flag Aron until Shaw begins to pull away from dogmatic Marxism. Even then, the Frenchman's presence is slight. Professor Shaw remarks that 'When I turned to war at the beginning of the 1980s, although I was much more influenced by Weberian ideas, I was aware of Aron but not really attracted to his work' (email of July 9, 2012). This is evident in the courses on *Modern Industrial*

---

19   Another perennial. Rex filled two niches simultaneously: that of a conflict theorist, that of a race/ethnicity theorist.

20   Though Joas (2003: 136) believes Aron's 'neo-Clausewitzian strategic realist' theory of war to be a dead end. On the topic of warfare, Joas compares Aron unfavourably with C. Wright Mills!

21   One Essex syllabus of Mann's is preserved in the archive (*Sociological Analysis* Summer 1976, Essex) but it has no mention of Aron.

Societies[22] and *Social Structures of Advanced Societies* that, during the 1980s and 1990s, Shaw shared with Colin Creighton. Creighton's sections of the course invariably cite Aron (for *Main Currents*), whereas Shaw's never do, even when they contain parts on war and the state. On the other hand, Shaw's edited collection on *War, State and Society* (1984) contained a major article by Hall on Aron's contribution to this area and Shaw's third year course for 1984/5, with the same title as the book, does mention two Aron (1958 and 1978a) pieces on war.

Conclusion

Reputational success, the formation of the so-called 'canon', is a common topic of sociological discussion. Reputational collapse attracts less attention (McLaughlin 1998; Turner 2007). This essay is a contribution to its study. When A.H. Halsey (2004: 169–79) conducted his 2001 survey of British chair professors (n. 255) and asked them 'Who have been the most important mentors in your career?' and 'In the world as a whole which sociologists of the twentieth century have contributed most to the subject', Raymond Aron appears in neither category.[23] In a subject teaming with influential continental writers – Beck, Bourdieu, Elias, Foucault, Habermas, Touraine – Aron no longer figures.[24] Various reasons may be adduced for this state of affairs. Aron was a liberal conservative in a leftist discipline.[25] His measured lucidity – 'a respect for the humble fact is one of the qualities that keep his prose permanently fresh' remarked Clive James (2007: 37) – collides with what British social theorists expect of their French counterparts: opacity, iconoclasm, promethean ambition. Yet, as this article has shown, Aron also failed to live up to what sociologists more generally expect of the discipline: digestible concepts; theoretical systems; methodological design; in a word, 'professionalism'. Aron was simply too broad ranging, too humanist, too unclassifiable to attract a critical mass of sociologists.

If, as Nietzsche said, some writers are born posthumously might others be posthumously re-born? Some renewed interest in Aron is certainly evident today.[26] Might that portend a larger reappraisal? We cannot know. Yet a nagging question hangs over anyone who takes the trouble to read Aron carefully in the context of

---

22   Before 1984/5 the course was *Modern Industrial Society*.

23   Halsey's citation analysis of British sociology journals shows Aron to be the ninth most cited author in the 1970s (175).

24   Aron's irrelevance to British sociology is evident by his absence in Scott (2007), Elliott (2009) and Blackhouse and Fontaine (2010).

25   Aron 2002b, 1969b, 1975. On the meaning of leftism among the left, see Aron 1979a: 49–50 and 1979b.

26   See the special issue of the *Journal of Classical Sociology* (Baehr (2011a, 2011b) and the work of Robbins (2011, 2012), Scott (2011) and du Gay and Scott (2010). More evanescently, see Alexander 1995: 6–64 and 211, n. 43.

our own age of hyper specialization, historical amnesia and ideological addle. Raymond Aron was a big thinker who asked big questions, straddled disciplines and challenged doctrinaire formulae from whatever quarter they came. He was a writer who put the highest store on intellectual honesty and political responsibility. When sociologists fail to read Aron because he does not conform to what they expect of a sociologist, is it Aron or sociology that is the bigger loser?

References

Albrow, M.C. 1969. 'Main Currents in Sociological Thought 2', *Sociological Review*, 17, new series: 112–14.

Alexander, J.C. 1987. *Twenty Lectures: Sociological Theory since World War II*. New York: Columbia University Press.

Alexander, J.C. 1995. *Fin de Siècle Social Theory*. London: Verso.

Anon. 1967. 'Economic Comparisons', *The Economist*, 24 June: 1364–5.

Anon, R. 1969. 'Nouvelle Critique?', *The Times Literary Supplement*, 19 June: 651.

Aron, R. 1950a. 'Social Structure and the Ruling Class: Part 1', *British Journal of Sociology*, 1(1): 1–16.

Aron, R. 1950b. 'Social Structure and the Ruling Class: Part 2', *British Journal of Sociology*, 1(2): 126–43.

Aron, R. 1958. *War and Industrial Society*, transl. Mary Bottomore. London: Oxford University Press.

Aron, R. 1961. *Introduction to the Philosophy of History*. London: Weidenfeld and Nicolson [First published Paris: Gallimard, 1938].

Aron, R. 1964a. *German Sociology*. Glencoe, IL: Free Press [First published Paris: Alcan, 1936].

Aron, R. 1964b. *La Lutte de classes: Nouvelles leçons sur les sociétés industrielles*. Paris: Gallimard.

Aron, R. 1965. *Main Currents in Sociological Thought Volume I: Comte, Montesquieu, Marx, Tocqueville*. New York: Basic Books [First published Paris: Centre de Documentation Universitaire, 1961].

Aron, R. 1966. *Peace and War: A Theory of International Relations*. New York: Doubleday [First published Paris: Calmann-Lévy, 1962].

Aron, R. 1967a. *Main Currents in Sociological Thought Volume II: Durkheim, Pareto, Weber*. New York: Basic Books [First published Paris: Centre de Documentation Universitaire, 1961].

Aron, R. 1967b. *Eighteen Lectures on Industrial Society*. London: Weidenfeld and Nicolson [First published Paris: Gallimard: 1962].

Aron, R. 1967c. *The Industrial Society: Three Essays on Ideology and Development*. London: Weidenfeld and Nicolson.

Aron, R. 1967d. 'Social Class, Political Class, Ruling Class', in R. Bendix and S.M. Lipset (eds), *Class, Status and Power*. London: Routledge & Kegan Paul Ltd.

Aron, R. 1968a. *Progress and Disillusion: The Dialectics of Modern Society*. New York: Frederick A. Praeger.

Aron, R. 1968b. *Democracy and Totalitarianism: A Theory of Political Systems*. New York: Praeger [First published Paris: Gallimard, 1965].

Aron, R. 1969a. 'Two Definitions of Class', in A. Béteille (ed.), *Social Inequality: Selected Readings*. Harmondsworth: Penguin Books.

Aron, R. 1969b. *Marxism and Existentialism*. New York: Harper and Row.

Aron, R. 1970. *An Essay on Freedom*. New York: Meridian Books [First published Paris: Calmann-Lévy, 1965].

Aron, R. 1974. *The Imperial Republic: The United States and the World 1945–1973*. Cambridge, MA: Winthrop Publishers [First published Paris: Calmann-Lévy, 1973].

Aron, R. 1975. *History and the Dialectic of Violence: An Analysis of Sartre's 'Critique de la Raison Dialectique'*, trans. B. Cooper. Oxford: Blackwell [First published Paris: Gallimard, 1973].

Aron, R. 1978a. 'War and Industrial Society: A Reappraisal', *Millennium*, 7(3): 195–210, with a Foreword by Ralf Dahrendorf.

Aron, R. 1978b. 'Thucydides and the Historical Narrative', in M.B. Conant (ed.), *Politics and History: Selected Essays*. New York: Free Press [First published Paris: Plon, 1960].

Aron, R. 1979a. 'On Liberalisation', *Government and Opposition* 14: 37–57.

Aron, R. 1979b. *In Defense of Decadent Europe*. Indiana: Regnery Gateway [First published Paris: Laffont, 1977].

Aron, R. 1983. *The Committed Observer: Interviews with Jean-Louis Missika and Dominique Wolton*. Chicago: Regnery Gateway [First published Paris: Julliard, 1981].

Aron, R. 1985a. *The Opium of the Intellectuals*. Lanham and New York: University Press of America [First published Paris: Calmann-Lévy, 1955].

Aron, R. 1985b. *Clausewitz: Philosopher of War*. Englewood Cliffs, NJ: Prentice Hall [First published Paris: Gallimard, 1976].

Aron, R. 1985c. *The Century of Total War*. Lanham and New York: University Press of America [First published Paris: Gallimard, 1951].

Aron, R. 1990. *Memoirs: Fifty Years of Political Reflection*, Foreword by H.A. Kissinger. New York: Holmes and Meier [First published Paris: Julliard, 1983].

Aron, R. 2002a. 'The Dawn of Universal History', in Y. Reiner (ed.), *The Dawn of Universal History: Selected Essays from a Witness to the Twentieth Century*, with an Introduction by T. Judt. New York: Basic Books [First published Paris: Plon, 1961].

Aron, R. 2002b. *Le Marxisme de Marx*, Preface and Notes by J.C. Casanova and C. Bachelier. Paris: Editions de Fallois.

Aron, R. 2010. *Mémoires: Edition Intégrale Inédite*, Preface by N. Baverez, with a Foreword by T. Todorov. Paris: Laffont [First published Paris: Julliard, 1983].

Ashworth, C.E. and C. Dandeker. 1986. 'Capstones and Organisms: Political Forms and the Triumph of Capitalism: A Critical Comment', *Sociology* 20(1): 82–7.

Ashworth, C.E. and C. Dandeker. 1987. 'Warfare and Social Theory: A Re-evaluation of Western European Development', *Sociological Review* 35(1): 1–18.

Badham, R.J. 1986. *Theories of Industrial Society*. New York: St. Martin's Press.

Baehr, P. (ed.). 2011a. Special Issue on Raymond Aron, *Journal of Classical Sociology* 11(2).

Baehr, P. 2011b. 'Marxism and Islamism: Intellectual Conformity in Aron's Time and Ours', in Baehr 2011a: 173–90.

Baehr, P. 2013. 'The Honored Outsider: Raymond Aron as Sociologist', *Sociological Theory* 31(2): 93–115.

Baldamus, W. 1967. 'The Industrial Society and Eighteen Lectures on Industrial Society', *British Journal of Sociology* 18(4): 455–6.

Barber, B. 1962. 'Dimensions de la Conscience Historique', *American Journal of Sociology* 67(5): 592–3.

Barbu, Z. 1968. 'Main Currents in Sociological Thought, Vol. II', *American Journal of Sociology* 73(6): 771–3.

Bendix, R. 1969. 'Progress and Disillusions', *Social Forces* 47(4): 481.

Bierstedt, R. 1967. 'Peace and War', *British Journal of Sociology* 18: 454–5.

Blackhouse, R.E. and P. Fontaine (eds). 2010. *The History of the Social Sciences since 1945*. Cambridge: Cambridge Univesity Press.

Bottomore, T.B. 1966. *Élites and Society*. Harmondsworth: Penguin [First published London: Watts, 1964].

Calhoun, C. 1989. 'Classical Social Theory and the French Revolution of 1848', *Sociological Theory* 7(2): 210–25.

Calhoun, C. 2012. *The Roots of Radicalism. Tradition, The Public Sphere and Early Nineteenth-Century Social Movements*. Chicago: University of Chicago Press.

Clignet, R. 1967. 'The Industrial Society', *Social Forces* 46(2): 296–7.

Collins, R. 1994. *Four Sociological Traditions*. Oxford: Oxford University Press.

Colquhoun, R. 1986a. *Raymond Aron: The Philosopher in History 1905–1955*, London: Sage.

Colquhoun, R. 1986b. *Raymond Aron: The Sociologist in Society 1955–1983*, London: Sage.

Coser, L.A. 1965. 'Main Currents in Sociological Thought, Vol. I', *American Sociological Review* 30(6): 948–9.

Coser, L.A. 1968. 'Main Currents in Sociological Thought, Vol. II', *American Sociological Review* 33(2): 303–4.

Du Gay, P. and A. Scott. 2010. 'State Transformation or Regime Shift? Addressing Some Confusions in the Theory and Sociology of the State', *Sociologica* 2: 1–22.

Elliott, A. 2009. *Routledge Companion to Social Theory*. London: Routledge.

Elster, J. 1983. 'Rules of the Game', *London Review of Books* 5(24): 6–7.

Elster, J. 2009. *Alexis de Tocqueville: The First Social Scientist*. Cambridge: Cambridge University Press.

Feuer, L.S. 1965. 'Main Currents in Sociological Thought, Vol. I', *American Journal of Sociology* 71(3): 331–2.

Gellner, E. 1961. 'Time Machines', *Time and Tide* 3 February: 176–7.
Gellner, E. 1966. 'On Democracy in France', *Government and Opposition* 1: 255–64.
Gellner, E. 1979a. 'From *the* Revolution to Liberalisation', in E. Gellner *Spectacles and Predicaments. Essays in Social Theory*. Editorial Preface by I.C. Jarvie and J. Agassi. Cambridge: Cambridge University Press.
Gellner, E. 1979b. 'Plaidoyer pour une libéralisation manquée', in E. Gellner *Spectacles and Predicament. Essays in Social Theory*. Editorial Preface by I.C. Jarvie and J. Agassi. Cambridge: Cambridge University Press.
Giddens, A. 1970. 'Recent Works on the History of Social Thought', *European Journal of Sociology* 11: 130–42.
Giddens, A. 1973. *The Class Structure of the Advanced Societies*. London: Heinemann.
Goldthorpe, J.H. 1971. 'Theories of Industrial Society: Reflection on the Recrudescence of Historicism and the Future of Futurology', *European Journal of Sociology* 12(2): 263–88.
Hall, J.A. 1981. *Diagnoses of Our Time: Six Views on Our Social Conditions*, London: Heinemann Educational.
Hall, J.A. 1984a. 'Aron's Principles', *Government and Opposition* 19: 423–37.
Hall, J.A. 1984b. 'Raymond Aron's Sociology of States, or the Non-Relative Autonomy of Inter-State Behavior', in M. Shaw (ed.), *War, State and Society*. London: Macmillan.
Hall, J.A. 1985. 'Capstones and Organisms: Political Forms and Triumph of Capitalism', *Sociology* 19(2): 173–92.
Hall, J.A. 1986. *Powers and Liberties: The Causes and Consequences of the Rise of the West*. London: Penguin.
Hall, J.A. 2010. *Ernest Gellner: An Intellectual Biography*. London: Verso.
Hall, J.A. 2011. 'The Nature of Sophisticated Realism: Raymond Aron and International Relations', *Journal of Classical Sociology* 11(2): 191–202.
Halsey, A.H. 2004. *A History of Sociology in Britain*. Oxford: Oxford University Press.
James, C. 2007. *Cultural Amnesia*. London: Picador.
Joas, H. *War and Modernity*. Cambridge: Polity.
Joas, H. and W. Knöbl. *Sociological Theory: Twenty Introductory Lectures*. Cambridge: Cambridge Univesity Press.
Kumar, K. 1976. 'Industrialism and Post-industrialism', *Sociological Review* 24(3): 439–78.
Kumar, K. 1978. *Prophecy and Progress: the Sociology of Industrial and Post-industrial Society*. Harmondsworth: Penguin.
Lemert, C. 1986. 'French Sociology: After the *Patrons*, What?', *Contemporary Sociology* 15: 689–92.
Lough, T.S. 1970. 'Democracy and Totalitarianism', *American Sociological Review* 35(3): 559–60.
Lukes, S. 1965. 'Aron Looks at his Legacy', *New Society*, 11 November 1965: 29.

Lukes, S. 1967. 'Politics and Industrialism', *New Society*, 22 June 1967: 928–9.

MacIntyre, A. 1968a. 'Future Unpredictable?', *New Statesman*, 16 August 1968: 203.

MacIntyre, A. 1968b. 'Sociological Ancestors', *The Observer*, 16 June 1968.

MacRae, D. 1967. 'Sceptic and Optimist', *New Society*, 17 August 1967: 234.

MacRae, D. 1968. 'Social Pioneers', *New Statesman*, 19 July 1968: 83–4.

Madge, C. 1962. 'Dimensions de la Conscience Historique', *British Journal of Sociology* 13(1): 78–9.

McLaughlin, N. 1998. 'How to Become a Forgotten Intellectual: Intellectual Movements and the Rise and Fall of Erich Fromm', *Sociological Forum* 13(2): 215–46.

Peretz, M. 1969. 'Progress and Disillusion', *American Journal of Sociology* 74(4): 436–8.

Poggi, G. 1966. 'Main Currents in Sociological Thought, I', *British Journal of Sociology* 17(2): 209–11.

Rex, J. 1968a. 'Guessing at the Future', *New Society*, 19 August 1968: 313–14.

Rex, J. 1968b. 'The Sociological Simenon', *New Society*, 24 October 1968: 613–14.

Robbins, D. 2011. 'Social Theory and Politics: Aron, Bourdieu and Passeron, and the Events of May 1968', in S. Susen and B.S. Turner (eds), *The Legacy of Pierre Bourdieu: Critical Essays*. London: Anthem.

Robbins, D. 2012. *French Post-War Social Theory*. London: Sage.

Robertson, R. 1966. 'Main Currents in Sociological Thought, Vol. I', *History and Theory* 5(2): 191–8.

Robertson, R. 1968. 'Peace and War', *Sociology* 2: 356–7.

Rodner, K. 1968. 'The Industrial Society', *American Sociological Review* 33(2): 302–3.

Runciman, W.G. 1967. 'Stock Questions', *New Statesman*, 7 July 1967: 23–4.

Runciman, W.G. 1968. 'The Last of the Unifiers', *The Listener*, 5 September 1968: 309–10.

Schnapper, D. 2005. 'A View from a French Sociologist', in A.H. Halsey and W.G. Runciman (eds), *British Sociology Seen From Without and Within*. The British Academy: Oxford University Press.

Scott, A. 2011. 'Raymond Aron's Political Sociology of Regime and Party', *Journal of Classical Sociology* 11(2): 155–71.

Shaw, M. (ed.). 1984. *War, State and Society*. London: Macmillan.

Scott, J. 1979. *Corporations, Classes and Capitalism*. London: Hutchinson.

Scott, J. 2007. *Fifty Key Sociologists*. London: Routledge.

Starr, J.M. 1971. 'The Elusive Revolution: Anatomy of a Student Revolt', *American Sociological Review* 36(1): 159–61.

Torrance, J.R. 1969. 'Main Currents in Sociological Thought 2', *Sociology* 3(2): 255–6.

Turner, S. 2007. 'A Life in the First Half-Century of Sociology: Charles Ellwood and the Division of Sociology', in C. Calhoun (ed.), *Sociology in America: The American Sociological Associations Centennial History*. Chicago: University of Chicago Press, 115–54.

Chapter 3

Two Men, Two Books, Many Disciplines: Robert N. Bellah, Clifford Geertz, and the Making of Iconic Cultural Objects

Matteo Bortolini and Andrea Cossu[1]

As individuals who 'specialize in the production of cognitive, evaluative and expressive ideas' (Camic and Gross 2001: 236), intellectuals are constituted by the practices and experiences taking place within more or less extended networks of other producers, critics, and publics.[2] Initially, would-be-intellectuals customarily undergo a period of learning and training as members of one group or 'school' within formal or informal venues. This apprenticeship, however, is bound to come to an end as they reach their 'maturity' and face crucial decisions regarding their positioning within the field of cultural production. According to Randall Collins (2002: 52–6), the very logic of intellectual distinction prompts the producers of cultural objects to determine whether to remain within the boundaries of their original networks and traditions or try to break with them in order to gain recognition as imaginative authors, scientists, or scholars.

Being already at the center of the profession, the best pupils of the best teachers will be pushed by structural and psychological factors to differentiate themselves proposing innovative and attention-grabbing ideas in forms that could be recognized as both groundbreaking and legitimate (ibid.; Frickel and Gross 2005). Within scholarly fields this often means abandoning the routine of normal science for that epistemological realm where the 'principles for the hierarchization of scientific practices' are discussed via the proposal of a

---

1 This chapter is the result of the joint work of both authors. The introductory section and the coda were jointly written by the authors. Matteo Bortolini wrote the following sections: 'Between Religion and Social Science: Robert Bellah, 1950–1970', 'Beyond Belief and its reception', and 'The Traps of Symbolic Realism' in the 'Books, Authors, Fields, Trajectories' section. Andrea Cossu wrote the following sections: 'The Uses of Diversity: Clifford Geertz 1950–1973', 'The Interpretation of Cultures and Its Reception', and 'Transcending Disciplinary Boundaries' in the 'Books, Authors, Fields, Trajectories' section.

2 We interchangeably use 'idea' or 'cultural object' to indicate any recognizable ideational object – discoveries, facts, theories, paradigms, methods, research programs, novels, ways of acting, paintings, songs, poems, and so on.

new paradigm, a new framework, or a new method (Bourdieu 1991). A key precondition of such a paradigm revolution is the creation of an 'exemplar', that is, an example of what can be done with the new method(s): how to construct problems, how to solve scholarly puzzles, how to relate different pieces of work within the new conceptual and methodological frame (Alexander 1987a). Well-crafted exemplars might be thought as would-be *iconic cultural objects* with which intellectuals and their positions may be identified by other participants in the field of cultural production (Bortolini 2012; Cossu 2012).

In this paper we try to further our understanding of processes of scholarly innovation and intellectual positioning by comparing the creation and reception of two collections of essays published in the early 1970s: Robert N. Bellah's *Beyond Belief* and Clifford Geertz's *The Interpretation of Cultures*. Both books were conceived as more than mere assemblages of texts: they were powerful statements of their authors' vision of the state of their field and the direction it should take from that moment on – they were both created as prospective iconic cultural objects advancing the cause of what later came to be called 'interpretive social science'. At the time of their publication, the two books were greeted with interest, respect, and enthusiasm. In the decade that followed, though, *The Interpretation of Cultures* became one of *the* founding texts of the cultural turn and was widely read across the disciplinary spectrum, while *Beyond Belief* lagged behind and ended up being little more than a repository of Bellah's most famous pre-1970s essays. If we take for granted that social processes other than the simple recognition of the 'best ideas' are at work, we should ask: what does explain the differences in the reception of the two books and their success as iconic cultural objects?

The comparison between *Beyond Belief* and *The Interpretation of Cultures* is made interesting by the remarkable affinity of their respective authors' early intellectual careers: a sociologist and an anthropologist, Bellah and Geertz studied together at the Department of Social Relations at Harvard under the mentorship of Talcott Parsons in the early 1950s. They were trained to an interdisciplinary approach to the social sciences and became full members of some of the most powerful scholarly networks of the time – structural-functionalism and modernization theory. Upon graduation, they got top academic jobs and developed similar research programs, often in close collaboration. In the mid-1960s, as they were approaching their forties, Geertz and Bellah quietly distanced themselves from Parsons and started working towards the creation of an interpretive social science, a distinctly hermeneutic approach to which coeval disciplinary boundaries made little sense. After a close description of *Beyond Belief* and *The Interpretation of Cultures* as performative cultural objects aimed at showing the full potential of interpretive social science as each man understood it at the time, we argue that successful interdisciplinary positioning can be accounted for by a combination of institutional conditions, autonomous cultural representations about the scholar and his work (perceived originality, stance against normal science, public image of the work as a 'turn'), and the penetrability of germane disciplines.

Between Religion and Social Science: Robert Bellah, 1950–1970

Born in Altus, OK, in 1927, Robert Bellah arrived at Harvard college in 1945 from Los Angeles. After one year of service in the army, he resumed his studies in social anthropology and graduated in 1950 – his honors thesis was published in 1952 as *Apache Kinship Systems*. He then enrolled in a PhD program in sociology and Far Eastern languages under the mentorship of Talcott Parsons and John Pelzel, studying the influence of reformist religious movements in Tokugawa Japan. He graduated in 1955 and, after a two year stint at the Institute for Islamic Studies at McGill University in Montreal, he went back to Harvard on a shared appointment at the Faculty of Arts and Sciences and the Divinity School. During graduate school Bellah befriended Clifford Geertz and established with him a solid intellectual and personal camaraderie, with Parsons being extremely active in fostering their collaboration.

Bellah's dissertation was published in 1957 as *Tokugawa Religion*. Reworking the Protestant ethic thesis via Parsonian systems theory, Bellah (1957) focused on the role played by religious beliefs and movements in setting the stage for the take-off of Japanese modernization. In his quest for an analogue to the inner-wordly asceticism Max Weber considered as crucial for the emergence of the spirit of capitalism, Bellah studied a spiritual movement, Shingaku, and its leader, Ishida Baigan. The book's roots in modernization theory were mitigated by a critique of the latter's crudest, most materialistic versions and a plea for a multidimensional analysis of industrialization founded on the causal autonomy of culture. *Tokugawa Religion* won Bellah international acclaim as a japanologist and a theoretician in the sociology of religion, and opened the doors of the most powerful networks in both modernization theory and area studies to him.

Bellah went to Japan on a Fulbright grant in 1960–1961, and upon his return he was promoted associate professor. At Harvard he was especially close to Parsons, Paul Tillich and, after 1964, his friend and mentor from his McGill's days, Wilfred Cantwell Smith. In the early 1960s, his theoretical and empirical work was divided between the attempt at establishing a paradigm for the study of religious meaning systems combining Parsons's systems theory and Tillich's theology of culture – 'Religious Evolution' (1964) – and a series of studies on Japanese and Chinese modernization – 'Values and Social Change in Japan' and 'Some Reflections on the Protestant Ethic Analogy in Asia' (1963) and the essays on Ienaga Saburo and Watsuji Tetsuro (1965).[3] As he approached his 40th birthday, however, Bellah quietly moved away from Parsonian functionalism for a complex synthesis of historical sociology and hermeneutics, which he termed 'symbolic realism'. As a method for studying myths and religious narratives, symbolic realism insisted on the *sui generis* nature of religious symbols as an irreducible way of grasping the ultimate conditions of human existence. In essays like 'Meaning and

---

3   Almost all these essays are now collected either in Bellah 1970 or Bellah 2002. See also Bellah and Tipton 2006.

Modernization' (1968) and 'Transcendence in Contemporary Piety' (1968) Bellah radicalized his crossdisciplinary posture and started to reflect critically on the untenability of disciplinary boundaries and positivist scholarly objectivism. This intellectual shift was also accompanied by a major existential change: in the spring of 1967 Bellah left Harvard to become a professor of sociology and chairman of the Center for Japanese and Korean Studies at the University of California, Berkeley, and an adjunct professor at the Berkeley Graduate Theological Union.

Shortly before his move to California Bellah published his best known essay, 'Civil Religion in America'. A description and interpretation of a non-denominational, abstract set of religious beliefs and practices which, according to Bellah, constituted the common religious backbone of the United States, the essay was published in the winter 1967 issue of *Daedalus*, the interdisciplinary journal of the American Academy of Arts and Sciences. One year later, it was reprinted in *The Religious Situation: 1968* along with commentary by historians and sociologists and Bellah's reply, where he defended himself from the accusation of nationalism and restated his prophetic conception of the civil religion as a higher moral standard toward which the nation and its leaders bore public responsibility (see Cutler 1968). Almost immediately 'Civil Religion in America' aroused a wide and raucous crossdisciplinary debate which took Bellah away from his Japanese interests and made him a well-known figure in American studies.

In 1970 Clifford Geertz was appointed as the first professor of social science at the Institute for Advanced Study at Princeton. Almost immediately he asked Bellah if he would like to join forces and create a full-fledged School of Social Sciences with the support of the IAS director, former Harvard economist Carl Kaysen. According to the documents prepared by Geertz to justify his choice, time was ripe for the social sciences to cross disciplinary boundaries and secure an alliance with humanists, historians and philosophers to study the relationships between ideas, institutions, and societal change. Bellah's official nomination aroused opposition from the majority of the permanent members of the Institute, and gave rise to an unusually harsh public quarrel. In the end Bellah decided not to join the Institute for personal reasons and went back to Berkeley (see Bortolini 2011). One of the main targets of Bellah's critics was *Beyond Belief*, his first collection of essays, published in 1970 as a recap of his past work and a statement of new things to come.

The Uses of Diversity: Clifford Geertz, 1950–1973

Clifford Geertz was born in San Francisco in 1926 and spent his childhood in Northern California. After World War II, he took advantage of the GI Bill and set off to Antioch college in Yellow Springs, OH, to study English literature and become a journalist (see Geertz 2000: 5 ff.). There, he met future sociologist and political scientist David Apter, with whom he was to establish a lasting, if somehow loose, association for the rest of his career (Apter 2007; 2011). Upon graduation Geertz enrolled in the anthropology program at Harvard, where he became recognized as one of the most gifted junior members of the retinue hanging around the Department of Social Relations. For example, he gave a distinctive contribution as research assistant to Alfred Kroeber and Clyde Kluckhohn's systematic attempt to review all existing definitions of culture (Kroeber and Kluckhohn 1952). In 1952–1954 he left Cambridge for Java to carry out his first extensive period of fieldwork. Back in the US, he obtained a position at Harvard before leaving again for Bali. Soon thereafter, he was often on the move (at Berkeley, Stanford, and again in Bali), before taking a position at the University of Chicago, where he landed in 1960 to work alongside Parsons's longtime associate, Edward Shils.

Geertz's early career was characterized by this sort of back and forth wandering between the field and prestigious academic institutions. Moreover, he entered anthropology in a period when the discipline's context was undergoing a tremendous change: the old colonial powers were retreating to their trenches in Europe, new independent states were being formed, and the new postcolonial elites were facing the twin challenge of democratization and modernization. This led also to the rise of a new figure of anthropologist, less acquainted with colonial officers and with the duties of colonial administration, and more involved in observing the dramatic cognitive and organizational changes shaking the foundations of the colonial infrastructure.

As a Parsonian by training and a Weberian by vocation, Geertz approached this changed context with a strong emphasis on culture, which allowed him to approach the issues at the core of modernization theory (social change and development) with a non-reductionist vision. His work from the 1950s shows an interest for ritual, symbols, and beliefs (Geertz 1956a; 1956b; 1957a; 1957b), and for the interconnection of this cultural dimension to the problems of economic and social change, an interest that became more prominent in the 1960s, a period when Geertz's more routine work often tackled issues *within* the framework of modernization theory (although with a Weberian flavor) rather than outside what was at the time a dominant paradigm.

Geertz's career was propelled by these early, remarkable achievements. He was appointed associate professor in 1962 and full professor in 1964. During the 1960s he also conducted ethnographies in Morocco and Indonesia and published a number of books: *The Religion of Java* (his dissertation, 1960), *Agricultural Involution, Peddlers and Princes* (1963a; 1963b), and *The Social History of an Indonesian Town* (1965a). This early phase of Geertz's work, by the mid-1960s, slowly changed into more reflexive, theoretically-laden work, in which – ironically enough – he entered the emerging critique of Parsonianism and its strong interdisciplinary program of unified social science by constantly reworking Parson's notion of 'cultural system'.

In 1964, he published 'Ideology as a Cultural System' in a collection edited by his former schoolmate David Apter (Geertz 1964). The following year one of the central texts of *The Interpretation of Cultures*, 'Religion as a Cultural System', saw the light in a preliminary version (Geertz 1965b). In its 1968, and ultimate, version, 'Religion as a Cultural System' originated a small family quarrel with Parsons (1968) and Bellah: the former criticized Geertz's particularistic view of singular 'religions' and voiced his preference for 'Religious Evolution' as a framework for comparative studies; the latter criticized his friend's epistemological bias in favor of the world of everyday life and affirmed his own conception of the religious world, 'which organizes the deeply unconscious fantasies on which both personality and society are built', as the paramount symbol system (Bellah 1968: 291).

At the same time, Geertz was taking decisive steps in the building of an hermeneutic methodology of his own. Like Bellah had done with 'Civil Religion in America', Geertz found in *Daedalus* an interdisciplinary venue for one of his master works. 'Deep Play. Notes on the Balinese Cockfight', published in 1971, described a seemingly trivial episode in the life of a Balinese village from which, thanks to its author's interpretive finesse, the whole pattern of Indonesian structural and symbolic social structure emerged. By then, many of the essays that were to become the bulk of *The Interpretation of Cultures* had been published. When the book finally appeared as Geertz's mid-career intellectual, conceptual, and methodological manifesto, it took anthropology by storm.

Beyond Belief and its Reception

Robert Bellah published *Beyond Belief. Essays on Religion in a Post-Traditional World* in 1970. His first collection included sixteen papers, slightly less than half of his publications up to that point. It was a carefully crafted cultural object aimed at positioning its author in the emerging field of religious studies: introduced by a preface and a long introduction, it was divided into three sections, each introduced by a short preamble; moreover, each text had its own footnote explaining when it had been written, its context, and how it related to Bellah's ongoing intellectual development. In this, *Beyond Belief* was incomparably more elaborated than both *The Interpretation of Cultures* and Parsons's own collections, such as *Essays in Sociological Theory* or *Social Structure and Personality*. The book included all of Bellah's most well-known papers: 'Religious Evolution', 'Civil Religion in America', and 'Meaning and Modernization', along with some more specific studies on Japan, China, and Islam.

The last section presented six papers, focusing on 'Religion in Modern Society', among which 'Transcendence in Contemporary Piety', an important essay where Bellah theorized the relationship between man and the symbols created to represent the intimate unity of all reality borrowing an insight from Wallace Stevens: 'To believe is a fiction, which you know to be a fiction, there being nothing else' (Bellah 1970: 203). In his review of Norman O. Brown's *Love's Body,* Bellah spoke of the book as an exemplary work that was 'at the same time religious and an analysis of religion' and reflected on its consequences for the *scientific* study of religion: if all symbolic forms spoke of of the same thing – that is, the human condition – then they were all legitimate to occupy the same terrain occupied by the social sciences. Methodological barriers should be 'flattened' so that the symbolic resources of religious thought would become 'vitally available' to the social sciences, with critical and, most of all, 'liberating' consequences (Bellah 1970: 233–5). Together, these essays indicated the direction of Bellah's future research, and his conviction that in the future social science would take the place of philosophy in providing 'the intellectual tools for religious self-reflection' (Bellah 1970: 191).

From another point of view, Bellah constructed *Beyond Belief* as an exemplar *in itself* of the strict, integral relationship between scholarly and personal life on which symbolic realism depended. In fact, the whole book was a dramatic and larger-than-life narrative of Bellah's shift from the 'Harvard complex' – scientism, structural-functionalism and modernization theory – to the 'Berkeley complex' – hermeneutics, religious experience and post-modern productive chaos. While in the preface Bellah declared his lack of satisfaction with the sociology of religion and promoted 'the crystallization of religion, broadly understood, as an independent field of reflection and research within the academic community' (Bellah 1970: x), the introduction tried to anchor his scholarly work dealing 'with the great collective myths which are dying and being born in our time' to his personal experience (Bellah 1970: xi). Bellah recounted his whole story up to the moment of his move to Berkeley, a place where he could feel 'the intensity, the immediacy, the openness and the precariousness of an emergent social order' (Bellah 1970: xvii). In his renewed commitment against 'any political totalism', Bellah embraced 'the playful radicalism of Norman O. Brown' and pleaded for a 'politics of the imagination, a politics of religion' (Bellah 1970: xvii). His short introductions to the reader's sections underscored his growing interest in symbolism within religious systems and his disillusion with a scientistic approach to social phenomena, his Weberian roots, and his optimistic concern for modernity's crisis of meaning (Bellah 1970: 1, 51, 191). The book closed with 'Between Religion and Social Science', Bellah's manifesto of symbolic realism, and its radical plea for a new understanding of religion which called into question the scholar as a whole human being: 'The radical split between knowledge and commitment that exists in our culture and our universities is not ultimately tenable. Differentiation has gone about as far as it can go. It is time for a new integration' (Bellah 1970: 257).

The book got rave reviews. In the *American Journal of Sociology*, Andrew M. Greeley (1971: 754) called Bellah a scholar of the highest quality and commented on the two book reviews included in *Beyond Belief* saying that 'my own inclination is to think that what Bellah has to say about Brown and Robinson is of considerable more interest than what Brown and Robinson themselves have to say'. One reviewer remarked the role played by Bellah in giving new life, and a higher status, to the sociology of religion in America (Gladden 1971: 733), while others underscored his interest for religious evolution and civil society. Most reviewers, however, focused on his personal introduction and his general attitude towards his *Beruf* as a scholar: the introduction was deemed as 'superb' and the quality of his essays was explained by pointing to his personal commitment. One reviewer, in particular, spoke of *Beyond Belief* as 'an autobiographical account of one sociologist's attempt to come to terms with the sociology of religion' and the essays as 'expanded expressions of that [individual] search'. Its interest, however, was more than biographical: Bellah's vision of the sociology of religion as a way of finding oneself religiously had methodological implications in that it highlighted 'the subjective nature of all contributions of sociology of religion' (Brendle 1971: 222–3).

The most appreciative review of the book, however, was published on the *Journal of the American Academy of Religion*. There, Samuel S. Hill, chair of the Department of Religion at the University of Florida, paired Bellah and Geertz as the most influential figures in the study of religion of the early 1970s and spoke of Bellah's 'uniqueness' in taking the widest possible array of roles: 'In addition to being social scientist, phenomenologist, and historian of religious-philosophical ideas (…) he is humanist, poet, mystic, and theologian' (Hill 1973: 448). Hill also praised Bellah's pluralism, radicalism, and open-mindedness, and concluded:

> No one should be surprised that his program sometimes meets with savage rejection. Yet, so intelligent, humane, and thoughtful a student of culture must be listened to. I have to conclude that he is a prophet (Hill 1973: 450).

As *Beyond Belief* came to be identified with symbolic realism, it followed its destiny. Influential sociologists of religion criticized Bellah's vagueness – the book lacked both one single theoretical statement on the study of religion and a precise methodological illustration of what the approach might accomplish, – his radicalism or, ironically enough, his hidden reductionism (Johnson 1977; Barnhart 1977). As the debate on symbolic realism quickly faded, *Beyond Belief* became a handy container for Bellah's most famous essays – especially 'Religious Evolution' and 'Civil Religion in America'. Later, its epistemological essays were somehow superseded by the more accessible appendix to *Habits of the Heart*, 'Social Science as Moral Philosophy', which became Bellah's new methodological manifesto – albeit a very different, and much less ambitious, one (Bellah et al. 1985). Upon Robert Bellah's death, obituaries generally cited 'Religious Evolution' or 'Civil Religion in America', *Habits of the Heart*, and *Religion in Human Evolution*, but almost no mention was made of either *Beyond Belief* or symbolic realism.[4] As a collection *and* a theoretical statement the book had been long forgotten.

---

4 Sam Porter, administrator of the website www.robertbellah.com, complied a list of 40 webpages with articles or obituaries published after Bellah's death: only 6 of them cited *Beyond Belief* at all, and only one spoke about it.

The Interpretation of Cultures and Its Reception

Few books have been able to make the interdisciplinary impact that *The Interpretation of Cultures* made upon its first appearance in 1973. All but one of the essays included in the collection had previously been published, but somehow its opening and closure – the long methodological essay on 'Thick Description' and the empirical venture into the world of Balinese cockfight – constituted a powerful couplet that, almost immediately, stood as a manifesto for interpretive anthropology. *The Interpretation of Cultures* also reconstructed Geertz's own intellectual path, signaling his reader that he could not be put easily into the cage of modernization theory.

Indeed, some of his essays dated back to the 1950s, and the majority had already appeared in the 1960s, when Geertz's clear interest was with the intertwined effects of culture and society onto economics and social change. Many of the essays included in the book represented Geertz's own attempt to come to terms with functionalism, and witnessed his move from a systemic understanding of culture to a more complex semiotic vision, influenced by the linguistic turn (Geertz 1973: ix), two definitions that are clearly visible in two of the major essays included in the book. In 'Religion as a Cultural System', Geertz made a step towards a univocal (and unified) notion of culture, trying to avoid the multiplicity of referents that Kroeber and Kluckhohn had reviewed in their work. To him, culture denoted

> an historically transmitted pattern of meanings embodied in symbols, a system of inherited conceptions expressed in symbolic forms by means of which men communicate, perpetuate, and develop their knowledge about and attitudes toward life (Geertz 1973: 89).

These symbols were tangible elements, 'concrete embodiment[s]' that qualified as 'social events' just like any other. At the same time, this symbolic dimension was also 'theoretically abstractable from those events as empirical totalities'. This conception of culture – and especially the notion that culture itself could be analytically isolated from 'the social' and 'the psychological' – was still a nod to Parsons's notion of the cultural system and to its implicit semiotics. From this point of view, Geertz's notion was semiotic in so far it established a relation between abstract symbolic meanings and expressions ('symbols'), even though he never went so far as to analyse in depth what kind of function this relation expressed.

Yet, in 'Thick Description' Geertz also moved forward, away from Parsons's homologies of the semiotic relationship within subsystems and among the operational workings of his generalized media of exchange. It is ironic that Geertz's contribution to the theory of culture, and then to the cultural turn, is wrapped in methodological preoccupations rather than in theory-building. The concept of culture presented in 'Thick Description' is 'essentially a semiotic one', an update of Weber's idea 'that man is an animal suspended in webs of significance he himself has spun', whose analysis is interpretive and whose understanding requires looking at what 'practitioners of it do': in a word, ethnography. The notion of thick description was therefore put forward as the solution to a methodological problem, building on the idea that observable behavior is grounded on structures of signification (Geertz 1973: 9) that become available (and only insofar as they are made available) in symbolic action.

Upon its publication, *The Interpretation of Cultures* was received with raucous praise in sociology, where culture was still a bad word, probably even more than it was in anthropology. In 1974, the book won the Sorokin Award of the American Sociological Association, while its author was the first recipient of the Talcott Parsons Prize of the American Academy of Arts and Sciences, an award endowed with a clearly interdisciplinary mission. As *The Interpretation of Cultures* gained its status mostly by word of mouth, it is indeed ironic to see – with a lot of hindsight – how problematic the first major reviews of the book were. Writing in *Science*, Ward Goodenough (1974) acknowledged that the book contained influential essays (like 'Religion as a Cultural System') as well as 'masterpieces' ('Person, Time and Conduct' and 'Deep Play'), but also wrote that Geertz's vision of culture was 'uncomfortably close' to Durkheim's idea of collective representations. Culture, therefore, became 'a system of Platonic ideals that [existed] in society as a kind of collective mind rather than in people'. In *Contemporary Sociology*, Elizabeth Colson (1975) recognized Geertz as 'one of the most original and stimulating anthropologists of his generation', while pointing out that his development as a scholar was making him more a 'philosopher' than an anthropologist. His work was 'an art, not a science'. As it had happened with Bellah, the most enthusiastic review appeared on *The Journal of the American Academy of Religion*, where William Shepherd (1975) marked the book as essential reading and 'the most significant anthropological understanding that we have of religious form and function in culture'.

Both critics and supporters praised Geertz's highly personal style, his irony, and his ability to move from the world of common sense to what he had called generalization 'within cases'. At the same time, they were clearly interested in his conversion from functionalism to semiotics and in the central role that methodological issues had played in this transition. The shift was 'brilliantly' argued and the result was 'an invaluable backdrop against which to understand his work on religion and on symbol, his ethnographic analyses, and his physical anthropology' (Colson 1975). Goodenough (1974: 436), for his part, wrote of thick description as 'an outstanding example of insightful and rich handling' of the problems arising from the public existence of ideal forms, somehow conflating Geertz's own semiotics and his implicit theory of the publicness of meaning, that he derived from the late Wittgenstein.

As we have seen, in the immediate wake of the book's appearance, rave reviews did not mean unanimous praise. Still, by the end of the decade, Geertz had established himself at the forefront of the cultural turn, praised equally by historians, sociologists, anthropologists, and literary theorists as well as philosophers. His interdisciplinary appeal resulted mainly from the reception of the two essays that ideally bracketed *The Interpretation of Cultures*, the methodological statement and its illustration by means of the masterful presentation of a case, the Balinese cockfight. All other essays, even the most influential ones, were forgotten save for specialists, shadowed by the iconic power of these two classic formulations.

To some extent, in fact, the two major essays of *The Interpretation of Cultures* became autonomous from both the context that had produced them, and from the book that contained them. One needed not be an expert of Balinese culture and society to read 'Deep Play' and get inspiration from the guidelines it provided for empirical analysis; nor did one need training in the philosophy of ordinary language to appreciate Geertz's Wittgensteinian seduction. Thus *The Interpretation of Cultures* became, almost overnight, an interdisciplinary cultural object, one that could be adapted to different fields witnessing the first changes brought by the cultural turn. What, then, are the underlying motives at the root of its success and appeal? And what is the social logic that makes an interdisciplinary object stick with a scholarly audience, to the point that it acquires the status of a classic?

Books, Authors, Fields, and Trajectories

The Traps of Symbolic Realism

Beyond Belief and *The Interpretation of Cultures* were meant as powerful scholarly statements that could push forward Bellah's and Geertz's programs for the interpretive renewal of social science. As it happened, they were also meant to seal their comradeship and collaboration, a project that failed when Bellah and his work became the epicenter of the intellectual controversy that prevented him from joining arms with Geertz at the Institute of Advanced Study. After the end of the 'Bellah affair' at Princeton, Bellah focused on the civil religion debate and, as the Bicentennial of the American Revolution approached, published *The Broken Covenant*, a hugely successful, deeply committed analysis of the nation's religio-political myths that won him the Sorokin Prize of the American Sociological Association for 1976. On the other hand, upon the publication of *The Interpretation of Cultures* Geertz gained enormous intellectual status. For many, his work became the epitome of the cultural turn in the social sciences, and a book that could serve well those who were trying a similar transition to interpretive social science, whether they came from the fragmented field of anthropology, or from the more positivistic milieux of sociology and social history.

What remains unexplained, though, are the differences in the intellectual trajectories of reception of these two books, which were similar in aim, if not in target and in their structure as proposed turning points in their respective fields. As much as one needs to approach the success of *The Interpretation of Cultures* by means of a careful reconstruction of its early reception and its interdisciplinary appeal, one needs to face the other side of the mirror; namely, why was a similar work left to disciplinary amnesia, and how did this different reception affect the image of the authors and, in the last instance, their reputation across the spectrum of disciplinary fields? Objectivist explanations based on the sheer quality of ideas do little to advance our understanding: by all measures *Beyond Belief* is a great book, and *The Interpretation of Cultures* has its flaws, which only the staunchest, less well-read, or strategically interested post-Geertzian culturalist would deny (especially those with little training in the kind of philosophy and 'semiotics' that Geertz was exposed to). We argue that what made the difference in the trajectories of the two books were (a) their transformation into compact symbolic objects – something that could be cited to nod at something that everybody knows – and (b) the structure of the fields within which they were launched and promoted as performative texts. The point is that a complex cultural object such as a collection of essays might be identified, or typecast, differently as one or more essays are taken to be its 'true core'; this identification, on the other hand, will 'encounter' a field structured around one (or more) symbolic opposition(s), in relation to which the work will make more or less sense and will be categorized either as a standard input to the field, an instanciation of an important idea, or even a groundbreaking work (Bortolini 2012). To be sure, the final outcome – i.e., the text assuming an iconic quality – depends on the combination of these two major factors together with other, lesser elements (its author's prestige, scientific or intellectual fads, its sheer availability, and so on).

As we said, in the early 1970s *Beyond Belief* came to be identified almost completely with symbolic realism – its most cited essays were 'Between Religion and Social Science' and 'Religion and Belief'. As such, its relevance depended on the force of Bellah's epistemological approach, one that had a paradoxical destiny. The sociology of religion was not ready to accept too radical a conception of interpretive social science denying the necessity of boundaries between the social sciences and the humanities. During the Postwar years, American sociologists of religion had fiercely struggled for the recognition of their sub-discipline as an objective, scientific and completely secularized scientific endeavor. Bellah's proposal, which depicted the scientific study of religion as yet another form of religious symbolism and called for a strongly personal involvement on the part of the scholar (Bellah 1970: 256–7), was too 'subjective' and anti-positivist to be accepted by his strictly scientist colleagues – to their ears, symbolic realism, and with it *Beyond Belief*, could be summarized in that infamous phrase, 'To put it bluntly, religion is true' (Bellah 1970: 253). Among the proponents of interpretive social science, Peter L. Berger proved to be more palatable for American sociologists of religion: not only did he clearly distinguish between sociology, theology, and religious studies, but he was at the forefront of the mainstream of secularization theory, which Bellah had often ridiculed from both a theoretical and an empirical point of view (see Bortolini 2014).

In fact, Bellah won most of his public in a field which, to a great extent, needed no hermeneutic revolution. As Donald Wiebe (1999: 97) wrote in his reconstruction of the politics of American religious studies, the study of religion after World War II was dominated by an unstable alliance of historians and theologians trying to establish itself as a 'clerisy, a secularized group who [expressed] great anxiety about modern developments in society and who [were] dedicated to protecting the soul and spirit of humanity'. From the point of view of the practitioners of religious studies, Bellah belonged to a wide front of 'offenders' who criticized the positivistic approach to the study of religion: Martin E. Marty, Mircea Eliade, Jacob Neusner, Michael Novak and Bellah's mentor and friend, Wilfred Cantwell Smith (see also Segal 1989: 57–62 and 126 ff.). In sum, as coeval commentaries show, Bellah's work was seen by sociologists as a capitulation to the humanities and by humanists as a welcome addition to an ongoing conversation between philosophers, theologians, and public spirited clergy from different denominations.

As Bellah was rejected by the sociology of religion and adopted by religious studies, the debate on symbolic realism subsided and the very structure of *Beyond Belief*, with its complex weaving of personal and scholarly themes, lost its main *raison d'être*. The book became, somehow, opaque to an overall reading as a cultural object in its own respect: when it was reissued by the University of California Press in 1991, reviewers noticed its personal character and criticized it on the ground that Bellah's own experiences as a 'religious scholar of religion' were 'not necessarily the stuff of academic scholarship' (Nossen 1993: 275). If *Beyond Belief* was *itself* an 'exemplar' of what could be done with symbolic realism it was both 'too much' (for conventional social sciences) and 'too normal' (for humanists and theologians).

Transcending Disciplinary Boundaries

The fate of *The Interpretation of Cultures* and its becoming a truly iconic cultural object can also be explained looking at the combination between typecasting processes and the structure of the different fields within which it circulated after its publication. To begin with, the condition of anthropology was quite peculiar, and undoubtedly different from that of religious studies. Cultural anthropology had benefited from the postwar expansion and was, by all standards, a complex and diverse field, with fuzzy boundaries, 'a range of places that could accommodate differences of theory and approach', and a tradition of scholarly hybridization (Silverman 2005: 283 ff.). As an eclectic modernization theorist who added a Weberian, 'cultural' twist to the study of economic and social development, Geertz was well-positioned when he began to elaborate his hermeneutical framework (Silverman 2005: 302 ff.). Quite rapidly, his position came to be recognized as one of the two poles along the materialist-culturalist continuum of cultural anthropology – with Eric Wolf, Marvin Harris and Marshall Sahlins occupying the opposite end.

At the same time, Geertz competed with others that were busy trying to redefine the anthropological notion of culture. He made a contribution to an area of scholarly reflection in which multivocality was the norm.[5] The field was therefore already permeable to the proposal of new ways to interpret culture, and the early reception of the linguistic turn provided a key for the recognition of a theoretical-cum-methodological proposal loosely based on a semiotic approach to culture, whether it came from French structuralism (Needham 1973; Sahlins 1976), Durkheimian sociology (Douglas 1966), or from American linguistics (Turner 1967). At the turn of the 1960s, to borrow two suggestive images from Victor Turner, the forest of symbols was indeed a forest, and anthropologists willing to penetrate the nuances of culture had better enter it and not stay sheepishly on the edge of the bush.

Geertz was first identified as a voice in a broader intellectual movement and then as the author of an original contribution to the cultural turn, especially the one he made explicit in *The Interpretation of Cultures*. Such a closeness between the author and his work (at the level of public perception) seems to be one of the factors at work in the making of a classic, i.e., that series of procedures of consecration (Bourdieu 1994) and sacralization (Di Maggio 1982a; 1982b) through which a peculiar kind of symbolic capital is bestowed upon a work. Classicization, however, goes one step further because, as Alvaro Santana-Acuña (2014: 98) has argued, it involves the autonomization of the work from the social conditions of its production. In particular, one element of the making of a classic involves a situation in which 'its contents are appropriated and considered meaningful by actors and organizations that had no share in their production'.[6]

Unlike *Beyond Belief* and other works by Robert Bellah, *The Interpretation of Cultures* was able to transcend both disciplinary boundaries and exert a cross-generational influence beyond both the circles in which the work was originally produced and the circles of those practitioners likely to refer to a work years after its publication. To this wider audience, *The Interpretation of Cultures* was not simply a theoretical statement, but most of all – and we may dare say, predominantly – an instruction manual that showed 'how to do things' with thick description. As an intellectual argument and as a cultural artifact it had a certain illocutionary force, inviting scholars to follow on the same path rather than simply taking a position in the area of cultural theory.

The recollections of prominent scholars support this idea. Harvard psychologist Jerome Bruner (2005: 22), who in the 1970s was pursuing his studies on language development from a strongly interactionist perspective, found that *The Interpretation of Cultures*, especially in the analysis of Balinese cockfights, demonstrated 'what you could do by keeping an eye firmly on the meaning-process'. Historian Natalie Zemon Davis, one of the first supporters of an interpretive vision in historical studies, explained Geertz's appeal as a reaction to the rejection of narrative and culture common among the majority of social

---

5   For a coeval review see Keesing 1974, which is an important document of the range of intellectual positions at the beginning of the cultural turn in one of its most strategic fronts.

6   For a perspective on this process see also Cossu 2012.

historians at the time. On the one hand, Geertz stressed the need to 'understand ceremonial, liturgical, festive and other forms of symbolic behavior', which 'social historians often ignored […] as "irrational", or reduced them to practical uses'. On the other, he was a perfect fellow traveller for micro-historians, thanks to his pendant for a focus 'on a limited space […] and an intensely significant and observable local event, out of which could be teased a world of meaning and an enduring style of living' (Davis 2005: 3839).

At the time, Geertz was not the only anthropologist that pursued the affirmation of a semiotic vision of culture and the development of methodological tools. At his best, Victor Turner (1974) offered a recognizable method (social dramatic analysis), an illustration of its application to historical events – his analysis of the assassination of Thomas Becket is as powerful as 'Deep Play', – and the promise of interdisciplinarity (see Moore and Myerhoff 1975; 1977). Yet, in the end, he remained dangerously close to narrative analysis and far from the kind of semiotic palace Geertz built. From this point of view, Geertz's characterization of culture as an 'acted document' could be easily appropriated by historians by focusing on the 'document', rather than on symbolic action. A document, indeed, counted already as an 'interpretation of an interpretation', an ethnographic account made from within one's culture of reference, rather than from without. The best case was perhaps put forward by historian Robert Darnton (1984: 6), who co-taught with Geertz a seminar at Princeton:

> It therefore should be possible for the historian to discover the social dimension of thought and to tease meaning from documents by relating them to the surrounding world of significance, passing from text to context and back again until he has cleared a way through a foreign mental world.

Darnton's formulation does sound like the hermeneutic circle, but also as an explicit appropriation of Geertz's methodological strategy. In a certain sense, the latter was ready made for historians and other practitioners in different disciplines in a way Bellah's wasn't – in fact, while Bellah was well-known among historians thanks to the American civil religion debate, *Beyond Belief* and symbolic realism gained no currency within the field of history. In a sense, symbolic realism was too radical, and at the same time too personal, asking for a personal involvement that meant 'going native' rather than seeing things 'from the native's point of view'.

Coda

Even in the top tiers of scholarly research, symbolic capital is distributed unequally, and barriers to circulation affect not only the early reception of a cultural object but also its interdisciplinary and intergenerational impact. In this chapter, we have tried to contribute to a growing body of studies on the dynamics of success and the mechanisms of consecration and classicization focusing on two works that had been carefully devised to become iconic cultural objects, *The Interpretation of Cultures* and *Beyond Belief*. In fact, only the former gained this enviable status, whereas the latter has been condemned to a subtle form of sociological amnesia.

Accordingly, we have identified a few reasons in the rise of Geertz's work: the permeability of his discipline, cultural anthropology, to the affirmation of a semiotic notion of culture, which resulted in early recognition of the merits of the work; the definition of a methodological proposal that was constructed in an interdisciplinary way and which called for interdisciplinary work, which resulted in understanding and appropriation outside his discipline; the production of an 'exemplar' in which this methodology was illustrated and tested. These conditions were lacking in Bellah's case, due to the shape of his primary area of research, the positivistic stance of practitioners in the area, and the problematic alignment between his methodological proposal and his best-known exemplar – 'Civil Religion in America'. This different fate calls for further research on the subject of how intellectual cultural objects achieve 'oneness' (Schwartz 2009), while others are forgotten.

References

Alexander, J.C. 1987a. 'The Centrality of the Classics', in A. Giddens and J. Turner (eds), *Social Theory Today*. Stanford: Stanford University Press, pp. 11–57.

Alexander, J.C. 1987b. *Twenty Lectures*. New York: Columbia University Press.

Apter, D. 2007. 'On Clifford Geertz', *Daedalus* 136(3): 111–13.

Apter, D. 2011. 'Clifford Geertz as a Cultural System', in J.C. Alexander et al. (eds), *Interpreting Clifford Geertz*. Basingstoke: Palgrave Macmillan, pp. 181–96.

Barnhart, J.E. 1977. 'Reductionism and Religious Explanation', *Perspectives in Religious Studies* 4(3): 241–52.

Bellah, R.N. 1957. *Tokugawa Religion*. Glencoe: The Free Press.

Bellah, R.N. 1968. 'Review of Part 2 of *The Religious Situation: 1968*', *Journal for the Scientific Study of Religion* 7(2): 290–91.

Bellah, R.N. 1970. *Beyond Belief*. New York: Harper & Row.

Bellah, R.N. 2002. *Imagining Japan*. Berkeley, CA: University of California Press.

Bellah, R.N. and S.M. Tipton (eds). 2006. *The Robert Bellah Reader*. Durham: Duke University Press.

Bellah, R.N., et al. 1985. *Habits of the Heart*. Berkeley, CA: University of California Press.

Bortolini, M. 2011. 'The 'Bellah Affair at Princeton', *The American Sociologist* 42(1): 3–33.

Bortolini, M. 2012. 'The Trap of Intellectual Success', *Theory and Society* 41(2): 187–210.

Bortolini, M. 2014. 'Blurring the Boundary Line', in A. Hess and C. Fleck (eds), *Knowledge for Whom?* Farnham: Ashgate, pp. 205–27.

Bourdieu, P. 1991. 'The Peculiar History of Scientific Reason', *Sociological Forum* 6: 3–26.

Bourdieu, P. 1994. *The Field of Cultural Production.* New York: Columbia University Press.

Brendle, M.R. 1970. 'Review: *Sociological Approaches to Religion, The Sociological Interpretation of Religion,* and *Beyond Belief'*, *Sociological Analysis* 31(4): 220–23.

Bruner, J. 2005. 'Celebrating Geertzian Interpretivism', in R.A. Shweder and B. Good (eds), *Clifford Geertz by His Colleagues.* Chicago and London: University of Chicago Press, pp. 20–23.

Camic, C. and N. Gross. 2001. 'The New Sociology of Ideas', in J.R. Blau (ed.), *The Blackwell Companion to Sociology.* Oxford: Blackwell, pp. 236–49.

Collins, R. 2002. 'On the Acrimoniousness of Intellectual Disputes', *Common Knowledge* 8(1): 47–70.

Colson, E. 1975. 'Review: *The Interpretation of Cultures'*, *Contemporary Sociology* 4(6): 637–38.

Cossu, A. 2012. *It Ain't Me, Babe. Bob Dylan and the Performance of Authenticity.* Boulder: Paradigm Publishers.

Cutler, D. (ed.). 1968. *The Religious Situation: 1968.* Boston: Beacon Press.

Darnton, R. 1984. *The Great Cat Massacre and Other Episodes in French Cultural History.* New York: Basic Books.

Di Maggio, P. 1982a. 'Cultural Entrepreneurship in Nineteenth-century Boston, Part I: The Creation of an Organizational Base for High Culture in America', *Media, Culture, and Society* 4(1): 33–50.

Di Maggio, P. 1982b. 'Cultural Entrepreneurship in Nineteenth-century Boston, Part II: The Classification and Framing of American Art', *Media, Culture and Society* 4(4): 303–22.

Douglas, M. 1966. *Purity and Danger.* London: Routledge and Kegan Paul.

Frickel, S. and N. Gross. 2005. 'A General Theory of Scientific/Intellectual Movements', *American Sociological Review* 70: 204–32.

Geertz, C. 1956a. 'Religious Belief and Economic Behavior in a Central Javanese Town', *Economic Development and Cultural Change* 4(2): 134–58.

Geertz, C. 1956b. *Religion in Modjokuto.* Cambridge, MA: Harvard University, PhD Dissertation.

Geertz, C. 1957a. 'Ethos, World-view and the Analysis of Sacred Symbols', *The Antioch Review* 117(4): 421–37.

Geertz, C. 1957b. 'Ritual and Social Change: A Javanese Example', *American Anthropologist* 59(1): 32–53.

Geertz, C. 1960. *The Religion of Java.* Glencoe: The Free Press.

Geertz, C. 1963a. *Agricultural Involution.* Berkeley, CA: University of California Press.

Geertz, C. 1963b. *Peddlers and Princes*. Chicago: The University of Chicago Press.

Geertz, C. 1964. 'Ideology as a Cultural System', in D. Apter (ed.), *Ideology and Discontent*. New York: The Free Press of Glencoe, pp. 47–76.

Geertz, C. 1965a. *The Social History of an Indonesian Town*. Cambridge, MA: The MIT Press.

Geertz, C. 1965b. 'Religion as a Cultural System', in W.A. Lessa and E.Z. Vogt (eds), *Reader in Comparative Religion. 2nd ed.* New York: Harper & Row, pp. 204–13.

Geertz, C. 1968. 'Religion as a Cultural System', in D. Cutler (ed.), *The Religious Situation: 1968*. Boston: Beacon Press, pp. 639–88.

Geertz, C. 1973. *The Interpretation of Cultures*. New York: Basic Books.

Geertz, C. 1988. *Works and Lives*. Stanford: Stanford University Press.

Geertz, C. 2000. *Available Light*. Princeton: Princeton University Press.

Goodenough, W. 1974. 'On Cultural Theory. The Interpretation of Cultures', *Science* 186(4162): 435–6.

Gladden, J.W. 1971. 'Review: *Beyond Belief*', *American Sociological Review* 36(4): 733–4.

Greeley, A.M. 1971. 'Review: *Beyond Belief*', *American Journal of Sociology* 76(4): 754–5.

Hill, Jr., S.S. 1973. 'Review: *Beyond Belief*', *Journal of the American Academy of Religion* 41(3): 447–50.

Isaac, J. 2009. 'Tangled Loops: Theory, History, and the Human Sciences in Modern America', *Modern Intellectual History* 6(2): 397–424.

Johnson, B. 1977. 'Sociological Theory and Religious Truth', *Sociological Analysis* 38(4): 368–88.

Keesing, R.M. 1974. 'Theories of Culture', *Annual Review of Anthropology* 4: 73–97.

Kroeber, A.L. and C. Kluckhohn. 1952. *Culture: A Critical Review of Concepts and Definitions*. Cambridge MA: Harvard University Peabody Museum of American Archeology and Ethnology Papers 47.

Moore, S.F. and B. Myerhoff (eds). 1975. *Symbols and Politics in Communal Ideology*. Ithaca: Cornell University Press.

Moore, S.F. and B. Myerhoff. 1977. *Secular Ritual*. Assen: Van Gorcum.

Needham, R. 1973. *Right and Left*. Chicago: University of Chicago Press.

Nossen, R. 1993. 'Review: *Beyond Belief*', *International Journal of Comparative Sociology* 34(3–4): 274–5.

Parsons, T. 1968. 'Commentary on Religion as a Cultural System', in D. Cutler (ed.), *The Religious Situation, 1968*. Boston: Beacon Press, pp. 688–94.

Sahlins, M. 1976. *Culture and Practical Reason*. Chicago: University of Chicago Press.

Santana-Acuña, Alvaro. 2014. 'How a Literary Work Becomes a Classic: The Case of One Hundred Years of Solitude', *American Journal of Cultural Sociology* 2(1): 97–149.

Schmidt, P.L. 1978. *Towards a History of the Department of Social Relations, Harvard University, 1946–1972*. Cambridge, MA: Harvard College,

Schwartz, B. 2009. 'Collective Forgetting and the Symbolic Power of Oneness: The Strange Apotheosis of Rosa Parks', *Social Psychology Quarterly* 72(2): 123–42.

Segal, R.A. 1989. *Religion and the Social Sciences: Essays on the Confrontation*. Atlanta: Scholars Press.

Sewell, W. 2005. *The Logics of History*. Chicago: University of Chicago Press.

Sheperd, W. 1975. 'Review: *The Interpretation of Cultures*', *Journal of the American Academy of Religion* 43(3): 635.

Silverman, S. 2005. 'The United States', in F. Barth et al., *One Discipline, Four Ways*. Chicago and London: The University of Chicago Press, pp. 257–347.

Turner, V.W. 1967. *The Forest of Symbols*. Chicago: Aldine.

Turner, V.W. 1974. *Dramas, Fields, and Metaphors*. Ithaca. Cornell University Press.

Wiebe, D. 1999. *The Politics of Religious Studies*. New York: St. Martin's Press.

Zemon Davis, N. 2005. 'Clifford Geertz on Time and Change', in R.A. Shweder and B. Good (eds), *Clifford Geertz by His Colleagues*. Chicago and London: University of Chicago Press, pp. 38–44.

Chapter 4

Erich Fromm: Studies in Social Character

Kieran Durkin

Introduction

An early member of the Frankfurt *Institut für Sozialforschung* (Institute for Social Research) who went on to enjoy a career as a leading intellectual figure in the middle-part of the last century, Erich Fromm is today largely forgotten. His theory of social character and applied social-characterological case studies, which were groundbreaking contributions to twentieth century social thought, have achieved at best a tentative assimilation into the sociological canon. In this chapter, I will look at Fromm's psychoanalytic social psychology and studies of social character within the context of the rise and consolidation of sociology as a discipline. As part of this study, I will discuss Fromm's largely under-acknowledged role in the early phase of the *Institut für Sozialforschung*, in which he and Max Horkheimer were the main drivers of an interdisciplinary programme which sought to unite the social sciences with philosophy in a long-lasting collaboration aimed at lessening the arbitrary injustice of social life. In addition to this, I will discuss Fromm's relationship to American sociology and, in particular, to the 'culture and personality' tradition which flourished there during the 1930–50s, as well as his break from Horkheimer, etc. and career as a 'public intellectual' following the publication of *Escape from Freedom*. Finally, I will look respectively at Fromm's more or less forgotten empirical social-characterological case studies of manual and white collar workers in Weimar Germany and of the inhabitants of a peasant village in Mexico.

Marx, Freud, and Social Psychology

Surveying the entirety of Erich Fromm's corpus, it is clear that it represents a complex body of social psychology, social philosophy, social commentary and politics – amongst other things – that, in many respects, escapes easy categorization. Whilst this is so, I have argued elsewhere that the various aspects that contribute to Fromm's thought can be most consistently and most adequately categorized as 'radical humanist' (Durkin 2014). As Fromm defines it in *You Shall Be as Gods*, radical humanism is 'a global philosophy which emphasizes the oneness of the human race, the capacity of man to develop his own powers and to arrive at inner harmony and at the establishment of a peaceful world. Radical humanism considers the goal of man to be that of complete independence, and this implies penetrating through fictions and illusions to full awareness of reality' (1966: 13). In an addition on the following page, Fromm stresses that radical humanism recognizes the fact that ideas, 'especially if they are the ideas of not only a single individual but have become integrated into the historical process, have their roots in the real life of society' (1966: 14). The quartet of clauses contained in this definition (three of religio-philosophical origin and a fourth taken from sociological or social-psychological thought) are connected on the basis of a developmental schema which works through the translation and retranslation of Judaic, Marxian, and Freudian elements (all interpreted humanistically) such that each new thought system successively develops the previous system without supplanting the core of that system. This core then works itself outward into the new system, where it interacts with the new elements in that system to progressively develop the basis of humanism itself (Durkin 2014).

Detailed discussion of this process is not possible in the present chapter, but suffice it to say that after concluding the absurdity of theology as a coherent intellectual endeavour in his mid-twenties (and thus breaking with the dominating feature of his life until this point) Fromm nevertheless sought to continue what he saw as the emancipatory thrust of the philosophical and hermeneutic traditions of Judaic thought by secular means – a continuation that he saw most clearly manifested in the philosophical and sociological thought of Karl Marx. Fromm saw Marx's concept of 'communism' and the whole emancipatory nature of his thinking as representing a form of secular messianism, his image of the communist society – to the extent that he offers one – paralleling the idea of 'Messianic Time' as found in the biblical prophets.[1] But not only this: Marx's materialism offers a crucial progression of the emancipatory thrust of the biblical tradition, his materialism seeking to invert and transcend the theological speculation of Hegel and Feuerbach and to thereby attain substantive, empirical knowledge of 'really existing active men' (Marx 2000: 191). In as much as this is the case, Fromm saw Marx as combining emancipatory and scientific concerns and thereby laying the basis 'for a new science of man and society which is empirical and at the same time filled with the spirit of the Western humanist tradition' (2006: 7).

The foregoing taken into consideration then, the social-psychological clause in Fromm's definition of radical humanism – which is of Marxian origin, in essence – can be seen to stem directly from the central radical humanist concern that characterizes Fromm's thinking. But it is with the adoption of Freud's insight into the forces in the psychological realm which direct us 'behind our backs' – the largely unconscious structuring of our passions and interests through discernible psychological mechanisms and tendencies – that Fromm's thinking takes on its most distinctive and determinate character. In the same manner that Marx

---

1   I do not have space here to deal with the controversial nature of this position, other than to say that the discovery of the *Economic and Philosophic Manuscripts of 1844* strengthened its viability.

represented a secular (or materialist) development of the messianic prophetic tradition for Fromm, the psychoanalytic theory and practice of Sigmund Freud represented, in certain crucial respects, a development of Marx's materialism, offering what Fromm saw as the basis of a 'science of the irrational' and, thus, a radical humanist conceptual instrument for more fully understanding really existing active persons. As such then, by combining Marx and Freud – completing Marx by supplying a formalized psychological basis to historical materialism, and correcting Freud by installing a more adequate sociological starting point for psychoanalytic theory – Fromm's thinking evolved into an epistemological and methodological materialism and, through this, into a sociopsychoanalytic programme which is directly relevant to sociology.

While working at the Frankfurt *Institut für Sozialforschung*, directly concerned with negotiating the theoretical and practical crossovers between psychoanalysis and historical materialism, Fromm formulated the essentials of this materialism, and, along with Max Horkheimer, laid down the specifics of the empirical programme of the early period of the Institut. Despite deciding against an academic career in favour of pursuing psychoanalytic training, Fromm was employed by the Institut on a part-time basis in 1929, becoming a tenured member and the most important theoretical influence next to Horkheimer himself two years later. Fromm had been introduced to Horkheimer by his schoolmate, Leo Löwenthal, an introduction which was itself facilitated by the fact the Psychoanalytic Institute of the South-West German Psychoanalytic Association, where Fromm was then based, was housed in the same building as the *Institut für Sozialforschung* (hereafter 'Institut'). As part of the Institut, Fromm was charged with the integration of psychoanalysis and sociology along the lines stipulated by Horkheimer in his inaugural lecture in January of 1931 – in this lecture, Horkheimer called for the fusion of philosophy and the various sciences, uniting in long-lasting interdisciplinary collaboration and focusing on 'the question of the connection between the economic life of society, the psychological development of its individuals and the changes within specific areas of culture' (Horkheimer 1989: 33). As such, Fromm was put in charge of an innovative empirical study of the attitudes of German manual and white-collar workers in relation to authoritarianism, which, although remaining unpublished until the 1980s, formed the conceptual and methodological basis for the Institut's more famous *The Authoritarian Personality* study some twenty years later.

Despite Fromm's central involvement in this early period of the Institut, he was for a long time effectively written out of its official history, being replaced by Herbert Marcuse, Theodor Adorno, and even Walter Benjamin in the 'Origin Myth' that went along with this history (McLaughlin 1999). Though this deliberate myopia has been challenged by Martin Jay, Rolph Wiggershaus and others, since the 1970s, the tendency to consider Fromm's role as minor, if to consider Fromm at all, often prevails. What is worth stressing here is that Fromm had, in fact, been working on the connections between psychoanalysis and sociology/historical materialism for some time prior to his involvement with Horkheimer. Whilst training as a psychoanalyst in Berlin, Fromm attended Otto Fenichel's famous '*Kinderseminar*', a gathering

point for young dissident psychoanalysts interested in exploring the relevance of
psychoanalysis for matters pertaining to socialism. During this time Fromm was an
acquaintance of Paul Federn, Ernst Simmel, Siegfried Bernfeld, and Wilhelm Reich,
all high-profile psychoanalysts and socialists with whom he shared ideas on the
connections between Marxism and psychoanalysis. Bernfeld and Reich in particular
are important here – Bernfeld's 'Psychoanalysis and Socialism', which originally
appeared in 1925, effectively acted as the introduction to the Freud-Marx synthesis,
whilst Reich's *Dialectical Materialism and Psychoanalysis*, which appeared in
1929, brought it to greater prominence. Fromm himself published *Die Entwicklung
des Christusdogmas, Eine Psychoanalytische Studie zur Sozialpsychologischen* in
1930 (translated as *The Dogma of Christ* in Fromm 1992 [1963]), as an attempt to
map the morphology of Christian Dogma by relating the ideas it conveyed, relative
to each stage of its development, as expressions of the socioeconomic situation and
psychic attitude of its followers. Although problematic in many respects – exhibiting
a somewhat cavalier attempt to render simple the complicated issues of Christology
and exegesis, and the problem of deep-historical attributions of psychic states – the
work was genuinely pioneering, being the first empirical example of the integration
of Freud and Marx. Two years later, Fromm published *Über Methode und Aufgabe
einer Analytischen Sozialpsychologie. Bemerkungen über Psychoananlyse und
historischen Materialismus* and *Die psychoanalytische Charakterologie und ihre
Bedeutung für die Sozialpsychologie* (translated as *The Method and Function of
Analytic Social Psychology* and *Psychoanalytic Characterology and its Relevance
for Social Psychology*, respectively, in Fromm 1970) as programmatic articles
mapping out the enduring fundamentals of his psychoanalytical social psychology
in the Intitut's periodical, *Zeitschrift für Sozialforschung*.

The Freudo-Marxist work discussed here is largely the development of the
critique of mechanical Marxism inaugurated by Karl Korsch and Georg Lukács
in the light of the failure of the German proletariat to realize the transition from
capitalism to socialism in the aftermath of the First World War. Korsch had seen
that this failure could be attributed to the social-psychological ill-preparedness of
the workers for revolution (Korsch 1974: 128) and Lukács had seen the general
need for Marxism to deepen its shallow empirical understanding of the subjective
experience of the working class, a realization reflected in his distinction between
'actual' and 'ascribed' class consciousness (Lukács 1971). But while this was so,
Korsch and, particularly Lukács were given to an anti-psychological view that
greatly limited their penetration into the subjective aspect. Going against this anti-
psychological position, Fromm and the other Freudo-Marxists sought to extend the
critique of mechanical Marxism into distinctively psychological, and in particular,
psychoanalytical territory. The thinking informing this extension ran approximately
thus: as society consists of nothing but individuals, and that as individuals are
subject to the laws and limits of the functioning of the psychological apparatus,
historical materialism needs to be able to say something about such laws and
their presence in the social process. What psychoanalysis could bring to historical
materialism (and, therefore, sociology), then, was the knowledge of the human

psychic apparatus and personality as a factor in the social process, considered next to and in connection with economic, financial, and cultural factors.

The proliferation of such Freudo-Marxist syntheses in 1920–1930s Germany was facilitated by a number of factors, most important of which being the following: 1) the socio-economic and political situation of the Weimar period (i.e., the failed post-war revolution of 1918/19 and the financial collapse of 1929); 2) the popularity of Freud's thinking; 3) and the particular development of German sociology. Sociology as a discipline was just forming in Germany when Fromm was a student, at the beginning of what Richard Münch describes as its 'consolidation phase' (Münch 1994) (Fromm studied what was then called 'national economics' at Karl-Ruprecht University, in Heidelberg, under Alfred Weber, Heinrich Rickert, and Karl Jaspers). To the extent that it existed as a coherent body of thought, sociology in Germany at the time represented a less autonomous and 'scientific' discipline than it did in France or North America. What characterized German sociology during this period was the combination of pronounced theoretical depth (the influence of Kant, Hegel, Marx, Nietzsche, and the Idealist tradition in general) and the *Verstehende* approach to social analysis that differentiated it from the Durkheimian tendency towards anti-psychology – a combination of influences best exemplified in the thought of Max Weber. Whilst Fromm clearly shares some of these influences with Weber, and whilst he relies heavily on Weber's historical sociology at points, his opposition to the kind of thoroughgoing nominalism and positivistic approach to value that characterizes Weber's thinking puts him at odds with what is now considered the mainstream of the sociological tradition. Fromm's social-psychological explorations are, nevertheless, certainly representative of definite trends in German sociology at this time. From the very birth of German sociology there were serious – if relatively unsystematic and amorphous – attempts to understand the individual as simultaneously individual and social: Wilhelm Dilthey, Georg Simmel, Alfred Vierkandt, and Max and Alfred Weber, amongst others (Karl Mannheim embarking on a similar programme in the 1930s). Precisely because of such a proliferation, we can see Fromm's social-psychological explorations as part of this wider phenomenon of sociology grasping for its object, passing beyond the stage in which it was merely a philosophy of history and trying to deal with the seemingly intractable issue of the relationship between the individual and the collective.

Escape from Freedom and the Rise and Fall of a Public Intellectual[2]

Political developments in Germany during the early 1930s meant that life was becoming increasingly precarious. Fearful of the prospect of deepening and long-lasting fascist rule, the Institut temporarily re-located to Geneva in 1933, before

---

2 In this section I have drawn extensively on the scholarship of Neil McLaughlin (1996, 1998, 1999, 2007), whose work on Fromm has been a crucial catalyst for much of the recent return to Fromm. Thomas Wheatland (2009) has also helped excavate Fromm's

moving on to the United States, settling in New York, at Columbia University in 1934. Part of the larger influx of European intellectuals that swelled the academic institutions of North America and rejuvenated the American intellectual scene at the time, the Institut were given generous office space and the recognition of a premier academic institution at Columbia. This support enabled the Institut to continue the interdisciplinary work it had embarked on in Frankfurt, this work evincing a shift of focus, however, from the earlier emphasis on research into the social-psychological connections between material and intellectual culture in relation to skilled and white-collar workers to the broader issue of the changes taking place in the structure of the family at a period of particularly severe economic crisis (Wiggershaus 1994: 137). *Studien über Autorität und Familie* (*Studies on Authority and the Family*), a 1,000-page preliminary report on this research, was published in 1936, containing a detailed social-psychological section by Fromm in which he elaborated on the connections between 'authoritarian forms of society' and what he termed the 'authoritarian character' (Fromm 1936).

All-throughout the period covering the move to New York and the preparatory work for *Studies on Authority and the Family*, Fromm was suffering from recurring bouts of tuberculosis which at various points severely restricted his ability for any sort of work beyond that of reading (Funk 2000: 81–2). The physical separation from the other members of the Institut that the illness brought about – Fromm was based at a sanatorium in Davos from 1932–1934, and was thereafter forced to regularly seek sea and mountain air to aid his recuperation – meant that he was removed from regular contact with Horkheimer and was generally unable to participate fully in the development of empirical programme. During this time, Horkheimer's attitude towards Fromm and towards the interdisciplinary project itself had begun to shift. Such a shift was to become evident in Horkeimer's rejection of a prospective article Fromm had written for the *Zeitschrift* in 1937 (the article has since been published, along with other previously unpublished works, by Rainer Funk under the title 'Man's Impulse Structure and Its Relation to Culture' in *Beyond Freud: From Individual to Social Psychology*, in 2010). In this prospective article, Fromm embarked on a fundamental re-examination of Freudian theory, accusing Freud of a bourgeois and patriarchal psychologism that confused the middle-class character with that of all humanity and, thereby, of thereby giving up 'the historical, that is to say, the social principle of explanation' (2010: 23). Fromm also put forward the idea of a revision of Freud's theory of the drives, in which the psychic structure of a person would be understood first and foremost by reference to the life-situation of that person rather than as the direct or sublimated product of the impulses themselves (2010: 46).

Horkheimer's rejection of the article is initially surprising, given his previous support for the interdisciplinary fusion of Marxian sociology and psychoanalysis that was the very basis of Fromm's position. Despite seeming to follow the logic of Marxian materialist analysis – based as it was on sociological and anthropological

---

true contribution to development of the 'Frankfurt School', and his role in the Institut's integration into the American academic establishment.

considerations that challenged the patently ethnocentric and biologically reductive aspects of Freud: the universality of the Oedipus complex and the psychosexual stages of libido development – Fromm's modification of Freud now drew accusations of 'revisionism' from Horkheimer, who had come to adopt a position in relation to Freud which closely echoed the position of Adorno. More and more intent on carrying out his long projected social-philosophical 'dialectics' work, Horkheimer was in the process of striking up an increasingly tight theoretical and personal relationship with Adorno, seeing in him an aggressiveness and a 'maliciously sharp eye for existing conditions' that he felt was lacking in Fromm (Horkheimer to Adorno, 8 December, 1936, in Wiggershaus 1994: 162). Horkheimer's move in this particular theoretical direction meant that Fromm was essentially surplus to requirements, and, therefore, a drain on finances which were certainly under some strain at the time. In addition to this, Horkheimer refused to publish the German worker study – the analysis of the questionnaires for which Fromm had been working through since 1935 (Funk 2000: 88). As the culmination of these developments, Fromm broke with the Institut in 1939, his departure depriving him of the funds, personnel and support that might have enabled the further development of his social-psychological research programme (whilst it has to be noted that such a development was perhaps an unlikely prospect, given Horkheimer's change of direction and refusal to publish the worker study, the Institut did return to interdisciplinary work in a series of empirical studies led by Adorno in the 1940s).

As it was, in 1941, two years after leaving the Institut, Fromm managed to secure publication of *Escape for Freedom*, a work which was in many respects the realization of the proposed psychological study of 'Man in the Authoritarian State' which had been listed as part of the research programme of the Institut prospectus of 1938 (Wiggershaus 1994: 272). Through this work, which consisted of a socio-historical and existential analysis of authoritarianism and conformism from the period between the Reformation to the present day, Fromm was to register on the American intellectual scene in a way that his Institut colleagues would not manage for two decades. On moving to New York, Fromm had made friends with thinkers such as Margaret Mead, Ruth Benedict, Edward Sapir, and the psychiatrist Harry Stack Sullivan, and was a regular attendee at Sullivan's Zodiac Club gatherings. *Escape from Freedom* received glowing reviews from Mead and people like Ashley Montagu, fitting in to the 'culture and personality' tradition that had grown up around Mead's studies and those of Benedict, Sapir, and Cora DuBois. Fromm's delineation of the idea of 'social character' developed here (the idea of a core character structure common to every group, class, or society), fitted alongside the idea of 'national character' developed in the accounts of the culture and personality authors and, in particular, to the idea of a 'basic personality structure' as developed by Ralph Linton and Abram Kardiner. Fromm's particular role in relation to sociology at this juncture was to help to bring depth-psychological insights to a tradition generally caught between grand systems theory on the one hand and abstract empiricism on the other (Mills 2000). *Escape from Freedom*, which is flawed as a historical sociological document but which was nevertheless a pioneering attempt to understand the historical interaction of emotional and characterological aspects as crucial elements in the social process, influenced thinkers such as Talcott Parsons and Robert Merton, who, much like Mannheim before them, attempted their own syntheses of social psychology and structuralism (McLaughlin 1998: 222). Parsons in particular made a concerted, if in fact somewhat limited, attempt to improve his account of the functioning of systems in this regard (Parsons 1950, 1964; and Parsons and Bale 1955). People like Gerth and Mills (1953) made an arguably more detailed attempt to carry this out, although, like Parsons and Merton, they generally opted for a more Freudian or Meadian version of psychology than the revised Freudian account that Fromm suggested in *Escape from Freedom* and in his next work *Man for Himself* (1947).

Fromm's popularity grew in the 1950s with the publication of *The Sane Society* (1955) and *The Art of Loving* (1956), the latter in particular becoming an international best-seller. Fromm's development of the notion of the 'marketing character' (which had first appeared in *Man for Himself*) and his critique of the affluent alienation of 1950s American market culture found resonance with other critics of social conformity, such as William H. Whyte, C.W. Mills, and Vance Packard. Whilst Fromm was increasingly reaching a wide public audience, and his reputation becoming cemented as a leading public intellectual, his work was also having a direct influence on later critical sociologists such as David Riesman, Robert Blauner, and Alvin Gouldner (McLaughlin 1998: 222–3). Fromm's popularity continued to grow over this period and into the 1960s where in *Marx's Concept of Man* (1961) he published what was at the time the most complete English-Language translation of Marx's *Economic and Philosophic Manuscripts of 1844*. During the 1960s Fromm was central to the growing radical movements that came to form the New Left, speaking to over sixty thousand people on a lecture tour of California in 1966 and taking on the role of speech writer in Eugene McCarthy's 1968 presidential campaign. In addition to this, Fromm was involved for a short period of time with the American Socialist Party-Social Democratic Federation (SP-SDF) and was a founding member of the influential anti-nuclear group SANE, a group which played a leading role in efforts at encouraging unilateral disarmament. In his recent biography of Fromm, Lawrence Friedman suggests that there is evidence that Fromm may in fact have influenced President Kennedy's June 1963 American University Commencement Address, a talk that was crucial in paving the way for disarmament talks between the Soviets and Americans (Friedman 2013: 210).

From the mid-1960s onwards, however, Fromm's appeal, both popular and academic, began to dwindle. By this time, the popularity of the culture and personality tradition had tailed off – Fromm in fact had been largely rejected by other culture and personality scholars since the late 1950s. Kardiner, who in particular disliked Fromm intensely, managed to disseminate, along with Ralph Linton, a negative view of Fromm's work through their well-attended culture and personality seminar at Columbia (McLaughlin 1998: 230). In addition to this – and despite being amongst the top 70 cited intellectuals in the social sciences between 1956–1965 (McLaughlin 1998: 244) – Fromm was increasingly seen as too unsystematic for mainstream sociology, which was embarking on a period of professionalization at the time. Fromm's ethical Marxian form of radical humanism was patently at odds with the sensibilities of most American sociologists, running up against the strict Weberian fact-value separation that had become one of the mainstays of social scientific thinking.

Ironically, at a time at which he was seen as too critical, too Marxian, by mainstream sociology, Fromm was increasingly opposed in radical circles by people like Sidney Hook and by his ex-Institut colleagues, particularly Adorno and Marcuse. These attacks centred on Fromm's apparent revisionist conformism – his stress on 'love' and 'humanism', and on practical steps to move towards the democratization of the political and economic spheres, essentially seen as the idealist and social democratic harmonising of social antagonisms. The critique of Fromm's positive, or 'identity' thinking provided by his ex-Institut colleagues, was simultaneously a criticism of Fromm's humanistic revisions of Freud. Marcuse, in particular, pursued this criticism in a very public spat with Fromm in *Dissent* magazine in 1955–1956 and in *Eros and Civilization*, accusing Fromm of 'the traditional devaluation of the sphere of material needs in favour of spiritual needs' (1966: 265). That these criticisms of Fromm do not hold up to rigorous analysis is not something I can go into here. Suffice it to say that Fromm's non-dogmatic flexibility and perceptiveness in his accounts of Marx and Freud – which, in fact, mirror the dominant interpretations of both thinkers today – meant that he was caught between two rigid, orthodox positions that were increasingly forced to assert themselves in the face of significant challenges to their authority at the time. Fromm's legacy naturally suffered as a result, the criticisms of Adorno and Marcuse being passed down and repeated by people like Russell Jacoby and Paul Robinson such that Fromm came to be superseded in popularity by Adorno and Marcuse and by a number of feminist, poststructuralist, and post-colonialist thinkers.

Studies in Social Character: Weimar Germany and a Mexican Village

In this section I want to focus on the previously discussed German workers study and on Fromm's subsequent study of a Mexican peasant village. As with his more well-known historical studies – *The Dogma of Christ* and, particularly *Escape from Freedom* – Fromm's empirical studies were also groundbreaking advances in sociological analysis. Like the more famous historical studies, the empirical studies sought to demonstrate the importance of emotional and characterological forces in social analysis, seeking to do so, however, through direct engagement with real, living individuals. But unlike the more well-known historical studies, these studies have received a lack of attention which is revealing in terms of making sense of Fromm's relative neglect and general exclusion from the sociological canon. Although it may be argued that it is Fromm's more well-known studies which ought be discussed here, it seems to me that focusing on these lesser-known empirical studies better enables the process of recovering the full relevance of his thinking for contemporary sociology.

The German workers study which Fromm led during the early period of
the Institut was published in German in 1980 as *Arbiter ind Angestellte am
Vorabend des Dritten Reiches. Eine sozialpsychologische Untersuchung* (it was
subsequently published in English as *The Working Class in Weimar Germany:
A Psychological and Sociological Study* in 1984). The study represents in
certain definite respects the continuation of a relatively short-lived period of
empirical sociological inquiry into the conditions and attitudes of German
workers before the outbreak of the First World War. In particular, it represents
the continuation of a study of the 'workers question' by Adolph Levenstein
in 1912 (Bonss 1984: 13). Levenstein's study, which was itself heavily
informed by an earlier working paper by Max Weber on the issues of surveying
workers in large-scale industry, was primarily concerned with the connection
between technology and the inner life of the workers, seeking to illicit data on
this connection through the implementation of a questionnaire consisting of
26 questions that probed on four particular themes: 1) the 'psychic relation'
to work and working conditions; 2) ideas on improvements of the material
situation; 3) the relationship to the 'social community'; and 4) attitudes to non-
occupational cultural and other problems (Bonss 1984: 13). Fromm's study
(which was largely carried out by Hilde Weiss) sought to develop Levenstein's
study, adding a level of psychological depth through use of an 'interpretive
questionnaire'. The questionnaire, which was distributed to 3,300 recipients,
consisted of a comprehensive open-ended list of 271 questions which would
collect data pertaining to 'the opinions, life-styles and attitudes of manual and
white collar workers', data which would then be analysed in accordance with
the basic psychoanalytic dictum that an individual's statement about his or
her thoughts and feelings cannot always be taken literally but must instead
be interpreted so as to try to unearth their deeper psychological motivation, in
order to illicit 'the relationship between the individual's emotional make-up
and his political opinions' (Fromm et al. 1984 [1980]: 42). In particular, the
study sought to determine 'the weight and reliability of political convictions'
amongst left-wing workers in relation to the rise of the Nazi Party (Fromm et
al. 1984 [1980]: 206).

Perhaps inevitably for such an exploratory exercise, there are some quite
considerable problems with the study: in addition to a flawed sampling strategy,
a response rate of only 33 percent (with only half of this number forming the
basis of the analysis) meant that as a picture of the attitudes and opinions of
the Weimar workforce it does not hold up as a representative account. Fromm's
stress on the fact they weren't trying to 'prove' certain hypotheses, admitting
that the material was 'both quantitatively and qualitatively much too sparse
to enable us to do this' (Fromm et al. 1984 [1980]: 42), only partly absolves
him here, for, as Richard Hamilton notes, Fromm at various points declared
the sample to be representative (Hamilton 1986: 83). As a result of this and
a number of other issues – the simplicity of the questions and the simplicity
of the cross-tabulations, amongst others – Hamilton questions the validity of

Fromm's contention that the study robustly demonstrated that it was only a small minority of the left-wingers who had deep anti-authoritarian convictions.

Whilst Hamilton's criticisms of the study are largely fair, there is a harshness and lack of charity to them at times that leads to his under-emphasis of the subtlety of Fromm's attempt to illicit unconscious material and of the overall significance of the project. For instance, whilst he is right to criticize Fromm's tendency to read his interpretation into the results with a conclusiveness which cannot always be justified, Hamilton overstates the occurrence of this phenomenon. As such, he downplays the more elementary point that the study did find empirical evidence in certain cases of the co-presence of conscious anti-authoritarian beliefs and apparently unconscious authoritarian convictions. In addition to this, from the point of view of the study itself, and of Fromm's overall social-psychological project, it seems clear that Fromm managed to find some evidence for what would later become his theory of social character and, thereby, for the idea of the much posited 'lag' that was reported to help explain the failed revolution of 1918–1919. By stressing the importance of judging it against the standards of today, then, Hamilton greatly underplays the significance of the study in the development of authoritarian studies and psycho-social analysis more generally. Fromm explicitly states in relation to the study that he was 'much more concerned with drawing the most appropriate theoretical conclusions from the evidence and with offering *a stimulus for new empirical and theoretical studies*' (Fromm et al. 1984: 42 – italics added). Taken on these terms, the study was unique, offering a level of critical depth in sociological analysis that had previously not been seen, and going some way to empirically validating Korsch's and Lukács's concerns over the simplistic standpoint of mechanical Marxism.

In the late 1950s Fromm started work on a follow-up to the German workers study, which would be published in 1970 under the title *Social Character in a Mexican Village: A Sociopsychoanalytic Study*. The work, which was co-authored by Michael Maccoby, was based on the fieldwork data gathered by a team of anthropologists and psychoanalysts between 1958–1963, in a village of 800 inhabitants near Cuernavaca, where Fromm had lived since 1956 (Fromm moved to Mexico City in 1950 due to the ill-health of his then wife). The stated aim of the study was 'the application of psychoanalytic categories to the study of social groups, by the minute examination of the personality of each member of the group, by the simultaneous and equally minute observation of all socio-economic data and cultural patterns, and, eventually, by the attempt to use refined statistical methods for the analysis of the data' (Fromm and Maccoby 1996 [1970]: 8). Vexed by criticism over the 'unempirical' nature of his theorizations in the field of social character, Fromm hoped the study would support his contention that specific social structures promote and are sustained by specific character types. As such, the preparatory work was more impressive than that of the German workers study. Unlike the workers study, the interpretative questionnaire in this case was administered to 95 percent of population. In addition to this, Rorschachs and Thematic Apperception Tests were administered to subjects drawn from the larger sample and the overall analysis was backed-up by a far greater level of collation and analysis of socioeconomic data and ethnographic material (the fact that there was a concerted effort to interact with the villagers over the course of a number of years was also significant).

In terms of substantive findings, the study sought to determine what happened to the peasant class (*campesino*) after the Mexican revolution in the 1920s. In particular, Fromm was interested in why it was that, despite being given land as a consequence of the revolution, levels of violence and alcoholism, for instance, rose among the campesinos. What the study purported to have found was the existence of three main village character types (based on Fromm's revised Freudian character typology) and their statistically significant correspondence to certain socioeconomic conditions: the *non-productive-receptive* character, corresponding with position of the landless day labourer; the *productive-hoarding* character, corresponding with the position of the free landowner; and *productive-exploitative* character, corresponding with the position of the new entrepreneur that had risen to prominence. The work here goes well beyond the workers study in terms of the psychoanalytical (as connected to a socio-economic) explanation for the analysis offered. Moreover, the study offers strong empirical support for the idea of social character as a 'character matrix' (i.e., a syndrome of character traits which has developed as an adaptation to the economic, social, and cultural conditions common to that group) – the particular social characters, as defined by Fromm and Maccoby, shown to be clearly correlated with economic activity (even down to the type of crops that were planted) and to cases of alcoholism. Fromm and Maccoby explain the differing fortunes of the respective social groups with reference to the idea of *social selection* through character adaptation to the objective conditions obtaining in the society, the idea being that 'those individuals whose character coincides with their class role tend to be more successful, provided that their class role objectivity allows the possibility of economic success', and that, therefore, 'when the economic situation of a class does not provide the basis for economic success ... only exceptional individuals whose character differs from the social character of their class can escape from a level of extreme poverty and dependence' (Fromm and Maccoby 1996 [1970]: 230). In the context of the study – although clearly potentially extendable beyond this context – Fromm and Maccoby show that an understanding of character can help us account for the increasing gap between richer and poorer villagers.

As with the workers study, there can be questions raised around the use of correlation, inference, and the level of 'proof' that the Mexican study provides. Perhaps the strongest criticism of both the village study and the earlier German workers study, however, pertains to the appropriateness of the methodological framework used. Given the nature of the material being sought (i.e., the dynamic and underlying dominant characters of the subjects under analysis) it could be argued, as Neil McLaughlin (2007) has done, that the studies might have been better conceived qualitatively, using in-depth open-ended interviews and offering a deeper ethnographic account than was the case. Interestingly, Michael Maccoby chose to move in this direction in his later studies into the character of managers of industrial companies in the United States (Maccoby 1976). Here Maccoby opts for a three-hour interview session through which he sought to determine the dominant character syndrome of each participant. He also sought to re-describe Fromm's character types in language that would appeal to the participants themselves, and not in the potentially condescending language that Fromm used. Other than Maccoby, and a few others who have worked with him and who knew Fromm in Mexico (Sonja Gojman and Salvador Millán, in particular), the kind of work pioneered in Fromm's Mexican study has more or less vanished without a trace. Fromm's increasing marginality, and the marginality of the culture and personality tradition itself, as well as the practical and financial demands of the nature of such interdisciplinary work, means that the study has become at worst completely forgotten and at best a relative curiosity at the very margins of the sociological tradition.

Conclusion

In any appraisal of the development of sociological thought over the past century or so, it seems clear that Fromm's psychoanalytic social psychology ought to be viewed as a genuinely pioneering contribution which has ultimately received insufficient attention. His attempt to bring about a fundamental rapprochement between psychology and sociology, effected through the melding of Marx and Freud, was innovative and exploratory, and played an important role in the development of German and American sociology – and of Marxian sociology more generally. But despite this, and despite his status as a leading intellectual figure in the middle-part of the last century, Fromm's work has largely come to languish on the forgotten margins of sociology – the result of personal, interpersonal, and cultural factors as much as the relative value, substance and promise of the work itself.

Looked at objectively and with an historical focus, it is clear that Fromm was at the vanguard of the social-psychological attempt to make sense of the social and historical forces that shape our individual and collective lives. His concept of social character was an attempt to reconcile the play of forces within the individual (elucidating the dividing line that separates the personal and the structural). Additionally, his introduction of the interpretative questionnaire to social-psychological inquiry opened up the ground for the empirical meeting of psychoanalysis and sociology which is being returned to today to a greater and greater extent. In terms of contemporary sociology, then, Fromm represents an example of how to bring psychological depth to sociological analysis and, thereby, to see emotional and characterological factors as contributory to a whole range of social phenomena. Although there are clearly potential problems with such an enterprise, to fail to try to understand the role of psychodynamic factors is to leave sociological analysis incomplete and potentially unsound at crucial points. Additionally, whilst culture and personality research has taken-off again in psychology, sociologists have been slow to return to it. This leaves much of sociological theory little better advanced in understanding these matters than it was during the middle-part of the twentieth century – an important development which goes some way to correcting this situation has, of course, been Bourdieu's concept of 'habitus' and its attempt to capture, at the individual level, the durable 'structuring of structure' (Bourdieu 1990: 53) characteristic of social groups and their dominant practices (it is noticeable, however, that the concept of habitus is developed by Bourdieu in relative disciplinary isolation, without explicit connection to psychology, as is the case in Fromm's account of social character). Returning to Fromm, therefore, offers the chance to deepen and broaden sociological thinking, to draw out the parallels and divergences between Fromm's social psychology and the perceptive sociology of Bourdieu, and to therefore more fully understand 'the laws that govern the life of the individual man, and the laws of society – that is, of men in their social existence' (2006: 5).

References

Adorno, Theodor, et al. 1982. *The Authoritarian Personality*. New York: W.W. Norton & Company.
Bernfeld, Siegfried. 1972. 'Psychoanalysis and Socialism', in Wilhelm Reich's *Dialectical Materialism and Psychoanalysis*. London: Socialist Reproduction.
Bonss, Wolfgang. 1984. 'Introduction' to *The Working Class in Weimar Germany: A Psychological and Sociological Study*. Cambridge, MA: Harvard University Press.
Bourdieu, Pierre. 1990. *The Logic of Practice*. Cambridge: Polity Press.
Durkin, Kieran. 2014. *The Radical Humanism of Erich Fromm*. New York: Palgrave Macmillan.
Friedman, Lawrence J. 2013. *The Lives of Erich Fromm. Loves Prophet*. New York: Colombia University Press.
Fromm, Erich. 1936. '*Sozialpsychologischer Teil*', in Max Horkheimer (ed.), *Studien über Autorität und Familie*. Paris: Felix Alcan.
Fromm, Erich. 1941. *Escape from Freedom*. New York: Farrar and Rinehart.
Fromm, Erich. 1947. *Man for Himself: An Inquiry into the Psychology of Ethics*. New York: Rinehart.
Fromm, Erich. 1955. *The Sane Society*. New York: Rinehart and Winston.
Fromm, Erich. 1956. *The Art of Loving: An Inquiry into the Nature of Love*. New York: Harper and Row.
Fromm, Erich. 1961. *Marx's Concept of Man*. New York: Continuum.
Fromm, Erich. 1966. *You Shall Be as Gods: A Radical Interpretation of the Old Testament and Its Traditions*. New York: Holt, Rinehart, and Winston.
Fromm, Erich. 1992 [1963]. *The Dogma of Christ and Other Essays on Religion, Psychology, and Culture*. New York: Henry Holt.
Fromm, Erich. 2006. *Beyond the Chains of Illusion: My Encounter with Marx and Freud*. London: Continuum.

Fromm, Erich. 2010. 'Man's Impulse Structure and Its Relation to Culture', in Rainer Funk (ed.), *Beyond Freud: From Individual to Social Psychology*. New York: American Mental Health Foundation.

Fromm, Erich and Michael Maccoby. 1996 [1970]. *Social Character in a Mexican Village: A Sociopsychoanalytic Study*. London: Transaction.

Fromm, Erich, et al. 1984 [1980]. *The Working Class in Weimar Germany: A Psychological and Sociological Study*. Cambridge, MA: Harvard University Press.

Funk, Rainer. 2000. *Erich Fromm: His Life and Ideas – An Illustrated Biography*. New York: Continuum.

Gerth, Hans and C. Wright Mills. 1953. *Character and Social Structure: The Psychology of Social Institutions*. London: Harcourt, Brace and World.

Hamilton, Richard. 1986. 'Review of Erich Fromm', *The Working Class in Weimar Germany*, *Society* 23(3).

Horkheimer, Max (ed.). 1936. *Studien über Autorität und Familie*. Paris: Felix Alcan.

Horkheimer, Max. 1989. 'The State of Contemporary Social Philosophy and the Tasks of an Institute for Social Research', in Stephen Eric Bronner and Douglas Kellner (eds), *Critical Theory and Society: A Reader*. London: Routledge.

Kessler, Michael and Rainer Funk (eds). 1992. *Erich Fromm und die Frankfurter Schule*. Tübingen: A. Francke Verlag.

Korsch, Karl. 1974. 'Fundamentals of Socialization', in Douglas Kellner (ed.), *Karl Korsch: Revolutionary Theory*. Austin: University of Texas Press.

Lukács, Georg. 1971. *History and Class Consciousness: Studies in Marxist Dialectics*. London: Merlin Press.

Maccoby, Michael. 1976. *The Gamesman. The New Corporate Leaders*. New York: Simon and Schuster.

McLaughlin, Neil. 1996. 'Nazism, Nationalism, and the Sociology of Emotions: Escape from Freedom Revisited', *Sociological Theory* 14(3).

McLaughlin, Neil. 1998. 'How to Become a Forgotten Intellectual: Intellectual Movements and the Rise and Fall of Erich Fromm', *Sociological Forum* 13(2).

McLaughlin, Neil. 1999. 'Origin Myths in the Social Sciences: Fromm, the Frankfurt School and the Emergence of Critical Theory', *Canadian Journal of Sociology* 24(1).

McLaughlin, Neil. 2007. 'Escape from Evidence? Popper, Social Science, and Psychoanalytic Social Theory', *Dialogue* XLVI.

Marcuse, Herbert. 1966. *Eros and Civilization: a Philosophical Inquiry into Freud*. Boston: Beacon Press.

Marx, Karl. 2000. 'The German Ideology', in David McLellan (ed.), *Karl Marx: Selected Writings*. Oxford: Oxford University Press.

Mills, C. Wright. 2000. *The Sociological Imagination*. Oxford: Oxford University Press.

Münch, Richard. 1994. *Sociological Theory. Volume 1: From the 1850s to the 1920s.* Chicago: Nelson-Hall Publishers.

Parsons, Talcott. 1950. 'Psychoanalysis and the Social Structure', *Psychoanalytic Quarterly*, June.

Parsons, Talcott. 1964. *Social Structure and Personality.* New York: The Free Press of Glencoe.

Parsons, Talcott and Robert F. Bales. 1955. *Family, Socialization and Interaction Process.* New York: The Free Press.

Reich, Wilhelm. 1972. *Dialectical Materialism and Psychoanalysis.* London: Socialist Reproduction.

Wheatland, Thomas. 2009. *The Frankfurt School in Exile.* Minneapolis and London: University of Minnesota Press.

Wiggershaus, Rolf. 1994. *The Frankfurt School: Its History, Theories and Political Significance.* Cambridge: Polity Press.

Chapter 5

From Literature to Sociology: The Shock of Celine's Literary Style and Viola Klein's Attempt to Understand It (With a Little Help from Karl Mannheim)

E. Stina Lyon

In his work on the history of sociology, *Between Literature and Science: The Rise of Sociology* (1988), Lepenies points to the lack of attention to the role of fiction as an important source of influence in the development of sociology. In the case of Viola Klein (1908–1973), the early experience of doing a sociologically informed linguistic study of a contemporary literary sensation – which aimed to provide a social commentary on the state of society in the wake of World War I – brought a lifelong attention to the significance of language in sociological argumentation. This paper presents a discussion of Klein's first, now forgotten, doctoral thesis on the literary style of the French novelist, Celine (Louis-Ferdinand Destouches) written at the University of Prague before her escape to Britain in 1938 (Klein 1936). Her second thesis, written under the supervision of Karl Mannheim at the London School of Economics and published as *The Feminine Character: History of an Ideology* (1946), is better known in the history of sociology. This thesis is now seen as one of the first attempts to apply Mannheim's conception of sociology of knowledge as a diagnostic tool in the analysis of a particular social issue – in Klein's case, that of the position of women in society – as a highly original critique of patriarchal constructions of knowledge.

Mannheim was not, however, her only source of intellectual influence. Her first thesis offers a textual analysis at the boundary between literary criticism, linguistics and the sociology of knowledge and culture. It throws light on her own intellectual journey during the 1930s, from literature, linguistics and philosophy to British empirical sociology, and also explains why she approached Mannheim for supervisory help. This was an ideologically turbulent decade across Europe with economic depression, political unrest, the rapid rise of fascism and anti-Semitism. Towards the end of the decade, a year after the completion of her thesis, Celine, a celebrated novelist and public intellectual, turned to virulent anti-Semitism and political support for German Nazi ideology. Klein, a Jewish woman journalist of left-wing persuasion, was at the same time forced to flee to Britain, leaving her parents behind in Czechoslovakia, both later to perish in concentration camps.

Klein brought to Britain a copy of her first dissertation, presently located in her archive at Reading University Library. But, there is no record of her referring to it again in her later works, nor has its content been discussed in other writings about her except as a curiosity (Sayers 1989; Deegan 1991; Kettler and Meja 1993). This dissertation became, for Klein, a case of self-imposed 'amnesia' about a work that started with high intellectual pretensions and ended in what can only be described as a failure to fully understand the complexity of her topic, a complexity which ultimately connects to the fate of her and her family. Nonetheless, one can trace its influence on her second thesis and her later commitment to a conceptually critical, non-typifying and empirically strong sociology – an approach that coloured all her later writings on women and made her a path breaker in the development of feminist sociological thought (Lyon 2007 and 2011).

After a brief summary of the biographical contexts of both Klein and her subject, Celine, the main part of the paper is devoted to a presentation of the structure and main content of her thesis and her attempt to combine a detailed linguistic analysis of Celine's use of speech and syntax with her own more general sociological analysis of the changing contexts of industrial mass society and its artistic and literary consequences as described by Celine. The paper will raise questions about how Klein's first dissertation, despite its theoretical weakness and failure to foresee the consequences of Celine's stylistic obsessions, nonetheless presents a powerful analysis of the syntactical tools and verbal tricks used in the populist language of Celine's fictional characters, a language later adopted in his still officially banned anti-Semitic writings. I outline what I consider to be the legacy of this work in terms of her relationship to Karl Mannheim and her second, sociologically more important, thesis on patriarchal ideology.

The Excitement and Tragedy of Celine

In choosing the language of Louis-Ferdinand Celine (1882–1961) as the topic for her thesis, Klein took on what has become one of the literarily and morally most controversial public intellectuals of the 20th century. Her choice was prescient of his continuing fame as a novelist, though not of his later notoriety as a ferocious proponent of anti-Semitism and a collaborator during the German occupation of France (Hewitt 1999; Jackson 2001; Callil 2006). There were many reasons why a progressive and politically engaged woman, knowledgeable in French, linguistics, Marxism and psychoanalysis, would have been intrigued about and attracted to his first novel, *Journey into the End of the Night*. Published in 1932, it was an acclaimed international success, especially amongst the socialist and communist left who saw the book as expressing Marxist and anarchist sympathies for a struggling proletariat. The book caused a literary furore because of its use of crude and offensive popular speech in vivid dialogue and descriptions of the misery, violence and abuse of power that characterized life during and after the First World War: on the battlefield, in factories, in hospitals, in domestic and sexual relations. In describing the adventures of the book's anti-hero, Bardamu, Celine drew on his own experiences as a young man in France during and after the First World War and on his travels across Europe, USA, and colonial Africa. Celine was a decorated soldier and a doctor of social medicine practising amongst the poor. For a brief period he held a Rockefeller grant in the US for medical research, and worked for the League of Nations (Hewitt 1999).

The first publication that stirred his literary talent and broke the frames of formal linguistic conventions was his medical thesis, a short biography of the Hungarian physician Philippe-Ignace Semmelweis (Celine 1952). An obstetrician in 19th century Vienna, Semmelweis discovered the cause of puerperal fever. His conclusion that women were infected by medical students, arriving fresh from the dissection of cadavers, led him to the simple recommendation of hand washing with disinfectant before assisting in child birth, advice rejected at the time by his medical superiors. Semmelweis was never given the recognition he deserved for his work, and his fate, alongside that of the infected women, became an illustration for Celine of the impossible obstacles of human indifference and cruelty that stood in the way of individuals seeking to ameliorate their effects. This became a recurrent theme in his novels. His first novel, largely pacifist in orientation and often highly humorous, gave no direct indication of his later dramatic shift to the anti-Semitic far right. The same year Klein passed her thesis, the first of Celine's violently anti- Semitic 'pamphlets' was published and widely disseminated. During the Vichy regime, he counted as his friends its most anti-Semitic supporters of National Socialist expulsion of French Jews to extermination camps (Calill 2006). After release from imprisonment in Denmark, he continued to work in France as a doctor of social medicine after the war. The refusal in France in 2011 officially to honour Celine on the half century of his death has more recently added to the continuing controversy about him and his work (Alliot 2012).

Thesis Work in Times of Conflict

Born in Vienna, Klein moved as a child with her family to Bohemia, then in Czechoslovakia. Having originally enrolled as an undergraduate at Vienna University in 1929, student violence kept her from attending and she instead spent a year at the Sorbonne in Paris before continuing her studies in Prague. Here she studied modern languages and philosophy. She worked as a teacher and journal editor before enrolling as a doctoral student in the Faculty of Philosophy at what was at the time the German University of Prague (now Charles University) in 1934. As part of her completion of the doctoral degree she sat two 'rigorous exams' in *Romanische Philologie* and *Deutsche Volkskunde* and a further one in Philosophy. She had her doctoral *Promotion* in March 1937. Her supervisors were Erhard Preissig (1889–1945), Professor of Roman Archeology and Epigraphics, and Friedrich Slotty (1881–1963), Professor of Comparative Indogermanic Linguistics. Both professors were of German origin and known in their field, but of

very different political persuasion. Preissig's earlier publications were on French
literature and language as 'thoughts of a people' (*Volkergedanke*). He was later
allowed to remain in post during the Nazi occupation. During the war he published
a book on pre-war French cultural 'propaganda' in Czechoslovakia (Preussig
1943), a work that systematically outlines the destructive presence of French
intellectual culture in Czech universities. It is particularly critical of concepts
derived from the French enlightenment such as universalism, human rights,
individualism, reason and rationality, at the time ideologically associated with the
'dangers' of Jewish cosmopolitanism. *Mitteleuropa* was then, as now, a contested
cultural domain, especially with respect to the position of minority groups across
the region, including both Jews and German speaking minorities (Vidmar-Horvat
and Delanty 2008). Slotty's publications, on the other hand, were technical studies
of the grammar and syntax of ancient languages. During the Weimar Republic
he was an active member of the Deutsche Democratische Partei and publically
opposed Hitler and the growth of National Socialism up till and on the occasion
of the invasion of Sudetenland in 1938. As a result he was immediately deprived
of his post and the right to publish. The tension between the two halves of her
thesis, between on the one hand generalizing national-historical and sociological
explanations of the context and location of a cultural *Zeitgeist*, and on the other
the logical, factual and critical details of the linguistic constructions and means of
expression of a particular creative individual, reflect these contradictions.

The Structure and Content of the Thesis

Klein structured the submitted version of her dissertation on Celine into two main
parts.[1] The introductory third of her 109 page thesis is devoted to the general social
and historical context of Celine's writings, the *Zeitgeist* of rapid industrialization
and total war. Here she cited her indebtedness to Mannheim's then recent book
Mensch und Gesellschaft im Zeitalter des Umbaus (1935), published the same year
Mannheim was forced, as a Jew, to relinquish his post as professor in Frankfurt.
In the second section, she offered a detailed linguistic analysis of Celine's use of
speech and syntax, quoting un-translated extracts from his first novel as evidence
of the ways in which his language could be seen to typify this new *Zeitgeist*.
Her list of references is brief and multidisciplinary, but, as was customary at the
time, she seldom referred to the sources in detail in the text. It includes a few

---

1   In the following sections, the translations both of Klein's German and Celine's
French are my own. My attempt to turn both of their writings into clear and readable
English is inevitably an 'interpretation' by myself as the 'author'. In undertaking the task of
trying to give a précis of her thesis, I have tried to stay as close to the original as possible.
There are many German concepts in this which themselves ask for a lengthy analysis as to
their meaning, such as *Zeitgeist* and *Volk*, but I have avoided the attempt to engage with this
in favour of a more immediate understanding of Klein's arguments.

texts in linguistics, amongst them Ferdinand de Saussure's posthumous *Cours de Linguistique General* (1922), a literary analysis of Emile Zola's novel *L'Oeuvre*, a philosophical text by Martin Heidegger and a text by the German art historian Wilhelm Pinder, a conservative nationalist whose writings on generational cultural shifts in European art history Mannheim saw as one of the departures for his own sociology of culture (Mannheim 1940: 41).

In introducing her topic, Klein made a biblical reference. In the beginning was 'the word', she wrote, and words have changed worlds, caused spiritual revolutions and affected the happiness and unhappiness of humanity. Words may have the power profoundly to affect human realities, but they are also the mental products of those same realities. Language, she argued with Saussure, is at the same time a living actuality, a *parole*, and a product of the past, a *langue*. For the writer, language is at the same time a tool box to be practically used and manipulated, and an expression of public consciousness, thus making the author both an individual artist and the voice of a particular concrete world in a specific historical situation. Language is both individual and social, and this paradoxical ambiguity is similar to that of sociological understandings of the individual in society. Thought, in both form and substance, changes with the situation it finds itself in, and with the social function it fulfils. With Mannheim she argued that major social change, such as had dominated Europe since the beginning of industrialization and modernity, had affected and changed cultural expressions, thought and understandings, without individuals knowing why. A writer like Celine, to be understood, must be seen both as a creative individual and as a mouthpiece of his time.

Celine in Social Context

What is this time, she asked, for which Celine and his linguistic style is the symbolic expression? Her answer comes first through an example from his novel *Journey into the Night*. Celine symbolized the epoch in which he writes through a vivid description of the young Bardamu's youthful experience of the Paris Exposition of 1900, one of mass humanity and brutality, '– of thousands of huddled feet in queues and trampling up escalators, all in awe in front of a gallery of machines in a glass cathedral, all fearful and stunned … of catastrophes in suspense. Modern life begins' (Klein 1936: 5. See also Celine 1989: 80–82 for full section in later English translation). The crisis of our time is one of machine idolization, argued Klein, and the accompanying spiritual crisis could be traced back to the simultaneity of contradictory elements: enormous technical and industrial progress without commensurate developments in the power and heart of human understanding. She described this discrepancy using Pinder's notion of the simultaneous presence of 'contemporaneity and the non-contemporaneous'. She illustrated this with a further analogy, this time one provided by Mannheim, of the technology of carpet bombing used to destroy a town of innocent civilians. The revaluation of values, a slow and socially uneven process, had fallen out of step with cataclysmic technological change. A form of thought that may once have been progressive emerges as counterproductive to societal well being. Her final literary analogy was taken from the satirist Karl Kraus: 'We are running a world transport system on narrow-gauge brain tracks' (Klein 1936: 7. This quote is taken from Kraus 1922: 7). The analysis of such change, she argued, required both detailed knowledge of the objective contexts of industrialization, political democratization, capitalism, and war but also of individual perceptions and their outcome in art and the written word. With Mannheim she came to see the heart of the social analytical enterprise as a diagnostic one, a study of knowledge and culture to be undertaken by a culturally informed and ideologically detached elite capable of dissecting the underlying factors affecting social understandings and expressing them in more socially informed and logically coherent ways. In her attempt empirically to apply such a theoretical framework to a complex author like Celine, she encountered many of the unresolved difficulties inherent in the sociology of knowledge and ideas and the ultimate disappointment of failing to foresee their consequences.

Klein did not write in terms of the turbulent party politics of the time. Hers instead was a passionate plea for greater intellectual understanding of the consequences of the 'machine age', drawing ultimately on Marx's concern for the fate of the growing proletariat. Modern production methods and their required centralization and detailed regimentation of work and planning, even of education, culture and the press, she argued, had left the lower middle classes of artisans, small traders and petty government officials in a permanent struggle, not just for an independent economic existence, but also for their particular forms of rational thought. This was the class into which Celine was born and whose lives he described. Her sympathy was probably enhanced by the fact that this was also a class whose hardships she knew from her childhood in Vienna and Bohemia. Fuelled by war, depression and unemployment, enmity against industrial rationalization had grown and become converted to hatred against all things associated with the elite and their hypocritical promulgation of an ideology of progress, ineffective politicians offering no social protection, and a rarefied culture inaccessible to the masses. The human propensity for irrationality, brought to public awareness by Freud, and previously reined in by religious doctrine and faith, had now turned to sport idolization, machine prowess, competition mania, and new modes of more emotional, populist linguistic expressions, as exemplified in Celine's crude literary style. It should be noted that when Klein wrote this the preparations for the 1936 Berlin Olympics and the 1937 International Paris Exposition were in full swing.

This 'double sidedness' between technical rationality and fanaticism had not so far, she argued, been as politically catastrophic in France as in countries overrun by mass totalitarian regimes, due largely to a longstanding French tradition of reason and rationality. This differed from the romanticism and mysticism characteristic of the 'Kleinburgertum' elsewhere in Europe. In so arguing, she anticipated later and ongoing debates about French 'immunity' in the politically turbulent decades preceding the Second World War (Kennedy 2008). At the time, however, this set of assumptions about 'rational' French resistance to fascism no doubt contributed to her benign assumptions about Celine's moral distance from his 'irrational' proletarian characters. It is noteworthy, that she offered no reflections on the growth of French anti-Semitism as an increasingly 'respectable' ideological response, both for the left and the right, and its expression in the thoughts and words of Celine's characters (Irvine 2008). It was an anxious time to be a Jew in a German speaking environment.

Celine's Language and Literary Style

Having briefly diagnosed the distinctiveness of Celine's social and cultural time, in the second and main part of her thesis, Klein turned to the question of what she saw as distinctive about Celine's literary style, and its capacity to shock and engage. Her linguistic skills came to the fore in a detailed analysis of Celine's use of popular speech (*Volksprache*) and the subtle ways in which his literary characters, drawn from 'an uneducated class', as Klein described them, get their meaning across through various creative but extra-grammatical linguistic means. Using such 'popular' spoken language to create his own individual literary style, Celine, she argued, aimed to contribute to the cultural and social revolution of his time. The power of his style to enrol the attention and sympathies of the reader, whilst at the same time shocking the literary sensibilities of the educated elite, had many elements: the use of loose and open-ended sentence constructions, the use of contrast to intensify expressions, repetitive emphasis, irony, satire, tricks of over emphasis and simplistically typecast characters and lives. She offered numerous detailed examples from his work, quoted in the original French, interspersing them with her own thoughts on the novelist and his motivations. Repeatedly she returned to the question of how to distance the author from his hero. One literary advantage of using *Volksprache*, she argued, is that despite using the 'I' form, the author almost never steps forward and it does not occur to the reader to identify him (Celine) with the narrator (Bardamu). Celine uses the mouth of *all* his many characters to describe his own varied life, love and travel experiences, thereby enhancing their colourful vividness, yet stands himself invisibly in the background. This 'distancing' is experienced through ironic nuances in the presentation of the main character. She makes a comparison with Chaplin's film *Modern Times,* released in 1936, in which Chaplin engages the audience by 'ironisizing' the many sufferings of his anti-hero through the means of situation comedy. Celine, she argued, does so through the ironic use of speech and with equal comic, yet powerful, effect shows the frustrations and dissolutions of a 'little man' in a false and brutal world beyond his control.

But forms of more 'sociological thinking' also entered into her linguistic analysis. Stylistically, argued Klein, Celine's resigned irony in the face of a sense of powerlessness in a collapsing world order is expressed through exaggerated extrapolation of absurd individual experiences into universal ones. Subjective and banal everyday judgements are, with ironic undertones, given the status and appearance of well established facts and causal relations. Klein referred to such verbal expressions as those of 'pseudo causality', by which she meant a kind of casual everyday 'wisdom' about what explains persons and events in the world, and which, if repeated often enough, became accepted as true social descriptions. Celine's frequent use of the impersonal French *on*, an all embracing totality and a depersonalization of personal experience, expressed, she argued, the tendency of ordinary persons to escape anxiety by generalizing their own experiences into what appears to be universally valid truths To give but one small example from her dissertation: Celine's use of an everyday expression such as: 'the streets are empty because of the heat', as expressed in conversation, can be read as a factual description of empty streets and the nature of the weather, but also, more sarcastically, of Parisians not at work in the summer, and thus also as a pseudo causal explanations and rationalization of why not, presented as fact (Klein 1936: 48). A highly personal picture thus becomes presented as if it were *the* picture of human motives, presented under the stylistic mask of irony, which for Klein was a clear sign of Celine's own literary distance, at least until she read his second novel and began to have doubts. The effect on the reader of the heavy use of such typifying generalizations, Klein argued, is seductive in the way that it creates a sense of fatalism, or 'resigned' determinism in a world where no one can escape their fate. Celine's characters have become imprisoned and determined both by their own muddled and contradictory minds and by the miserable proletarian environment in which they find themselves. Through the transition from a more specific *nous* and *vous* to the generalized *on* the reader is brought into a community in which what counts as truth for the teller also includes the reader in a shared language. Here Klein saw the problem of 'the simple man' as one of not having been given the linguistic means to express particular and complex feelings, but instead having to rely on general descriptions of human anxiety, insecurity and vanity. Her repeated references to Celine's 'ordinary characters', including Bardamu, as 'the uneducated', point to her own tendency to separate 'them' from 'us'. This leaves both Klein, and the well educated Celine, creator of the words, as reflecting thinkers positioned 'outside' the scene, yet, it is Celine's own experiences that are described. Not once in the thesis does she offer a linguistic experience or encounter of her own, either as a woman or a Jew, subjectivities she would have felt inappropriate for a research thesis.

Alongside the use of *Volksprache,* Klein described Celine's style as one characterized by the use of 'free indirect speech' (*erlebte Rede*), a concept she took from the work of the linguist E. Lorck (1921). This describes impressionistic writing using a stream of consciousness of third person narration alongside first-person direct speech. Klein showed in detail how Celine consistently makes public the content of subjective deliberations to give his readers an experience that is as alive as that experienced by the author and his characters as it happened. The speech is of the moment, unedited, incomplete and loose ended. Thus, a mixture of voices are presented without clear contours, yet offering an atmospheric whole. Such a style, she argued, does not reflect a logical thought process, but only a mixture of emotion, interpretation and commentary. Whereas Proust used an impressionistic style to express the mental differentiations and emotional sensibilities of the intellectual, she argued, Celine's impressionist use of language is 'folksy' and represents a different social stratum with a fundamentally different world view, incoherent thought, and a totally different language in which to express it. The muddled thoughts of the 'simple man' give Celine the excuse for a frequent use of drastic juxtapositions in which there are only 'rich and poor', 'humans and animals', 'leaders and followers'. This is also exemplified in the 'bagatellizing' of dramatic contrasts between ordinary situations and horrendous experiences, as when the blood from a severed head is compared to an overflowing pot of jam, or burning villages during the war to fireworks on a jolly festival night. The 'simple man' cannot make a big fuss about his feelings, but sticks to irrelevances, and Celine, she argued, makes of this emotional primitiveness an artistic style.

Finally, Klein richly exemplified Celine's use of grammatical manipulation for emotional effect. To mention only a few: expressions and explanations suddenly withdrawn for an opposite afterthought; the second part of a sentence used as a commentary on the first; rich use of supplementary brackets and sub-clauses to fill in previous omissions; expressive use of double negatives; onomatopoetic summary lists of objects and adjectives; overemphasis of particular pronouns; loosely connected memories appearing in an associative manner creating a sense of unbalanced restlessness; making verbs passive or excluding them altogether. Such linguistic restlessness she saw as a valid expression of the high speed modernity of the time, expressing human fates out of control. She referred to Karl Kraus when she argued that 'style' is not the 'what' but the 'how' of seeing. She also here made a brief socio-cultural comparison with artistic culture in Germany when she argued, presciently as it turned out, that Celine's style was a break away from an old French tradition of logical clarity in favour of a more Germanic style of emotional literary expression. In retrospect it is surprising, though politically understandable, that she offered no discussion of the contemporary French and German artistic styles of expressionism and surrealism, styles closer to that of Celine than her frequent comparative references to impressionism and Proust, but also at the centre of the national-socialist charge of 'degeneracy' at the time (Johnson and Johnson 1987).

Behind the Mask of Celine the Intellectual

Celine's second novel, *Death on Credit* (1936), published in the final year of Klein's thesis preparation, received only a brief mention in her thesis. It was recommended to Klein by Celine himself, but did not quite 'fit' with her earlier arguments. In this novel, Celine gives the main character his own name, Ferdinand, and the story is told as auto-biographical memory. Klein observed a change of style here towards greater brutalism and unrealistic exaggerated fantasy in the description of the down trodden masses and the experiences of Ferdinand growing up amongst them. She quoted from a public speech given by Celine in 1933, at an event honouring Zola, in which he described the world as stuck in an incurable war psychosis, a collective death wish for destruction with all political parties, liberals,

Marxists, and fascists offering only one solution – more soldiers and war. With the old literary realism of Zola no longer convincing only symbols and dreams remain. She noted how the heavy use of popular speech mannerisms in this second novel was even more emotional, underpinned by an even greater use of three full stops delineating unfinished sentences. His linguistic style had become as recognizable as that of impressionists like Manet or Renoir, a comparison she felt confirmed her initial proposition of a particular literary 'style': the artistic expression of a particular, socially located, mind revealed in a particular form in accordance with patterns of social change, and articulated as a contribution to such change.

But Celine's second novel must also, alongside his letters to her, have given an indication of the difficulties inherent in drawing inferences from a particular personal literary style to the psychology, political motivations and class alignment of its creator. Klein sought help with some of her questions by writing directly to Celine. His four replies, dated between May and October 1936, are included as an appendix to the thesis. The first two of his replies are gallant: he is 'absolutely (totally) flattered that my work could be the object of your thesis' and 'completely at your disposal in giving all the desired information' (Klein 1936: 106). But he warns her that he feels incapable of reasoning about literature and has a natural hatred of all commentary. 'I execute or I keep quiet.' He offers to send her a revised version of his medical thesis, which, he tells her, will help explain his style. This would have her reference to it in the thesis, but also points to his continued identification with the victimhood of Semmelweiss. Celine, who had many women friends across Europe, encourages her to seek out his friend in Prague, the psychoanalyst Anny Reich (the ex-wife of Wilhelm Reich and a member of the Vienna Psychoanalytic Society). Later in July, a further letter charmingly, but rather patronizingly, addresses Klein as 'Cher Demoiselle' and invites her to Paris for a 'personal conversation', offering her hospitality in his home 'if that would suit her better'. In August he replied more fully, but in a much angrier tone. Today more is known about Celine's tempestuous personality, but these were not the kind of answers Klein might have expected, given her assumptions about Celine as an admired novelist and a committed doctor to the poor. Celine had by now been exposed to a very critical reception of his second novel, both from the intellectual left who saw it as a demeaning attack on the proletariat, and the intellectual traditionalist right, who saw its style as an insult to French culture. He now rants in a style similar to that of his books. On his manner of working he explains that he 'knows nothing of literature but likes to make his page sing like Chopin on his piano ... he is a *failed* poet who only does what he can ... . He has never read Joyce ... is only interested in emotional expressions ... singing ... the organic ... he finds such "aimless meandering", like those of Proust, repulsive, and would really like to write popular songs' (Klein 1936: 107). He proclaims himself 'fundamentally, absolutely, radically an *anarchist* ... one must strangle all leaders ... *All that which commands* is *ipso facto* rotten, harmful, criminal, repugnant, only worthy of death ... Language is a whore, she enjoys being raped, caresses leave her cold'. In the final letter he simply states: '*I do not know ... I have a* profession in medicine and earned my living ... Poetic impulses? I do not know. It is indecent to speak of such things. These are things one must never say, nor write. All that is shameless and disgusting ... Here is my advice ... Men and especially writers do not behave as modestly as they should' (Klein 1936: 108).

We now know that, having exposed in his novels the horror of capitalism, imperialism, militarism and, after a visit to Stalin's Russia, communism, he was now in the process of embracing virulent anti-Semitism and about to publish his first propagandistic pamphlets. Celine's fictional characters, awful as they are with words, but to whom the reader is invariably drawn, provided the tools, on which Celine sharpened his pamphleteering style in the defence of an ideology with already visible murderous effects. 'Klein' was one of the Jewish names on the long lists of such names he assembled to support his attack on them, and Proust and Joyce figured prominently as examples of 'degenerative' Jewish influence on 'genuine' French popular culture and art (Celine 1937).

A Failure of Interpretation?

Klein's attempts to socially contextualize and explain Celine and his literary style were more complex than she appreciated at the time. A more contemporary psychoanalytical approach to the work of Celine concludes that there is no valid way of making inferences from his literary writings to his motivations and personality. Such interpretations invariably become as much a reflection of the analyst as an account of the mind of Celine (Coen 1982). Klein attributed to Celine a detached 'intellectual wisdom', of being like 'us', like her, like Zola, or Chaplin or even Mannheim: educated and cultured individuals with reason and logic and a demand for accuracy of judgement behind them. But the occasional expressions of anti-Semitism and racism Celine puts in the mouths of his proletarian characters were also at the time deeply embedded in him and in French elite culture generally (Irvine 2008). Her simplistic sociological assumptions about the cultural uniformity of class, and her view of Celine as a 'detached' intellectual using populist language to elicit sympathy for the underclass, were plainly wrong. She may have seen Celine's fictional character of Bardarmu as the mouth piece for the 'little man', as in Chaplin's film *Modern Times* (1936), but Celine the author was not as detached as Klein assumed. So why, in the light of all this should Klein's first thesis not remain forgotten? Even if in one respect this thesis was a failure, there are reasons to conclude that her analysis of the social contexts and manipulative uses of language in the creation of prejudice, cynicism and hatred is as relevant today as it appeared to her when after the tragedy of World War II she was faced with writing a second dissertation to compensate for her unmentionable first.

A brief read of Celine's anti-Semitic language shows Klein's insights. Celine's three notorious anti-Semitic texts remain banned in France. The first, *Bagatelles pour un massacre* (*Trifles for a massacre*) (1936), has been translated into English and is available on the net. In this, the stylistic techniques used by Celine in the process of directly engaging the reader in his narrative, so carefully analysed by Klein, are brought to the fore with even greater power and intensity than in his first novels. Celine here expresses his own views, using his distinct literary style so carefully dissected by Klein. His breathless style, including what she calls 'energy saving' grammatical devices that force the reader to fill in missing bits, thus becoming sucked in as a co-creator of the meaning of the text, leaves the reader no time to think about content, or step back for any kind of critical detachment. Through the use of imagined intimate conversational dialogue between the author and various friends, emotive and verbally rich descriptions, sudden dislocating shifts of tone and even more rapid ad hoc pseudo-causal connections, the reader is purposefully led down narrow allies and dark basements of anxiety and hatred, but also into a seductive sense of identification. He does not tell us what to think, but through engagement with this rapid and loose ended narrative we become sucked into a particular kind of pseudo-experiential knowledge. Which is subjective or objective, which experiences belong to author, or are just fictitious inventions based on rumours assumed to be shared by the reader? Celine does not distinguish. From a starting position of expressing his own hatred of critics, publishers and literary agents for turning against his work, Celine rapidly, and repeatedly, moves to an identification of all his personal opponents as Jews or sympathetic to Jews. He then turns these enemies into a fictitious homogenous universal group, ever present and always in control, particularly where there are communists, capitalists, freemasons or militarists responsible for revolutions and wars against the common people. He is the only one courageous to stand up to their conspiracy. With ad hoc lists of random names and organizations, selective quotes and totally dubious statistics from popular publications and newspapers, including clearly misrepresented Jewish ones, and fictitious ones like the *Elders of Zion*, the writing gives the air of being respectably historically and sociologically 'factual' rather than the rants of a fictitious character in a proletarian novel. His irony and sarcasms are no longer 'detached', but used as propaganda in what, today, can only be described as incitement to hatred.

The Importance of Words: The Making of a Critical Sociologist

In one of her first letters to Mannheim after gaining her refugee scholarship, Klein self-effacingly 'confesses' that she has not yet done 'any preparatory studies worth mentioning' (VKA 16.9.41, Lyon 2011). But her proposed problem formulation on the issue of women's emancipation in democratic post-war 'reconstruction' brings to mind ideas discussed in her first thesis and borrowed from her earlier readings. She points to a culture and a reality out of joint, for which she gives the example of the political and psychological attraction of the 'back to hearth' policies of the German National Socialist Party, and its simultaneous failure to implement such reactionary principles in practice, given industrial demands for labour. In a democratic future based on the ideals of liberty and equality such contradictions need to be addressed, she argued, with studies about what values to preserve and what changes are necessary to facilitate the adoption of these democratic ideals.

But half a year later her tone in addressing Mannheim is less anxious to please, and her topic gained a sharper focus. She now wrote that what people think of as typical female characteristics are not based on factual observations, but on prejudice and ideology. She aims to prove that the 'scientific attitude' is 'not less than any other way of regarding experience subject to the influence of surrounding culture and or personal bias' (VKA 30.5.42). Klein already knew the difficulties in trying to understand the linguistic, and illogical, means by which a fictional character like Bardamu articulated his prejudices, and the even greater difficulties in trying to discern where a respected author like Celine drew a line between the ill-informed prejudices of his characters and his own views. The task she was now setting herself was to expose how well-known seemingly rational social scientists in pursuit of *the* scientific truth about women, fell into similar prejudicial, typifying and poorly evidenced pseudo causal traps, with little critical self-awareness of their very damaging effect on individual women's search for equality and freedom.

She pursued this task in a critical, at times literary and journalistic, style that owed less to Mannheim than to her own earlier intellectual trajectory. When he sent her long and highly eclectic literature lists, or suggested she do major overviews of literature on women's cultural and social change and their psychological consequences, she was grateful, but stuck to her own search for critical clarity. After a broad general sociological introduction on the changing position of women, she focused on a series of specific authors, amongst them Freud, Haverlock Ellis, the Vaertlings and Otto Weiniger (not only patriarchal in his categorizations, but also anti-Semitic), whose works she meticulously criticized with respect to conceptual, theoretical and logical inconsistencies, weak methodological strategies, poor empirical accuracy and doubtful validity of findings, spurious and tendentious descriptive and pseudo causal generalizations, lack of regard for comparative counter evidence, and assumptions about 'ideal type' norms (Klein 1946). In the first edition of the book she included an analysis of a 'generational' novel about women as evidence of the reflection of social change in literature (Klein 1946). Such biased assumptions can, she believed, only be explained by the pervasive patriarchal ideology based on conceptually simplistic binary contrasts seductive to an audience in search of false certainties. In the introduction to the book version of her thesis she was anxious to dispel the notion that such critical contextualizing of scientific writings was an expression of relativism, or a belief that 'objectivity' in the social sciences was not possible, only that it required a lot more self-criticism of one's own perspective than she observed with respect to these 'scientists' of women (Klein 1946).

But when, towards the end of her supervisory period, Mannheim suggested that she include a comparison between women and intellectuals in her thesis, she forcefully pointed out that too close a comparison between free-floating intellectuals, women and minority groups was unwarranted. Her reply to Mannheim, as conclusion to this story of an intellectual journey, is worth quoting in its entirety. It gives us some insight into the hard lessons that she had learned whilst working with, and on, 'free floating intellectuals' and literary wordsmiths during one of the most cruel periods of recent European history and how the experience had sharpened her sociological understandings:

> With regard to the "freischwebende Intelligenz" it does not seem to me to fall into the same category as those marginal groups I mentioned. It is characteristic of the intelligentsia to be socially unattached – while all those types I mentioned are characterized not by detachment, but by *dual* loyalty; both to their own, subordinate group and to the prevailing standards of the dominant group. The intelligentsia does, moreover, not share the two essential characteristics common to women, Jews, foreigners, Negros, etc.: they have not got that sense of solidarity and unity which, for want of a better expression I called "collective consciousness"; they have, on the contrary, a very marked "Sinn fur den Wert der Eigenpersonlichkeit", and are not subject to inferiority feelings and compensatory mechanisms as intellectuals. A Jew, qua Jew, a woman qua woman, a Negro as a Negro, feel inferior; but I do not believe that even in Nazi Germany with its proclaimed contempt of the intellect, an intellectual will ever on that account feel inferior. The marginal position may in many cases contribute to make a person an intellectual; the constant shifting of perspectives will heighten his critical judgement and increase sensitivity. But the intelligentsia, as a group, does not share the characteristics of the other "marginal" groups mentioned in my chapter and I do not think I can include it, except, if you think right, in a footnote, emphasizing the differences between this and the other unstable groups (VKA, letter to Mannheim, 25.4.1944).

References

Alliot, D. 2012. 'Presence Celinienne', *Special Celine* 4: 5–8.
Callil, C. 2006. *Bad Faith: A Forgotten History of Family and Fatherland.* London: Jonathan Cape.
Celine, L.-F. [1924] 1952. *Philippe-Ignace Semmelweis.* Paris: Gallimar.
Celine, L.-F. [1932] 1977. *Journey into the End of the Night.* London: John Calder Publishers Ltd.
Celine, L.-F. [1936] 1989. *Death on Credit.* London: John Calder Publishers Ltd.
Celine, L.-F. [1936] 1937. *Bagatelles pour un massacre* (anonymously translated as *Trifles for a Massacre*, available on the net as .pdf).
Coen, S. 1982. 'Louis-Ferdinand Celine's Castle: The Author–Reader Relationship in its Narrative Style', *American Imago* 39: 343–68.
Deegan, M. (ed). 1991. *Women in Sociology: A Bio-biographical Sourcebook.* New York: Greenwood Press.

Jackson, J. 2001. *France: The Dark Years 1940–1944*. Oxford: Oxford University Press.

Hewitt, N. 1987. *The Golden Age of Louis-Ferdinand Celine*. Leamington Spa: Berg Publishers Ltd.

Hewitt, N. 1999. *The Life of Celine: A Critical Biography*. Oxford: Blackwell Publishers.

Irvin, W. 2008. 'Beyond Left and Right, and the Politics of the Third Republic: A Conversation', *Historical Reflections/Reflexions Historique* 34(2): 133–46.

Johnson, D. and M. Johnson. 1987. *The Age of Illusion: Art and Politics in France 1918–1940*. New York: Rizzoli International Publications, Inc.

Kennedy, S. 2008. 'The End of Immunity? Recent Work on the Far Right in Interwar France', *Historical Reflections/Reflexions Historique* 34(2): 25–45.

Kettler, D. and V. Meja. 1993. 'Their "Own peculiar way": Karl Mannheim and the Rise of Women', *International Sociology* 8(1): 5–55.

Klein, V. 1936. *Stil und Sprache des Louis Ferdinand Celine*. Viola Klein Archive, Reading University.

Klein, V. 1946. *The Feminine Character: History of an Ideology*. London: Kegan Paul, Trubner & Co, Ltd.

Kraus, K. 1922. 'Apokalypse' (First published in 1908), Kraus, K., *Untergang der Welt durch Schwarze Magie*. Wien: Verlag Die Fackel.

Lepenies, W. 1988. *Between Literature and Science: The Rise of Sociology*. Cambridge: Cambridge University Press.

Lorck, E. 1921. *Die 'Erlebte Rede': Ein Sprachliche Untersuchung*. Heidelberg: Carl Winter.

Lyon, E.S. 2007. 'Viola Klein: Forgotten Emigre Intellectual, Public Sociologist and Advocate of Women', *Sociology* 41(5): 829–42.

Lyon, E.S. 2011. 'Karl Mannheim and Viola Klein: Refugee Sociologists in Search of Social Democratic Practice', in Shula Marks et al. (eds), *In Defense of Learning: The Plight, Persecution, and Placement of Academic Refugees 1933–1980*. Oxford: Oxford University Press.

Mannheim, K. [1935] 1940. *Man and Society in an Age of Reconstruction*. London: Kegan Paul, Trench, Truber &. Co., Ltd.

Preissig, E. 1943. *Die Franzosische Kultur-Propaganda in der Tschechoslowakei 1918–1939*. Stuttgard and Berlin: W. Kohlhammer Verlag.

Sayers, J. 1989. 'Introduction', in Viola Klein, *The Feminine Character: History of an Ideology*. London: Routledge.

Vidmar-Horvart, K. and G. Delanty. 2008. '*Mitteleuropa* and the European Heritage', *European Journal of Social Theory* 11(2): 203–18.

VKA, Viola Klein Archive (MS1215), Reading University Library (List of dated content available on request.)

Chapter 6

Olive Schreiner, Sociology and the Company She Kept

Liz Stanley

Olive Schreiner and Sociology: Opening Thoughts

The South African feminist writer and social theorist Olive Schreiner (1855–1920), who lived in Britain for long periods as well as South Africa, was in her day one of the world's most famous people.[1] The 'company she kept' in a literal network sense included many well-known figures in Sociology and other social sciences and her analytical concerns are clearly of sociological import – and yet there were at the time and still are now issues concerning where and how to locate her in relation to Sociology as a body of ideas and a way of thinking, and also as a discipline. In exploring the whys and wherefores of this, the 'company she kept' will also be explored in more complex figurational terms of her associational connections and their political and ethical grounding.

Schreiner's publications convey the range of her concerns and indicate the analytic connections shared with Sociology.[2] These include a ground-breaking novel (*The Story of an African Farm*, 1883), two collections of socialist and feminist allegories (*Dreams*, 1891; *Dream Life and Real Life*, 1893), a powerful critique of Cecil Rhodes and his imperialist activities in a scandalous 'magic realist' novella (*Trooper Peter Halket of Mashonaland*, 1897), a number of ground-breaking political economy essays (*The Political Situation*, 1896; *An English South African's View*, 1899; *Closer Union*, 1909) and a best-selling volume of feminist theory (*Women and Labour*, 1911), and they put her firmly on the international intellectual and political map. After Schreiner's death, posthumous publications included two more novels (*From Man to Man*, 1923; *Undine*, 1929), another collection of allegories (*Stories, Dreams and Allegories*, 1923) and a volume of essays analysing the racial dynamics of polity and economy in South Africa (*Thoughts on South Africa*, 1923).

Schreiner wrote in and across a number of genre forms, with all her publications containing a strong element of social theorising, as also do her nearly 5,000

---

1 For background and Schreiner as a proto social scientist, see Stanley, 2002.

2 For bibliographic information on all Schreiner publications, see the Essential Schreiner/Schreiner's Publications page of the *Olive Schreiner Letters Online* at www.oliveschreiner.org.

extant letters (published in full in the *Olive Schreiner Letters Online* at www. oliveschreiner.org; see also Stanley and Salter 2014). Schreiner's political and social as well as literary contributions were widely praised by contemporaries, including Herbert Spencer, W.E. Gladstone, Charles Dilke, Keir Hardie, and later J.A. Hobson, Leonard Hobhouse, Bertrand Russell and Norman Angell in Britain and Jane Addams and Charlotte Perkins Gillman in the US; and were also acknowledged by those on the receiving end of her social analysis and critique, including Cecil Rhodes, Jan Smuts and Lloyd George. Schreiner's analytical concerns include the economic base and its implications for divisions of labour; the relationship between political, economic and social hierarchies; the three great 'questions' of labour, gender and 'race'; imperialism and its violent exploitations; forms of governance and their implications for libertarian politics; autocracy and the causes and consequences of increasingly industrial forms of warfare; and social justice and how a better future might come into being.

These matters are undoubtedly also among the concerns of Sociology, with the sociological company Schreiner kept featuring some high-profile names. They include: Hebert Spencer, whose *First Principles* she was initially influenced by and later recoiled from and with whom she later maintained a friendly relationship while she lived in England and subsequently. Karl Marx, who she met via his daughter Eleanor during the last months of his life and with her social care theory of value in *Women and Labour* in some measure a rejection of the Marxian one. Karl Pearson, a friend in the days of his socialist as well as social science concerns with social ethics, but whose emotionally frozen rationalism she disliked. John Atkinson Hobson, an economist-cum-economic sociologist with whom she shared many ideas about imperialism, war and pacifism. Leonard Hobhouse, regarding his critical engagement with imperialism, including in *Democracy and Reaction* (1904) and *Liberalism* (1911). And the US sociologist W.E.B. Du Bois, whose ideas about 'race' were a particular influence on her thinking in the mid 1900s.

At her death, Schreiner's reputation and stature seemed assured. Subsequently, in some areas of UK Sociology her work, particularly regarding imperialism (her influence on Hobson's theory of imperialism, and his on Lenin's) and also women and work, had considerable impact. Indeed, as late as the 1970s, *Women and Labour* appeared on some undergraduate Sociology reading lists, together with her younger friend Alice Clark's (1919) *Working Life of Women in the Seventeenth Century*, and Hobson's *The War in South Africa* (1900) and *Imperialism* (1902), with Hobson's *War* featuring an interview with Schreiner (concerning the actual feelings of the Boer population, rather than as reported in the press). But with hindsight this was a swan-song occurring in departments with strong economic sociology inclinations, like Manchester University's Department of Sociology, where I encountered it in the late 1970s as a new lecturer. Few sociologists between then and now would have placed Schreiner's work within the expanding sociological canon because, ironically, it was displaced from reconsideration by contemporary feminist writings at the very point when reassessment might have occurred.

Subsequently, however, the decline of a 'commanding heights' view of Sociology and accompanying rise of diversity and areas of specialism has enabled a broader range of sociological ideas and positions to be recognized, and to some extent Schreiner's work has benefitted from this. Indeed, in terms of intellectual distinction on an international and interdisciplinary level, Olive Schreiner is clearly 'a winner', with new editions of her major books still appearing supported by an international interdisciplinary industry of Schreiner interpreters at work within contemporary academic feminism. But while a good case can be made for the relevance of her theorizing, she is still largely forgotten as a sociologist, or rather as someone who might, or might not, 'belong' to Sociology, both as constituted across the period of her life-time, and also in the present-day. But of course this begs the questions of what Sociology was and is and where its boundaries lie – and who is seen as legislating these matters and consequently who is seen to produce key sociological ideas.

What follows explores these matters of borders, boundaries and not/belonging regarding Sociology and the relationship of this to 'the company she kept', focusing on Olive Schreiner and her work. The discussion starts with her links with Spencer, Hobson, Hobhouse and Du Bois.

Sociological Company She Kept

The earliest known intellectual influence on Schreiner was sociological in character and came from Herbert Spencer's (1862) *First Principles*. She encountered this in 1871 while staying with her aunt Elizabeth, married to the missionary Samuel Rolland. The Rollands lived at Beersheba on the frontier of the now-Lesotho, and a chance passing visitor left his copy of *First Principles* with her. Its impact was profound although not perhaps quite what Spencer might have wanted, for in 1895 Schreiner wrote to a friend that, while it had showed her that systems of political and ethical thought could replace religious ones, she had rejected its mechanism and had to 'transmute' this into workable ideas (OS to Betty Molteno, 24 May 1895; see *Olive Schreiner Letters Online*) The 'social organism' aspect of Spencer's thinking and his ideas concerning increasing social complexity attracted Schreiner. However, *contra* Spencer, she rejected a 'progress' view of social change over time, with her eye remaining on what she termed the 'backwards' and 'downwards' movements that also occurred, while the strong individualistic emphasis in Spencer's thinking and his rejection of state 'interference' are poles apart from Schreiner's communitarian and socialist-federalist stance (Stanley 2002; Mingardi 2013; Francis and Taylor 2014).

During the first period she lived in Britain (end 1881 to late 1889) and on subsequent visits, Schreiner and Spencer became personally acquainted and she remained grateful for her early encounter with his work. Later, each referred appreciatively to the other's public rejection of Britain's provocation of war in South Africa (1899–1902), and Schreiner valued Spencer's linking of imperialism with war. Spencer's last public activities included his active opposition to the war in public statements and writings, while Schreiner's many high-profile writings and political activities in this respect led to her confinement under martial law for most of the war's duration (Spencer 1902; Stanley and Salter 2014: 130–60). The appreciation was mutual, shown by Spencer donating to the fund that helped Schreiner when her Johannesburg house was destroyed in 1900 by fire-bombing, with Schreiner appreciatively commenting, 'that dear old Herbert Spencer who has meant so much to me since I was a girl, should have contributed' (OS to Mary Brown, 9 January 1901; see *Olive Schreiner Letters Online*); and in 1903 when Spencer was dying, he had favoured passages in *The Story of an African Farm* read to him.

The South African War witnessed other connections between Schreiner's social theorizing and Sociology, through her links with Leonard Hobhouse (Owen 1975) and John Atkinson Hobson (Cain 2002), both then working for the *Manchester Guardian*, the major anti-war British newspaper of the day. Among other things, overtures were made for Schreiner to act as a special correspondent and, via Hobson's involvement in the South African Conciliation Committee, an invitation was issued for her to carry out an anti-war speaking tour (for health reasons, she refused). The social reformer Emily Hobhouse became a friend of Schreiner's and Schreiner certainly communicated with and shared some political views with Leonard Hobhouse, Emily's brother, who in 1907 became Britain's first professor of Sociology. However, the closer political and intellectual affiliation, and the one with greater longevity, was with Hobson.

This is indicated with Schreiner's literal presence in Hobson's *The War in South Africa* of 1900, and also because her thinking underpins the analysis in his *Imperialism* of 1902. Hobson's intellectual contributions were cross-disciplinary in approach and interdisciplinary in formation, with important conceptual ideas including under-consumption, marginal productivity and the concept of imperialism in its academic formulation owed to him. Although Hobson is often described as an economist, he can with equal justification be termed an economic sociologist. By the 1920s and 30s, his closest associations were with economic sociology and the sociology of work, and he was closely involved in pre-1939 planning to expand Sociology around economic sociology, an academic and government venture foiled by the outbreak of World War II (Dugdale 1937).

While mutual influences can be traced around how the thinking of both Schreiner and Hobson developed concerning imperialism in general and in southern Africa in particular, it was the relationship of such things to war that provided the long-term bond. Both opposed the South African War in very public ways. But unlike many who did so, it later became apparent that they shared absolute pacifist views regarding war generally and rejected any involvement with its conduct. Later, during the 1914–1918 Great War, Hobson was a leading figure in the Union of Democratic Control (UDC) and also an opponent of the introduction of conscription, while Schreiner became involved with the No-Conscription Fellowship (NCF), publishing open letters supporting conscription-resistance in its pamphlet series and also anti-war writings in a journal associated with both organizations, *War & Peace* (Stanley and Salter 2014: 321–64; Kennedy 1981).

Another, rather different, influence on Schreiner from Sociology came through the work of W.E.B. Du Bois, which she described as changing the way she conceived of matters of 'race' and racism. Schreiner and Du Bois never met face to face and do not seem to have had links outside of the impact that reading his *The Souls of Black Folk* (1903) had on her. However, Schreiner was invited to and almost attended (again, ill-health intervened) the Universal Race Congress in London in 1911 that Du Bois was an important presence at, and she wrote letters of support and gave her name to various of its public documents (Spiller 1911). So a meeting between them came tantalizingly close.

There were two things in particular that impressed Schreiner about *The Souls of Black Folk*. The first was that Du Bois was clearly her equal in education and insight and his book expressed how he saw and directly experienced the world as a black man. This was something different in crucial respects from how well-intentioned whites (she mentions Harriet Beecher Stowe in *Uncle Tom's Cabin* and herself in *Trooper Peter Halket*) represented this, and she thought self-representation of fundamental importance. The second was a longer-term influence, starting with her powerful reaction to one of Du Bois' essay in *Souls*, 'Of the passing of the first-born'. This was written as a bereaved father and, among other things, he comments that his deceased son would never learn to lower his head in the face of prejudice or hatred. The same sentiment had been written by Schreiner some years earlier concerning the death within hours of birth of her daughter, and reading and assimilating it led her to draw direct (both experiential and political) comparisons between the situations of women and black people. Eventually it influenced her thinking about the women and 'race 'questions', and her analysis of social movements and their challenges to the autocratic forms of governance characterizing the imperial powers.

Schreiner's links with some sociologists and sociological writings as outlined here are interesting and suggestive. In network terms, she has clear sociological connections. However, looking more closely suggests that all of them, not just the encounter with Spencer and *First Principles*, became 'transmuted', the word Schreiner used in her 1895 letter to Betty Molteno referenced above. The abstract systemic approach of *First Principles* became transmuted into Schreiner's appreciation of Spencer as a public intellectual and essayist opposing war, with Schreiner playing a similar public role herself. A shared analysis of imperialism transmuted into her long-term connections with Hobson in the context of both of them having an absolute pacifist opposition to all war. The overlaps between the 'classic' liberal analysis of democracy and imperialism of Hobhouse (Morefield 2004) and her own more radical stance faded, perhaps not coincidentally with Hobhouse later becoming a supporter of Britain's involvement in the Great War. The conviction that black people should represent their own experiences and that the different social movements for justice and social change shared fundamental human and political principles, brought home by the work of Du Bois, became central for Schreiner and among other things can be traced in her *Closer Union* (1910) and *Women and Labour* (1911), and also her never completed 'The Dawn of Civilization', discussed later.

More Company: Networks or Figurations?

The idea of figurations and figurational or process sociology is central to the work of Norbert Elias (1939, 1970). Figuration is sometimes used – in my view misused – as though synonymous with network and thus being what fills the conceptual divide between the individual on the one hand and society on the other, with figurations seen as the 'small social worlds' of networked individuals (eg. Malerba 2014: 127–8; Depelteau and Hervonet 2014: 179–81, 189–90). There are, however, important network/figuration differences. Figurations involve unfolding processes and flows, and are perpetuations with accruing differences (and shifting power-ratios) over time. But, while some new departures in thinking about networks, in particular actor network theory (Latour 2007), aspire to similar temporal longitudinality and processual complexities, the mainstream of social network analysis remains wedded to a cross-sectional 'snapshot' approach (Scott 2012: 139–46). Turning to Elias (1939: 482–3) on figuration, his use of the analogy of a dance in explaining it confirms the difference, for the participants in a dance join and leave although the dancing continues, and they may have little personal or network links with each other apart from their figurational presence, their involvement in a shared enterprise.[3]

Succinctly, networks involve links between persons at particular points in time, while figurations are over time social enterprises with common frameworks which people variously join and leave; and those involved may or may not have shared inter-personal connections with each other but are nonetheless part of the mutual enterprise. Another way of thinking about this is that figurations depend on functional, emotional and dynamic interdependences of a kind that networks need not imply, with Elias (1987) helpfully discussing such matters in his *Involvement and Detachment*. In this connection, Schreiner's network links with some sociologists and sociological writings have been explored above, but pinning these down is quite tricky, for while the network links are demonstrable, and that they involve sociologists is apparent, they frequently over time transmuted into other kinds of allegiance and association. It is these associational connections of Olive Schreiner's that are figurational in character and connected with but not reducible to her network links that I now want to explore.

Schreiner and Hobson met when he visited South Africa in late 1899 around two closely connected matters, imperialism and the role of international finance capital, and the provocation of war. The context was the events leading to the South

---

3   Elias (2007) on the naval profession provides a detailed example for thinking through figuration/network overlaps and differences.

African War (1899–1902). For both, there were deeper processes at work and the dynamics involved here also played out in other contexts, not just regarding these particular events. Another close friendship originated at this time and for similar reasons, with exploration of this opening up more of the figurational associations at work. This was with Frederick Pethick-Lawrence, now best known for his involvement with his wife Emmeline Pethick-Lawrence in the women's suffrage organization, the Women's Social and Political Union, and later as a Labour Government Secretary of State for India. In the run-up to the South African War, Fred Pethick-Lawrence was a newspaper owner and journalist of increasingly radical views and came to know Schreiner in the context of a fact-finding visit to South Africa. Their friendship was maintained through letters, a joint Pethick-Lawrence visit to South Africa, and then after Schreiner's return to Britain from late 1913 to mid 1920, in face-to-face ways.

During the Great War (1914–1918), Fred Pethick-Lawrence became Treasurer of the UDC (in which Hobson was closely involve too) and he was also an opponent of conscription when introduced in Britain in 1916. Emmeline Pethick-Lawrence was one of the few British women who managed to arrive at The Hague for the feminist peace congress that established the pacifist Women's International League for Peace and Freedom (WILPF) (Confortini 2012), with Schreiner becoming a member of its International Committee. Schreiner's friendship with Fred was straightforward and admiring, although her relationship with Emmeline had earlier been problematic because of the latter's interjections in South African suffrage matters during 1907–1910 by promoting votes for women there on the 'same terms as men'. In context, this meant a racial franchise, as only white men were fully enfranchised, something Schreiner strongly opposed (Stanley and Salter 2014: 207–68). However, over the period of the Great War, Emmeline's absolute pacifist credentials stood out and the breech was healed to the extent that Schreiner could see the Pethick-Lawrences' views as largely her own.

Another long-term friendship was cemented by shared opposition to the South African War, with the socialist feminist Isabella Ford, who Schreiner had first met in the 1880s (Hannam 1989). Ford was even more outspokenly anti-war than Schreiner, which caused some difficulties regarding both censorship and the effects of martial law for Schreiner during the South African War. Later, Schreiner together with various other radical or liberal South African expatriates supported members of two black delegations to Britain in 1914 and 1919 to protest its unfolding race politics following the 1910 Union of South Africa and the passing of highly retrograde legislation there (Stanley and Salter 2014: 321–3, 344–8). Ford was one of the few British radicals involved in supporting the delegations' activities and also a wider anti-racist platform. In addition to involvements in both the UDC and the NCF during the Great War, Ford was active in the WILPF and one of a relatively small number of Schreiner's friends to adopt an absolute pacifist stance. 'Lost' friendships with people who stopped short of this and gave degrees of humanitarian and other support to wartime activities included Edward Carpenter, Havelock Ellis, Mohandas Gandhi and Emily Hobhouse.

This was not simply a matter of old friendships continuing or becoming less close, although something of this was involved. It was more that the changed circumstances were responded to by many people as politically and morally *in extremis* ones, and this pointed up levels of agreement or disagreement not fully realized before. This in turn led to the 'transmuting' of relationships, the term used earlier, with Schreiner in each case emphasizing figurational association and pacifism over network links and sociological connections. As the Great War started, so the divisions quickly became starkly clear between those who objected to particular wars, those who objected to war but accepted aiding combatants in humanitarian ways, and those who objected to all war and rejected giving their support to any aspect. What was revealed, both to Schreiner and to many (former) close friends, was that for her anti-war associational ties had been the basis of many close relationships, but these were sometimes grounded in the misapprehension that the friend in question objected to all war and all war absolutely.

Whether Schreiner's associational tie with Herbert Spencer – founded on his analysis of imperialist autocracy and its provocation of wars and in particular the South African War – might have been loosened or ended in the Great War context, given his somewhat different approach to defensive wars, is merely speculative, as he died in 1903. What is certain is the weakening of a whole swathe of Schreiner's relationships; and of those connected with Sociology discussed so far, only that with Hobson remained strong (another, with Jane Addams, is discussed later). At the same time and in spite of Schreiner's increasingly debilitating heart condition, some older friendships took different form and a range of new associations and related activities came into prominence in her life. The changed character of her relationship with Emmeline Pethick-Lawrence has already been noted around her and Fred Pethick-Lawrence's involvements in absolute pacifist causes and organizations, as has Schreiner's association with Hobson in this regard.

The level of Schreiner's own involvement in pacifist activities is marked. When legislation for compulsory conscription was introduced in Britain, Schreiner was one of the leading figures who published an open letter in the *Times* on 12 January 1916 opposing this and supporting Sir John Simon's attempts to prevent it passing into law, with other signatories including Pethick-Lawrence and Hobson. The impetus here probably came from Bertrand Russell, a high-profile absolute pacifist active across a range of wartime initiatives and organizations (Vellacott 1981). Russell and Schreiner established a political friendship and he seems to have been a source for some of her information about war matters. Schreiner's relationship with Norman Angell, one of the founders of the UDC and a later Nobel Peace Prize winner, also came about at this time (Ceadel 2009). This probably occurred through anti-Conscription Bill meetings and is discernible through various lunches and meetings with him noted in her letters and also her publications in the journal that Angell's Foundation sponsored, *War & Peace*.

Schreiner's absolutist convictions and her profound sense of the injustice of military tribunals scapegoating men who resisted both conscription and humanitarian forms of service led her to most closely support the NCF. The analysis in *Women and Labour* of 1911 suggests that if everyone, both women and men, had social care responsibilities, then aggression and violence would decline. However, this stance had given way by 1915, leading to Schreiner's attempt to write the fragmented and barely started 'The Dawn of Civilization, Stray Thoughts on Peace & War', intended to result in an absolute pacifist analysis of the well-springs of human aggression. By 1915 her conviction, based on many everyday wartime experiences, was that women and men shared equally in animalistic aggression but because of social conventions the expressions of this took different gendered forms. Thus while Schreiner's support for the WILPF was strong and active, this was around her understanding that no special relationship existed between women and peace or men and war.

Many women involved in the WILPF shared Schreiner's absolute pacifism (although not always her rejection of a binary view of the gendered character of aggression and violence), with Emmeline Pethick-Lawrence already mentioned in this respect. Also, high level WILPF members Aletta Jacobs and Jane Addams were friends of Schreiner. Aletta Jacobs was the first Dutch woman doctor and a leading member of the International Woman Suffrage Alliance, and she and Schreiner had first met in 1911 when Jacobs was in South Africa as part of an IWSA tour. However, it was Jacobs' absolute pacifism during the Great War that became the prime link between them. The US activist, sociologist and reformer Jane Addams was, with Ellen Gates Starr, the founding presence in Hull House, a centre for social research as well as social reform in Chicago. And here too, it was Addams' role in absolute pacifist activism that formed the major bond between Schreiner and her, not Sociology.

Hull House was closely if uneasily connected with the University of Chicago's Sociology Department, with Addams a charter member of the American Sociological Association and a university extension lecturer on Sociology topics. Hull House personnel and activities received a less than positive response from some male sociologists at Chicago and were side-lined or vanished in various subsequent accounts of Chicago Sociology (Deegan 1988). However, Addams has more recently been reclaimed as 'key sociologist' (Deegan 2006) and there is certainly now a greater acceptance of a broad church approach to 'the discipline' and the presence within it of more policy-oriented and social reformist strands, in the UK as well as the US and elsewhere.

However, it was not Addams' Sociology credentials or publications that Schreiner was influenced by and nor does she mention these in her letters. It was instead Addams' absolute pacifism, in particular her leading role in the pacifist movement in the US and also in relation to the WILPF and its Peace Committee (which toured the world successfully commanding meetings with national leaders in many of the combatant countries) that attracted Schreiner. Rather than network links and Sociology, it was the associational connections of absolute pacifism and the international peace movement that led to the flourishing of friendship between Schreiner and Addams and their meetings when the latter was in Britain on WILPF business. Another way of putting this is that, rather than understanding the 'sociology of ideas' in terms of academic contexts, ideas and networks, in Schreiner's case it was instead the political-ethical pacifist connections and the social analysis that went with them which was primary, with intellectual-ethical affinities providing a kind of social glue holding these relationships together.

The discussion so far has brought to sight two strands of important relationships in Schreiner's life, and shown that while there were strong interconnections, these were by no means coterminous. Schreiner's strong analytical inclinations and the range of social and political concerns that engaged her are clear and there are definite network links with some sociologists and some Sociology key works. At the same time, she had, for instance, very different responses to different components of Spencer's writings and political interventions, and her recognition of important overlaps between her thinking and Hobson's did not lead her to follow his particular intellectual boundary crossings. The developing thread of her intellectual, political and ethical concerns departed from these network connections around her unfolding analysis of social organization, the economic base, forms of governance, imperialist and autocratic expansionism, and violence and war, with the latter an increasing emphasis from the 1890s on. Regarding this, another set of links developed, with some of the same people and ideas but others too, and these were engaged in concerning associational co-presence, with her Great War relationships with, for example, Addams, Russell and Angell being cases in point.

So how, then, is Olive Schreiner to be characterized in relation to Sociology, its boundaries, domain ideas and people? At this point it is helpful to remember that Herbert Spencer was not only a social theorist but also a prominent public intellectual, and to think about whether Schreiner is 'in' or 'out' when considering that perhaps more porous boundaries existed between public intellectuals and Sociology than did so between Sociology and other kinds of boundary-crossing, such as regarding feminist work.

The Public Intellectual and Public Moralist

In earlier work, I have described Schreiner as a social analyst who was a cultural entrepreneur, someone who used her analytic activities to fuel her active engagement with contributing to processes of change at individual, interpersonal and also social movement levels, particularly in relation to cultural and political domains (Stanley and Dampier 2012; Stanley, Dampier and Salter 2010; Stanley and Salter 2013). She did so around a strong sense of the need for social justice and equality, with her writing having an emphasis that was both realist and utopian regarding the future, with an attention to the unfolding character and effects of events in the present and how these contributed to this future state. However, Schreiner can equally well be characterized as a public intellectual, positioning herself at the intellectual and political margins, so as to analyse and comment on the social fabric. In her case, these margins were habits of mind rather than the literalist ones sometimes invoked, that the '... real or true intellectual is, therefore, always an outsider, living in self-imposed exile, and on the margins of society' (Said 1994: 142). In addition, Schreiner can be seen as part of the public moralist discourse that Collini (1993) sees as a prominent feature of British civil society from the 1850s to the 1930s, signifying the existence of an intellectual class, a figurational grouping, rather than particular individuals and their pronouncements.

The figures Collini identifies in public moralist terms are John Stuart Mill, Matthew Arnold, John Maynard Keynes and F.R. Leavis. In the Britain context Herbert Spencer and Olive Schreiner should certainly be seen as among their ranks, as key producers of ideas harnessed to social critique and ethical demands for greater social justice. This is a notion of the public intellectual as not only a public moralist in Collini's sense, but also as having a *modus operandi* that placed them 'between philosophy and politics', to use the sub-title of Melzer, Weinberger and Zinman's (2003) discussion, and in a context where an intellectual class or figuration was in existence, rather than just lone individuals speaking out.

Achieving the status of a public intellectual and public moralist had already been established at the beginning of the period Collini discusses as something that could be legitimately if awkwardly aspired to and sometimes achieved by women. The novelist George Elliot (Mary Ann Evans) is one case in point, and the journalist and social commentator Harriet Martineau another (Hill and Hoecker-Drysdale 2003). However, as invoking Martineau points up, women's presence in academia was another matter, as a still resolutely male preserve and with Sociology not so much present within as on or beyond the margins and admissible mainly via Philosophy or Psychology. Thus while in the Britain of Schreiner's young womanhood the representative figure of 'the sociologist' was Spencer, Martineau has claims as good as his, as the translator of Comte, author of Sociology's first text on observational methods (*How to Observe Manners and Morals* of 1838), a major figure in publishing popular works of economic sociology both in the *Times* newspaper and in book form (*Illustrations of Political Economy*), and a leading figure in the National Association for the Promotion of Social Science (NAPSS).

In the British intellectual landscape of the 1880s as Schreiner experienced it, it was Spencer and his colleagues and peers around and within the university system who constituted 'the social sciences', including in Schreiner's milieu Karl Pearson, initially a socialist ethicist with an equal interest in German literature, later a mathematician and statistician turned eugenicist (Porter 2006). Schreiner drew her distance from the concerns and habits of mind thus configured, referring to the aridity of Spencer's social theory, and Pearson's humourless and emotionally-denuded rationalism. In her maturity in South Africa, her relationship to Sociology and the other social sciences was more simple, for while there was some 1900s interest in Comte and Spencer, a course in Sociology was not taught until 1919 (at the University of South Africa [UNISA]) and departments were not founded until the 1930s (Jubber 2007).

In the contexts of Britain in the 1880s of Schreiner's young womanhood, and South Africa from the 1890s to the 1910s of her maturity, it would not have been possible for her to 'be a (professional) sociologist', then. Nor would it have been possible for her to have had the freer-floating intellectual and academic career of Hobson, moving in and out of academia and working with ideas that could legitimately if controversially cross nascent disciplinary boundaries. In Britain and South Africa, for 'sociologically-minded' and boundary-crossing women of Schreiner's generation and earlier, the outlets were social reform, and/or a public moralist role, and/or by writing works of fiction. However, although such comments are a useful reminder of academic boundaries and patterned exclusions, confining the discussion to this would beg some important questions and reservations.

Firstly, there is the important matter of whether Schreiner might have ever seen herself as, or wanted to be, part of the configurations of either Sociology or the academia of her day. The evidence firmly suggests no. She had a developed critique of the then current academic way of thinking and deportment, expressed in particular in comments about Pearson's approach, which was not a rejection of analysis but of the particular masculinist mode he represented. Also, apart from late teenage hopes that a brother's foray into diamond-mining might produce sufficient funds to send her to a women's college in the US and a subsequent short-lived (for health reasons) attempt to train in midwifery, there is no sign that Schreiner thought of herself in terms of 'a career' outside of writing.

Secondly, there were important gains from Schreiner's position 'outside', a position that resulted from her particular habits of mind as well as barriers of gender and education. These habits of mind are intertwined with the aesthetic and analytical principles set out in the well-known 'Preface' to *The Story of an African Farm*. They involved Schreiner focusing on the everyday and emergent, interweaving emotion and reason, crafting cross-genre and mixed genre ways of writing, combining political commitments with measured analysis, and developing innovative modes of presentation. Recognizing this, and thinking about the work of Spencer and Hobhouse in comparison, points up both differences and gains, for it is highly doubtful that Schreiner could have produced and published what she did within the narrower frameworks accepted by Spencer and Hobhouse (and recognizing these two were positioned rather differently from each other in time-period and academic location).

And thirdly, thinking about Schreiner *vis a vis* the older Harriet Martineau in Britain and slightly younger Charlotte Perkins Gilman in the US is helpful in considering the role of temporality and context here. Martineau is in some respects a more 'respectable' and mainstream figure than Schreiner, because of what was possible for independent women to be and do during Martineau's young womanhood and maturity, also because of her particular family, class and religious background. Martineau nonetheless was an experimentalist in genre and an intellectual boundary-crosser and achieved considerable acclaim as a writer and public intellectual. But by comparison Schreiner seems less fettered, more wide-ranging; and because of the changing times she moved in, women in metropolitan contexts at least had a wider range choices available than had existed for Martineau. However, the colonial context of the Cape that Schreiner returned to in late 1889, remaining until late 1913, was very different. She experienced it as limited in intellectual and political terms, while a series of events which started with invasion and massacres in the then Matabeleland and Mashonaland by Cecil Rhodes' Chartered Company (the topic of her *Trooper Peter Halket*) and eventuated in the Union of the white settler states in 1910 and the rapid introduction of racially retrograde legislation, absorbed much of her analytical energy.

Charlotte Perkins Gilman was also an experimental writer and genre-crosser (Lengermann and Niebrugge-Brantly 2013). Gilman, a friend and colleague of Jane Addams, identified as a sociologist, taught sociology courses, published some work in the *American Journal of Sociology* and like Addams was a charter member of the American Sociological Society. However, Gilman's certainly closer relationship with institutional Sociology was still somewhat problematic in spite of disciplinary patrons who sought to help and promote her and her work. This may have been connected with her allying herself strongly with Lester Ward's gynocentric ideas about gender relationships, while her ideas about domestic labour failed to reckon with how class and 'race' issues made professional women's liberation reliant on 'specialists' who would carry out childcare and domestic work. However, it was also connected with the US's disciplinary associations, including the American Sociological Society (later Association), being both active and open to women, but with institutional Sociology in colleges and universities still struggling with co-education and its ramifications. The result was that the possibilities regarding Sociology were somewhat greater for Gilman (and Addams) than for Martineau or Schreiner, although jobs and disciplinary acceptance remained elusive.

Clearly 'the times' and the context were important regarding what kinds of boundaries existed, impacting on who was seen as 'in' and 'out', including where Sociology itself was located, as well as influencing these three women's relationships to it. However, associational concerns and habits of mind still have to be acknowledged and reckoned with. Given the importance of both for Schreiner, it is difficult to envisage her wanting to enter the portals of any discipline, let alone any university, while it is extremely easy to imagine an Olive Schreiner without asthma or heart disease as a leading figure in a social movement or political context as well as a public intellectual one.

The Small Matter of 'Forgetting'

Forgetting is something humankind does well: we forget almost everything we have ever done or experienced, and what we do remember is often wrong. However, sometimes forgetting is strongly patterned and maps onto such structural matters as age, gender, 'race' and class. The strange 'forgetting' of the connections of key women producers of ideas with Sociology is one such instance. A combination of the fetishizing of the small handful of 'founding fathers', coupled with a frequent marked presentism in how Sociology is written and taught, clearly has something to do with it. However, beyond noting the problem, explanations lie outside the concerns of this chapter. What is within its remit, however, is to emphasize what is lost, lost *to Sociology*, when a producer of ideas of the stature of Olive Schreiner is 'forgotten' in the ignored sense. Schreiner did not aspire to be 'a sociologist', disliked the academic mode, and her style of theorizing traversed genre boundaries; but the power and reach of her analysis, its international significance and close connections with key sociological concerns, ensures that her work remains of high relevance to Sociology. What Sociology was, and where it was located, in the period of Schreiner's lifetime from approximately 1850 to 1920, is complicated, no matter what inter/national context this is explored from. There is accordingly no good reason to exclude from consideration women such as Schreiner who produced internationally recognized social theory, for her complicated relationship to Sociology and sociologists and even stronger associational concerns and connections is the name of the game, just as with Spencer, Hobson and Addams. Canon-revision needs to open its eyes to such matters.

Acknowledgements

My grateful thanks to the ESRC (RES-062-23-1286) for funding the Olive Schreiner Letters Project. Thanks also to the Sociology Department at the University of Pretoria, South Africa, where these ideas were formulated, to the Sociology Department at the University of the Free State, South Africa where the final draft was written, and to Emilia Sereva from Edinburgh Sociology.

References

Ceadel, Martin. 2009. *Living the Great Illusion: Norman Angell 1872–1967.* Oxford: Oxford University Press.
Cain, Peter. 2002. *Hobson and Imperialism.* Oxford: Oxford University Press.
Clark, Alice. 1919/2014. *Working Life of Women in the Seventeenth Century.* London: Routledge.
Collini, Stefan. 1993. *Public Moralists: Political Thought and Intellectual Life in Britain 1850–1930.* Oxford: Oxford University Press.
Confortini, Catia. 2012. *Intelligent Compassion: Critical Feminist Methodology in the Women's International League for Peace and Freedom.* New York: Oxford University Press.
Deegan, Mary Jo. 1988. *Jane Addams and the Men of the Chicago School.* New Brunswick, NJ: Transaction Books.
Deegan, Mary Jo. 2006. 'Jane Addams', in John Scott (ed.), *Fifty Key Sociologists: The Formative Theorists.* London: Routledge, pp. 3–8.
Depelteau, Francois and Ronan Hervonet. 2014. 'The Metamorphoses of the Dacha', in Tatiana Landini and Francois Depelteau (eds), *Norbert Elias and Empirical Research.* New York: Palgrave Macmillan, pp. 179–96.

Du Bois, W.E.B. 1903/1989. *The Souls of Black Folks.* New York: Penguin.

Dugdale, J. 1937. *Further Papers on the Social Sciences: Their Relations in Theory and Teaching.* London: Le Play House.

Dunning, Eric and Jason Hughes. 2013. *Norbert Elias and Modern Sociology.* London: Bloomsbury.

Elias, Norbert. 1939/2000. *The Civilising Process.* Revised edn. Oxford: Blackwell.

Elias, Norbert. 1970/1978. *What Is Sociology?* London: Hutchinson.

Elias, Norbert. 1987. *Involvement and Detachment.* Oxford: Blackwell.

Elias, Norbert. 2007. *The Genesis of the Naval Profession.* Dublin: UCD Press.

Francis, Mark and Michael Taylor (eds). 2014. *Herbert Spencer, Legacies.* London: Routledge.

Hannam, June. 1989. *Isabella Ford.* Oxford: Blackwell.

Hill, Michael and Susan Hoecker-Drysdale (eds). 2003. *Harriet Martineau: Theoretical and Methodological Perspectives.* New York: Routledge.

Hobhouse, L.T. 1904. *Democracy and Reaction.* London: Fisher Unwin.

Hobhouse, L.T. 1911. *Liberalism.* Oxford: Oxford University Press.

Hobson, John A. 1900. *The War in South Africa: Its Causes and Effects.* London: James Nisbet.

Hobson, John A. 1902. *Imperialism: A Study.* London: Allan and Unwin.

Jubber, Ken. 2007. 'Sociology in South Africa', *International Sociology* 22: 527–46.

Kennedy, Thomas. 1981. *The Hound of Conscience: A History of the Non-Conscription Fellowship.* Fayetteville: University of Arkansas Press.

Latour, Bruno. 2007. *Reassembling the Social: An Introduction to Actor-Network Theory.* Oxford: Oxford University Press.

Lengermann, Patricia and Gillian Niebrugge-Brantley (eds). 2013. *Charlotte Perkins Gilman.* Farnham: Ashgate.

Malerba, Jurandir. 2014. 'The New Style: Etiquette during the Exile of the Portuguese Court in Rio de Janeiro', in Tatiana Landini and Francois Depelteau (eds), *Norbert Elias and Empirical Research.* New York: Palgrave Macmillan, pp. 127–8.

Melzer, Arthur, Jerry Weinberger and M. Richard Zinman. 2003. *The Public Intellectual: Between Philosophy and Politics.* Lanham, MD: Rowman and Littlefield.

Mingardi, Alberto. 2013. *Herbert Spencer.* London: Bloomsbury.

Morefield, Jeanne. 2004. *Covenants Without Swords: Idealist Liberalism and the Spirit of Empire.* Princeton, NJ: Princeton University Press.

Owen, John. 1975. *L.T. Hobhouse, Sociologist.* London: Nelson.

Porter, Theodore. 2006. *Karl Pearson: The Scientific Life in a Statistical Age.* Princeton, NJ: Princeton University Press.

Said, Edward. 1994. *Representations of the Intellectual.* New York: Vintage Books.

Schreiner, Olive. Olive Schreiner Letters Online www.oliveschreiner.org.

Schreiner, Olive. Olive Schreiner Letters Project www.oliveschreinerlettersproject.ed.ac.uk.

Scott, John. 2012, *Social Network Analysis.* 3rd edn. London: Sage.

Spencer, Herbert. 1862. *First Principles*. London: Williams and Northgate.

Spencer, Herbert. 1902. *Facts and Comments*. London: Williams and Norgate.

Spiller, G. (ed.). 1911. *Papers on Inter-Racial Problems*. London: P.S. King.

Stanley, Liz. 2002. *Imperialism, Labour & the New Woman: Olive Schreiner's Social Theory*. Durham: sociologypress.

Stanley, Liz and Helen Dampier. 2012. '"I just express my views & leave them to work": Olive Schreiner as a Feminist Protagonist in a Masculine Political Landscape with Figures and Letters', *Gender and History* 24: 677–700.

Stanley, Liz, Helen Dampier and Andrea Salter. 2010. 'Olive Schreiner Globalising Social Inquiry: A Feminist Analytics of Globalization', *Sociological Review* 58(4): 656–79.

Stanley, Liz and Andrea Salter. 2013. 'Olive Schreiner, Epistolary Practices and Microhistories: A Cultural Entrepreneur in an Historical Landscape', *Cultural & Social History* 10: 577–97.

Stanley, Liz and Andrea Salter (eds). 2014. *The World's Great Question: Olive Schreiner's South African Letters*. Cape Town: Van Riebeeck Society.

Vellacott, Jo. 1981. *Bertrand Russell and Pacifists in the First World War*. Basingstoke: Palgrave Macmillan.

Chapter 7

Lucien Goldmann's Key Sociological Problems and His Critical Heritage: From the Hidden God to the Hidden Class

Bridget Fowler

I address here the work of Lucien Goldmann (1913–1970), at present removed from both the sociological canon and the curriculum, but once acclaimed by Alasdair MacIntyre as an 'original philosopher of great powers [... whose] "untimely death in 1970 robbed us of the finest and most intelligent Marxist of the age"' (1971: 79). It will be argued that Goldmann is worthy of consecration not just as the originator of a powerful theory of cultural production but as a key contender to hegemonic structuralism and post-structuralism (1981: 55–74). His *genetic structuralism* is rooted in Kant, Hegel, Marx, the young Lukács and Piaget[1] rather than in Spinoza and Levi-Strauss. It has contributed towards the abandonment of a simplistic base-superstructure theory (Williams 1977: 75–82). As Raymond Williams concludes, this was a huge gain for a non-mechanistic historical materialism (1971: 11). Goldmann kept alive a rich, non-Stalinist Marxism at a time when the very idea of *the subject* was being devastatingly revoked. Two highly-distinguished works are crucial in this respect: *Immanuel Kant* and *The Hidden God*. His many other contributions elucidate the theoretical ideas behind these, whilst also demonstrating his grasp of the German phenomenological tradition and advancing the sociology of the novel. Although exposed to withering criticism by some of his sociological peers, I shall claim, alongside Sami Naïr and Michel Löwy (1973) and Mitchell Cohen (1994) that his oeuvre represents an enduring achievement, especially in the historical sociology of cultural production. More surprisingly, as we shall see, even some vigorous detractors, like Pierre Bourdieu, have constantly evoked his memory.

----

1 We might be tempted to see Goldmann's homage to Piaget as a repayment of an early debt incurred in World War II when the young man was sheltered by Piaget in Switzerland as a penniless Jewish Rumanian, fleeing from a concentration camp in occupied France. But this would be a mistake: Goldmann's adoption of a genetic structuralism was fired throughout his life by Piaget's constructivism (1972). This he regarded as an empirically-based epistemology and social theory of human adaptation, organized around the flux of structuration and destructuration. He regarded this theory as all the more precious for its corroboration of his own ideas because of its *non-Marxist* scientific origin.

But first we assess his historical sociology of the Enlightenment, with his work on the French rationalists (1973), and on the philosophical roots of Lukács and Heidegger (1977). Here Goldmann's most sustained and lasting accomplishment is without question *Immanuel Kant*, his original Swiss PhD thesis.

Part I: Goldmann's Studies of the Tragic Vision: Kant, Racine and Pascal

Kant

Immanuel Kant (2011 [1945]) analyses Kant's philosophical works, from the pre-critical writings to the three critiques: of pure reason, practical reason and judgement. Goldmann emphasizes the importance of Kant's 'Copernican Revolution' which was founded on his antagonism to Humean atomistic empiricism and deepened by his relational conception of the human community (2011: 14). Fundamental to this is Kant's understanding of knowledge as based on a priori synthetic judgements, as well as on experience. Goldmann argues plausibly that it was partly because Kant lacked an adequate conception of the collective, or transindividual, subject that he instead attributed the categories of synthetic judgement to '"the divine understanding"' (2011: 62–3). Be that as it may, his formulation of the a priori categories (space, time, causality etc.) certainly provided an early initial conception of a social consciousness (2011: 71). Hence for later writers, such as Goldmann himself, the transcendental element was ultimately vested solely in the social, following thinkers such as Durkheim and Piaget, with their social and genetic epistemology (2011: 14).[2]

For Goldmann, it is Kant's 'anthropological' conception of 'universitas' – humankind, the emergent human community – that founds the '*task of creating a world*' (2011: 57). This is based on reason and law, of course, but also peace and cosmopolitanism; in contrast to the rationalists, it moves beyond possessive individualism (2011: 83–5). Unlike the Romantics, Kant's community is directed at a 'universitas' founded on both individual autonomy and the general will: a hope Kant formulated by 1764 and which he maintained in his mature thought (2011: 125–6). Yet he also realized with great poignancy that all such rational projects were *at present* unattainable. For Goldmann this produced Kant's subsequent tragic vision:[3] '[C]ritical philosophy became one of the great expressions of the tragic

---

    2   Goldmann notes that in some respects Kant was Durkheim's great predecessor. For example Kant pointed out that death was both based on natural laws but also on human freedom, that might lengthen or shorten life. Goldmann regards this as *Suicide*'s central insight, as long as human freedom is interpreted broadly (Goldmann 2011: 77).

    3   Goldmann clarifies this by adding that Kant considered a community as presupposed when he established knowledge as based on synthetic a priori categories – space, time, number etc. Moreover, empirical knowledge, using the categories, aids humans in the forging of communities (2011: 163). Nevertheless, he did not see a community based on

visions of the world [...] it became a "metaphysics of tragedy"' (2011: 170). Such a historically-recurrent view, Goldmann noted, was especially strong where the forces bearing the Enlightenment were blocked – like Elias on the 19th century, Goldmann derives the tragic vision from the historical impasse of the weak and divided German progressive bourgeoisie in the face of Prussian authoritarian rule (Elias 1996).

Goldmann's approach to Kant and his heritage is sharply differentiated from his appropriation by the Marburg neo-Kantians. As Cohen has astutely observed, his is based on 'a post-Kantian, humanist, Marxist reading [...] rather than a Lukácsian (Hegelian), Marxist one' (1994: 117). Goldmann's interpretation makes Kant a sympathetic figure for sociologists due to his break with Cartesian atomism. His unusual reading of the categorical imperative[4] envisages it as based not on an eternal collision between virtue and happiness but on a contingent tragic clash in contemporary society, in which duty or obedience to law must at present triumph over pleasure. Indeed, it is Goldmann's more generous view that Kant, the greatest thinker of the German Enlightenment, had come too early to see the material and social prerequisites emerge for a community such as he imagined it, virtuous, just and happy. One striking piece of evidence for this is the ageing Kant's salutation to the French Revolutionaries as having 'broken the bars of their prison' (1971: 220). Under the Revolution's influence, Kant founded (although failed to elaborate) a philosophy of history:

> Kant opened the way to a new philosophy which unites the Christian idea [...] with the immanence of the ancients and the philosophers of the seventeenth and eighteenth centuries in considering the intelligible world, the totality, as a human task, as the object of the authentic destiny of man and the product of human action (Goldmann 2011: 225).

The Hidden God (1964 [1956]) *and Racine* (1956)

Lucien Goldmann's linked studies of Jansenism, *The Hidden God* and *Racine,* together bestow us with one of the most valuable scholarly analyses of the sociology of literature. Goldmann not only shows how Pascal and Racine break with earlier thinkers, such as Aquinas and Descartes, but illuminates how they are linked to wider social groups in so doing. Thus they express a *world-vision* elaborated through distinctive philosophical and artistic forms – the fragment (Pascal's *Pensées*) and tragic drama (Racine). Such a world-vision or significant structure is a 'reality which goes beyond them as individuals [and] which finds

---

common human activity as existing in the present, acknowledging instead individuals' largely instrumental action, or, alternatively, the 'folly' of clashing nationalisms (2011: 24n, 154–5).

    4   Goldmann translates this as 'Act only on that maxim through which you can at the same time will that it should become a universal law' (cited 2011: 166), acknowledging that Kant recognized that at present this was consigned to a highly formal character.

expression in their work […] in the particular case of [these] authors, a tragic vision' (1964: 15).

Resting as it does, on a 'transindividual subject', this claim is not without its controversial elements. Indeed, the literary historian, David Caute, ridiculed the very idea of any collective authorship, dismissing Goldmann's author as merely the 'midwife' of a social group (1971). But this is to misread Goldmann: he never denied that authors might contribute original and distinctive elements; these derive from the writers' singular histories, and are potentially illuminated by Freudian psychoanalysis (1970a; 1981). Thus Caute's individualist default position missed the wider significance of the author: his/her capacity to express in the most unified and coherent fashion the (possible) consciousness of a group when faced with practical problems of living. In elaborating on this, Goldmann (1964) pioneered a new method: first, he interprets the writings of Pascal and Racine, linking their most ideal-typically 'pure' works together as underpinned by a tragic world-view; secondly, these most unified and coherent works are understood in terms of the 16th and 17th century development of Jansenism; a history clarified by Goldmann's own discovery of an 'extremist' doctrinal fraction around Barcos, with his unearthing of the latter's letters. Finally, Jansenism – and the Barcos fraction as its most oppositional wing- can only be explained by an existential and material crisis on the part of a whole social group. The State's legal officers or noblesse de robe, faced with being suddenly marginalized by the royal turn to absolutism, represented such a declining group or class fraction.

What then was radical Jansenism? Goldmann locates this in an ascetic movement within the Catholic Church, founded on the Augustinian belief that salvation required both sufficient and efficaceous grace. Certain Jansenist religious houses were highly influential here, particularly the convent of Port Royal, where the orphaned Racine was later to be educated. Crucially, Goldmann distinguishes three currents of Jansenism, whose fluctuating fortunes cannot be entirely separated from developments in the political world. These are, in his terms, first, the 'moderates', notably, Arnauld, St Cyran and Nicole ('moderate' despite St Cyran's arrest and death in prison); second, the 'extremist Jansenists' – Mère Angelique and Barcos, who demanded that believers refuse the world and retreat into monastic seclusion; and third, the 'radical Jansenists', for whom refusal meant remaining within the world but saying 'yes' and 'no' to it. Goldmann links Pascal's *Les Provinciales* and Racine's tragedies of 1667–1670 – *Andromaque, Britannicus* and *Bérénice* – to the *second* strand of tragic thought. Much more austere was the radical rigour of the third current – expressed solely in the *Pensées* of Pascal and Racine's tragic *Phèdre*. What was dominant here was a notion of a 'hidden God', and therefore of a deep paradox within social reality. Pascal's distinctively tragic ethos, crystallized in the most condensed form in the paradoxes of *Pensées*, is illuminated both by Goldmann's internal textual analysis and also by his historical detection of hitherto-missing writings.

The quintessential tragic world-view derived from 'the God of Pascal being like that of Calvin, […] a transcendental God, inaccessible and mysterious, who has absented himself from the world' (Lovell 1973: 314). His absence explains human wretchedness and the unendurable 'weight of the world' – yet his presence is also evident, especially in humans' continued search for justice and truth (Goldmann 1964: 63). For Pascal, the world had to be rejected and humans had to live by perpetually seeking to reconcile opposites. Far from God being Descartes' watchmaker who started off a whole efficient global mechanism, God's existence could only be grasped through a wager – it was a 'perpetually unprovable possibility' (Pascal) (1964: 63). Hence, at best, humans were 'justes pécheurs' (justified sinners): 'those who seek God with groans and anguish without being able to find him' (*Pensées*, quoted 1964: 163).[5]

Parallel to this were Pascal's actions at his bleakest, towards the end of his life, which epitomized both the pursuit of absolute ends and a turn to innerworldly asceticism. Meanwhile Racine was producing plays at court, in the heart of the Beast, so to speak. His *Phèdre* – the most pure of his tragic plays – pivots on the irresolvable opposition between Phèdre's transgressive love for her stepson, Hyppolyte, and her regal awareness of her precious public reputation. Thus rather than the monstrous figure whom some see in her, Racine's Phèdre is an ideal-type 'righteous sinner', who finds herself irrevocably abandoned by her closest friends and the world. His other tragic heroines in pursuit of love – such as Andromaque and Bérénice – are cast into a dizzy vortex of political passions where men with power are portrayed as acting like wild animals.

But what was the engine of this tragic vision? Goldmann produces a highly-compelling account of a social group that might have motivated the garnering of such an extraordinary harvest from its suffering. His detailed analysis proposes that this is the rise and fall of the noblesse de robe – a meritocratic State Nobility of law officers which had gathered strength throughout the 17th century, only to clash with the centralizing monarchy's royal intendants, a new bureaucratic stratum. These officials 'de robe' varied as to whether or not they were legally ennobled. But from the 1630s they all suffered from social devaluation, including the removal of their heirs' inheritance of their offices on payment of a tax (la paulette) and the degradation of their skills following the establishment of the new intendants and the 'conseils de roi'. Significant numbers of this group turned to Jansenism, especially from the Paris Parlement, which they staffed (Cohen 1994: 167–9; MacIntyre 1971: 82). Theirs was suddenly a socially-paradoxical position, structurally correspondent to the theological, moral and artistic paradoxes of *Les Pensées* and *Phedre*.

---

5 I am unconvinced by MacIntyre's explanation of the idea of the justified sinner. This does not mean – as MacIntyre suggests – that a just man may well be deprived of God's grace. Rather that (in certain interpretations) possessing predestined grace, one can sin and still not lose salvation *whatever act is committed*. It is this interpretation that is at stake in the 18th century Scottish novel, *A Justified Sinner* (Hogg). This is surely another of the paradoxes to which Pascal alludes in his onslaught on Descartes.

There remains one puzzle: if Racine could be appointed court dramatist, an Academician and one of only two royal historiographers, how could he be simultaneously the bearer of such an austere and uncompromising Jansenist tragic vision? This is a curious enigma given the quite different drama of Corneille and Molière, which – although sometimes expressing disenchantment – lacks the crushing necessity running through Racine's tragedy. For it appears that both Molière and Racine were central members of court society, yet Goldmann sees Molière as closest to the noblesse de cour (the pacified nobility of the feudal military aristocracy) while Racine expresses the outraged indignation of the noblesse de robe. As Viala (1985) elaborates, this enigma is heightened by the fact that the 17th century witnessed the first beginnings of an autonomous literary field, occupationally committed to freedom from State and Church control, which established certain new literary institutions such as the (writers') Academy (1635). Goldmann himself acknowledges Racine's membership of the Academy. Perhaps only such a well-placed and protected position could explain the room for manoeuvre that allowed the playwright to advance the discomfortingly tragic vision of *Phèdre* – his last and most uncompromising play.

Goldmann's wider solution to this puzzle is convincing. He argues that the orphaned Racine, brought up at Port Royal, turned sharply away from extreme Jansenism as an adolescent. He broke with Barcos as his spiritual father via a letter, and through him, with the entire convent community (1970b: 66). Indeed, unable to find other work, Racine turned transgressively back to the court as a dramatist. He not only married an actress but – flouting the Jansenist sexual ethic – made various other liaisons, all with actresses. Yet, despite appearances, Racine at court was not the 'fish in water' that this suggests. Openly a renegade from Jansenist authority and engaging in a literary form which was anathema to Jansenism, as a dramatist he never entirely gave up this inner commitment, even when writing to Louis XIV's wife (Mme de Maintenon) to expressly deny any active connections with Port Royal. Towards the end of his life, the resumed persecution of the Jansenists and the narrow conformism of the absolutist court turned him into an 'internal refugee'. Using Goffman's terms, we might say that Racine became an expert at 'passing'. It is this that is responsible for Racine's conflictual 'double vision', turning him into an extraordinary dramatist who:

> had brought together in his works the two principle traits of progressive literature: implacable realism and the defence of oppressed innocence (Goldmann, 1970b; 134, my translation).

Both Calvinism and Jansenism held a doctrine of predestination and a saved elect (Lovell 1973: 315). Why did predestination in the one instance produce an *inner-worldly activism* whilst in extremist Jansenism, with the exceptions above, it produced flight – being in but not of the world?[6] Here the different class-fractions that adopted the beliefs seem crucial, as Terry Lovell so lucidly argues. The rebuffs to the once ascendent noblesse de robe, described vividly both in Goldmann and in Perry Anderson's *Lineages of the Absolutist State,* induced their demoralized refusal. Having lost their semi-independent role they either had to join the Third Estate or retreat (Lovell 1973: 309). Their political and material situation thus contrasted sharply with the improved position of the urban merchant and industrial masters who, as Weber and others described, took up Calvinism.

These different responses are much more explicable now we possess Elias's phenomenological experience of everyday life in Parisian court society (2006). In particular the rise of the 'royal mechanism' (Elias) created not just the ruin of the noblesse de robe, but the forced domestication at court of the former noblesse d'épée (military nobility), their 'weapons reduced to words' (Elias 2006: 231) This stopped any potential for the traditional nobles' regionally-based rebellions against the kingly centre, but it created a new 'game' from which even the king – whom it benefited – was not exempt. This was organized around conspicuous luxury at court, in other words, a life dedicated to idleness, fashionable consumption and gambling, all activities funded by the peasants' raised taxes. It created a deepened gulf between the world of the court and plebeian society since both peasants and servants now became seen, in Elias's words, as a racialized other (Elias 2006: 53).

As Goldmann emphasizes, Pascal was himself an original social theorist, not just a theologian of Christian belief and ethics. More surprisingly, he was also an exemplary mathematician and, indeed, the inventor of roulette. We now have a greater understanding of what his distinctiveness was in terms of the parallel emergence historically of probability theory, for instance, in the playing of games of chance such as cards or dice. It is argued that this leap forward in statistics could only have come from the dawn of modernity and especially from the growth of a mercantile bourgeoisie, who instigated the first era of collective mutual insurance (Reith 2002: 28–9). This is not to deny anything that Goldmann wrote; yet the new historical studies of chance, probability and risk heighten even more acutely the paradoxes that Goldmann identifies as at the centre of Pascal's thought.

Part II: *Towards a Sociology of the Novel (1975 [1964])* and *Method in the Sociology of Literature (1981)*

As many have commented, Goldmann appeared subsequently to lay aside the theoretical approach of *The Hidden God,* for example in his studies of the 20th century novel (Cohen 1994; Eagleton 1976; Evans 1981; Orr 1977). His declared method is rather to adopt an internal analysis of the novels in order to discover

---

6   As Lovell points out, Calvinism was already a heresy, thus only Jansenism was effectively open to the noblesse de robe – subsequently, it would be deemed heretical as well (Lovell 1973: 320)

their significant literary structures, and then to explain these structures by showing
their homologies with the historical development of the structures of capitalism
itself. More specifically, he distinguishes between three stages: laissez-faire,
market-based capitalism with its emphasis on individual autonomy (1800–1910),
the First World War and interwar crisis of capitalism (1910–1950), and the period
of post-war 'organized capitalism' with State intervention and technocratic
authority (1950–1969). Thus he refers to certain wider literary motifs, such as the
dissolution of character associated with the inter-war period (in Kafka, Joyce, and
Musil) or the emergence of the nouveau roman or 'chosisme' (representations of
a reified world, without heroes) with post-war writers such as Robbe-Grillet and
Sarraute. But he typically omits both the social and literary groups in which the
novelists are situated. In other words, while these writers are chosen because their
works possess unusual thematic depth and aesthetic coherence, Goldmann fails
to clarify which social groups or 'transindividual subjects' are the bearers of their
work.

What, then, does Goldmann say about method? He does acknowledge that
these particular studies are 'internal' alone – i.e., that they display 'comprehension'
of the text but 'explication' only by means of reference to the changing nature of
capitalism (1975: 124). Elsewhere, endorsing Sartre's view that Valéry's poetry
cannot be *explained* by being located as the work of a petit- bourgeois writer,
Goldmann emphasizes that we must examine how this class fraction at a given
point develops a set of categories that are then elaborated with a notable coherence
and rigour through the richness of Valéry's writing (1970a: 249–50). But he does
not himself undertake this for the novel, via, for example, dissecting the plight and
contradictory pressures experienced by the petit-bourgeoisie.

Goldmann's analysis of Robbe-Grillet's experimental fictions is certainly a
telling advance over Lukács's wholesale dismissal of modernism as mere 'literary
subjectivism'. But in his *Novel* studies he fails to openly pose questions of his
authors' places either within the literary institution or within the field of power.
In the absence of this, his method here could be said to be, in John Orr's words:

> [a] mechanistic reflection of the changing nature of the economic system, in
> which social consciousness, as the third element, plays only a secondary role
> (Orr 1977: 35).

What then is his strategy with his extended study of the interwar novels of André
Malraux (1901–1976)? These are all shown to have the same significant structure:
a problematic hero who searches for authentic existence (Enlightenment values)
within a degraded universe. Unlike the epic form, his heroes fail to find these
enshrined in a viable community; or, more specifically, they may find an authentic
community but lose their lives in identifying with it.

The precise structures of Malraux's fictional works change along with his own
trajectory within the interwar period, undergoing transformation from surrealist
novellas to various types of realist narrative. These are organized round heroes

caught up in the history of French imperialism in Indo-China and the Chinese revolution. Several of these novels are set in Shanghai; they represent a very different world from, say, Ballard's *Empire of the Sun*: that of workers faced with oppressive structures very close to those of colonialism.

In Goldmann's view, the most powerfully organized and innovative of Malraux's novels are *Man's Fate* (1933) and *Man's Hope* (1938). *Man's Fate* is set in the industrialized region of China but is orchestrated around a Chinese couple, Kyo and May, who are members of the Shanghai revolutionary workers group. They in turn are dependent on the strategic decisions of the Chinese Communist Party leaders. The action revolves around the deliberate sacrifice of the Chinese revolutionary group by the Howkow Communist Party leadership, apparently in the interests of discipline but in fact to protect Soviet socialism from exposure to any danger via China. Thus *Man's Fate* ends with the betrayal and imprisonment of the vulnerable revolutionary group. Kyo and May are bound by their love as a couple, not by the exploitative eroticism depicted in earlier Malraux novels. But they finish by committing suicide. Sharing their cyanide pills, they cheat the otherwise inevitable torture before death that the Leadership's action has brought upon them, but, of course, at the cost of their lives.

Love appears once again in Malraux's last novel centring on revolution, *Man's Hope*, organized, like the earlier *Days of Wrath* (1935), around the engagements and defeats of the Spanish Civil War. This is a love remembered later in the person of the revolutionaries' child, who was born in Czechoslovakia, where they escaped Nazism. In *Man's Hope*, as in *Man's Fate*, Malraux depicts an emergent and non-problematic organic community and 'the supersession of solitude' (1975: 79). But in *Man's Hope* – haunted by Nazism and the consequent defence of the Soviet Union – there is an unequivocal celebration of the Communist Party as well as of the Republican revolutionaries, despite also introducing thematically the austere discipline of the Party. Its heroes would not die in vain but would be remembered as martyrs (1975: 80).

We can summarize Goldmann's key oppositions in his sociological analysis of Malraux by drawing on another of his works: *Lukács and Heidegger* (1977). Whilst crediting Heidegger with a critique of the sometimes superficial or even trivial nature of Western modernity, as well as acknowledging his incisive grasp of the phenomenological experiences of time and the omnipresence of death, it is Lukács who is viewed as offering a more democratic return to the values of the Enlightenment – in other words, liberty, tolerance, solidarity. These he combines with a model of an unalienated community. Heidegger on the other hand, is ultimately only concerned about the small elite community of creative individuals: in this sense, he is a Nietzschean philosopher.

In terms of novel structures, we could gloss Goldmann further by noting that Malraux's early literary works, up to and including *The Conquerors* (1927), are underpinned by Heideggerian or reactionary modernism. By *Man's Fate* Malraux has moved instead into the Lukácsian orbit of a pursuit of progressive values: an existence lived out in a tragic bid for a just social order. In this schema, *Man's*

Fate and *Man's Hope* are the equivalent of Pascal's *Pensées* and Racine's *Phèdre*: the most radical form of Malraux's tragic vision. In the intervening novel, *Days of Wrath*, he abandons a tragic vision, but maladroitly, and merely as the lesser of two evils. For Goldmann then, the development of the novel by this author is highly distinctive: 'Malraux is the only writer, apart from Victor Serge, to make the proletarian revolution an important structural element in his novels' (1975: 35).

Are there in fact groups to whom this literary structure can be linked? If we read Goldmann closely we notice that he criticizes Trotsky's interpretation of Malraux's 1928 'novel of the break', *The Conquerors*, as suffering from Stalinist blind-spots. Despite protests to the contrary, Goldmann in fact interrogates Malraux's novels in terms of their political or ethical structures and the political fractions underlying them. For this reason, for Goldmann, *Man's Fate* is the supreme example of the proletarian revolutionary novel because its realism possesses the perspective of the Russian Workers' opposition. *Days of Wrath*, on the other hand, is less powerful. Here Malraux gave up both the realist insights and the painful (even tragic) vision that he had possessed earlier, in order to depict the revolutionary couple making common cause with the Soviet Union in the Resistance.

In other words, beneath the surface, Goldmann's actual practice is to locate Malraux's entire fictional works in terms of their alternation between divergent literary groups. These groups are segregated first, by their *political world-visions* – including their reaction to the changing policies of the Soviet-dominated Communist Party in the context of the rise of Nazism. But they are also divided, secondly, by their *literary form*, especially surrealism versus realism.[7] The sociology of literature that has best extended this analysis of form and meaning is perhaps Sapiro's brilliant study (*La Guerre des Ecrivains* [1999]), which shows how French writers' political and literary stances within the Second World War were structured by the places they occupied within the various opposed regions of the literary field (Académie, Goncourt prize-winners, poets in small surrealist magazines etc).

We might add that in the 1930s, the novel of political revolution or of what Lunacharsky called the 'proletarianization of the Enlightenment' (Fitzpatrick 1970) stretched beyond the path-breaking contribution of Malraux. Indeed – with varying degrees of literary power – it underpinned the central literary structure adopted by numerous writers across the world, including Agnes Smedley, James Hanley, Tillie Olsen, Jean Guéhenno, Georges Navel, Lewis Jones and Grassic Gibbon (Klaus 1985: 106–27). Unlike Malraux, these novelists were of working-class origins.[8] But they participated, along with many educated writers from

---

7   Similarly, Flaubert's 'formalist realism' or 'pure novel' measured its distinctive universe within the literary field against Victor Hugo's earlier Romantic 'social art' and 'morality' (Bourdieu 1996 [1992]: 73, 111, 134–5, 237).

8   Malraux's father was a stockbroker; when bankrupted by the 1929 Crash, he committed suicide, as his maternal grandfather was suspected of having done.

the middle-class – such as Steinbeck, Dos Passos, and Malraux himself – in representing a socialist world-vision that had become truly global in scope.

There are two more points that should be made here. First, I would argue that it is essential to analyse the type of education (or cultural capital) that these various revolutionary writers possessed in order to elucidate the nature of the form they chose, the precise social meanings they represented and the composition of their alliances. This poses questions that obviously overlap with the concerns that Bourdieu has raised in relation to writers' necessarily slow acquisition of craft and experimental skills in modernist movements (1993; 1996). In brief: the more experimental the form, the longer the literary apprenticeship to master it.

Second, as David Harvey has suggested (1989: 275), a 'dialectical' (or progressive) world-vision has constantly alternated with regressive modernism.[9] The most recent period, since Goldmann's death, has produced a further variant of such a regressive modernism with an anti-historical, even anti-ethical turn to aesthetic formalism (Harvey 1989: 336, 338–42). If this is right, then the alternating shifts in artistic movement in the 19th century between the realist bohemia and the modernist bohemia, described so vividly by Bourdieu in *The Rules of Art*, have *continued* as oscillating artistic structures into the 20th century. It is only by pursuing both these aspects of the internal structuration of the literary field that we can find the deeper 'mediating' groups Goldman's critics searched for. Such mediating groups *appear* to be totally absent from *Towards a Sociology of the Novel* but Goldmann's schematic political comments surely beckon us towards them.

Goldmann's study of Genet's plays clarifies these issues further (1970c; 1981). Genet, in Goldmann's words, is the 'poet of the sub-proletariat' (1970c: 11). But he is also described by Goldmann as a poet whose mastery of form has entailed a reaching out to wider social groups – to progressive workers, the intelligentsia of the left, even the cultivated bourgeoisie (1970c: 13). More precisely, as with Pascal and Racine, it is necessary to identify, with Goldmann, different periods in Genet's drama and to notice over time a shift from a tragic vision – in which the contest for power merely produces a circulation of elites (*The Maids, The Balcony*) – to a more transformative vision (*The Screens*, and to a lesser degree *The Negroes*). Thus, for example, in *The Screens* the colonized Algerians are represented successfully staging a revolt against their colonizers, without immediately sinking into a pale reflection of their oppressors. Of course, there is a fidelity, too, to his early ideas of the outsider (*Querelle of Brest, Our Lady of Flowers*). But Goldmann is right to argue that if the earlier plays express the disillusionment of the working-class and the political Left with State socialism, the later plays return to a reworked version of this, with a new conception of a 'possible consciousness' and an alternative social reality.

---

9   Goldmann's essay (1959) on Kraus shows that a writer can be a "reactionary" in the non-deprecating sense of a thinker committed to 18th century Enlightenment ideals at a time of 20th century war and Depression.

This is not merely Goldmann's genetic structuralist reading of *Genet's* literary position-taking but it also epitomizes in certain key respects the development of *Goldmann's* own mature world-view, as noted perceptively by Cohen (1994: 199–200). For shortly before his death, Goldmann expresses the hope that the new combination of realism and 'optimism of the will' might be seen as the first swallow in the spring that will presage the summer. Genet's *The Screens* (1959) is symptomatic of this: the Events of May 1968 were also enactments of such hopes (1970c: 34). Goldmann distances himself from some of Genet's views, identifying this 'summer' with the model of workers' control in general, and the ideas of the Yugoslav Praxis group at their Korkula conference in particular (1970c: 34). Cohen reports that Goldmann went on to develop both concrete and detailed arguments for democratization, for example in the form of a film he made which owed much to Proudhon and to Spanish anarchism (Cohen 1994: 268–73). Here he finds fresh and suitably complex modes for confronting and detailing the transformation of the social world.

Part III: Goldmann Faced with the Crisis of Working-class Transformative Agency

Following Lukács's *History and Class Consciousness* (1971), Goldmann had conceptualized the working-class as the class most subjected to reification in capitalism and thus as the revolutionary force that would act as grave-digger of the entire economic and political system (1959; Naïr and Löwy, 1973: 37). Later, in the 1960s, deeply influenced by changes in contemporary capitalist organization, Goldmann questioned that classical position. He saw both Stalinism in Eastern Europe and the higher levels of material consumption in the West as having deeply undermined revolutionary dispositions (1970a: 296). Cohen has aptly expressed this as a move from *The Hidden God* to the Hidden Class (1994: Ch. 8).

However, against what he called Marcuse's 'pessimism', Goldmann never gave up the notion that humans develop *wider* aspirations when their material ones are satisfied (1970a: 280, 287); they crave further democratization at work, whilst they continue to possess and exercise powers of resistance against unjustified outcomes. Hence his attraction to the 1960s Yugoslavian factory-democracy reforms, to the ideas of the Praxis group such as Heller and Fehér, and to the thought of 'progressive workers' (1970a, 1970c: 13). But hence also his revaluation of *limited* market elements as a source of actors' autonomy:

> The great conquest of Yugoslav socialist democracy, *workers' control* ("autogestion") is, from a theoretical point of view not solely the means of assuring effective democracy, but [it is] also the union of an extensive socialization of the [...] means of production [...] which permits the end of the exploitation of man by man [...] and the maintenance of production for the market, facilitating the foundation of a real and authentic development of

"liberty from", the humanist values of liberty in general, the liberty of expression in particular and of individual dignity (1970a: 310, my translation; 1974).

I have no space here to debate the issue of market socialism. However, Goldmann's revisions of classical Marxist theories of proletarian opposition are worth further comments. In order to evaluate better such theories of the making – and remaking – of the working-class, we are now able to address the recent research undertaken by Satnam Virdee (2014). Whilst focusing particularly on Britain, this work has wider implications for the West as a whole. For it is Virdee's claim that from the 1880s on, the mainstream of the English working-class was *incorporated* within the British nation, via the ideology of social imperialism. It was only racialized outsiders who consistently resisted this turn – notably Irish-Catholic workers (racialized in the course of the 19th century), as well as Jewish, Indian, Caribbean and African migrants:

> [...] their attachment to the British nation tended to be less firm, whilst their participation in subaltern conflicts gave them a unique capacity to see through the fog of blood, soil and belonging so as to universalize the militant yet often particularistic fights of the working-class. In this sense, they acted as a leavening agent nourishing the struggles of all, informed by their unique perspective on society (2014: 164).

This suggests that a structural position exists which has been veiled both by the doctrinal historiography of classical Marxism and the retreat made by the Frankfurt School, most spectacularly by Adorno and Horkheimer. In contrast, Virdee is persuasive in noting the continued salience and radicalism of marginalized outsiders within the working-class from the 1880s on, particularly in relation to anti-imperialist and anti-fascist movements. It was they who offered the greatest resistance to Britain entering World War I and, much later, they who challenged racialized divisions in the 1960s. This argument merits extended analysis elsewhere, especially in relation to Goldmann's characterization of 20th century Western societies.

Since his death in 1970, some of Goldmann's later stances demand re-evaluation for different reasons. In particular we need to interrogate his conclusion that capitalism has overcome the *inherent tendencies to crises* in its earlier history (see also Evans 1981: 143–5). Writing in the Keynesian period, for him economies appeared to be haunted no longer by mass impoverishment and precarisation. Consequently the main issues now were different: they were the degradation of labour and the reification inherent in '[...] a society that threatens to deprive human life of all spiritual content' (1973: 95).

After forty years of neoliberal doxa and finance capitalism, in which it is largely the bourgeoisie that has acted in and for itself (Boltanski 2008), we need an expanded notion of the working-class or 'labour'. Following Goldmann and Mallet, this should include not just the 'new working-class' (educated technicians) to whom he referred, but nonmanual workers more broadly, who are devoid of significant power. We also need an unflinching recognition of the changes within capitalism since 1979, not least the return to social inequalities *on the same level as those of the pre-World War I Edwardian period*. Goldmann was rightly sensitive to changes in capitalism following Labourism and social democracy. But subsequent developments within the global capitalist world system – which he could not have foreseen – have recreated precarity and instability on a much more widespread basis (Harvey 1989: 328–35). In particular, new and well-documented research shows deepened gaps in class life-chances in terms of both income and returns from capital since the late 1970s. These buttress conjectures of a decline in social mobility and the success of a 'conservative revolution' (Piketty 2014: 246–50, 484–5, 549).

Yet if Goldmann had some justification in the late 1960s for detecting a decline of mainstream working-class activism, his rootedness in his time in other respects has since been laid bare. It is much to his credit that he broke with Lukács's repudiation of modernism. Yet his silence on other questions that have since moved to the fore is all too evident: the issue of patriarchy and gender divisions, for example, despite having Julia Kristeva as his doctoral student. In his work on Genet, he keeps to his drama alone, omitting the early novels that would require debating Genet's creative play with gay identities. Except for considering Genet's *The Negroes* and *The Screens* in terms of the liberation from colonialism, he never addresses Eurocentric perspectives[10] (1970c). Lastly, despite Cohen's justifiable praise for the flexible nature of his thought, in normative terms his theorizing of radical humanism is somewhat schematic, especially in comparison with writers such as Erich Fromm, Eric Olin Wright or Lawrence Wilde.

Yet despite these omissions, we should remember that it was Goldmann who from an early period stood up against linguistic structuralism, challenging the hegemony of Foucault's archaeology of knowledge – especially the provocation that 'Man is an invention of a recent date. And one perhaps nearing its end' (Foucault 1970 [1966]: 387). It was Goldmann, too, who consistently lamented Althusser's failure to address issues of agency or the future (see, for example, Goldmann 1981: 50, 87–8). He was fond of quoting a student who wrote on a blackboard in the midst of the May 1968 Events 'Structures don't take to the streets' (Goldmann 1981: 50).

Part IV: Goldmann and Bourdieu

Finally, I return to the disputed question of Goldmann's legacy. He has been rightly lauded as a sociologist of culture, both in Williams's striking obituary (1971), and more recently, Mitchell Cohen's thoughtful and erudite study (1994). Yet Williams's general assessment also raises persuasive critical arguments –

---

10   He briefly criticizes Malraux's Eurocentrism within his novels set in Indochina and China (1975).

does Goldmann's model of homology allow enough for the specific nature of the imaginative *literary* works which are 'a simultaneous realisation of and response to [...] underlying and formative structures' (1971: 14)? Williams argues cogently that orthodox Marxist conceptions never allowed sufficiently for the imaginative constructions of the writer. In contrast, the 'practical criticism' and the emergence of Leavis and 'Left Leavisism' had acknowledged the distinctive intensity of the literary response to new experiences and emergent social relations.[11] Goldmann was moving away from such a reductive approach, but his concept of form was still too abstract. The notion of a problematic hero pursuing authentic values in a degraded world was over-general. a philosophical legacy of Lukács's early *Soul and Form* and of the bipolar split between the abstract rationalist and empirical arguments in *History and Class Consciousness*. More close-up microscopic analysis of social tensions and contradictions was necessary, especially more awareness of differences within the novel as a genre, and a greater focus on novels outside the French tradition (Williams 1971: 15).

A similar point had been made cogently by Henri Lefebvre when he argued that Goldmann's methodological preference for works that exhibit great coherence is in danger of neglecting the registering of contradictions. 'Doesn't Goldmann tend to overestimate the importance of *coherence* and neglect the existence of contradictions in the works?' (Goldmann et al. 1967: 215, my translation and emphasis).

More combatively, reading Pierre Bourdieu's repeated criticisms of Goldmann, it might be thought Goldmann had left *no significant legacy in the sociology of culture* (1993: 56–7, 180–81; 1996 [1998]: 83, 202–3, 350n.2, 383n.24). Yet closer observation reveals that the issues are more disputed than that. It is clear that the evolution of Bourdieu's own master-concept of 'habitus' shared a dependence on the notion of 'collective consciousness' and 'homology' (see Goldmann 1970c: 37; Bourdieu 1968). Both authors became firm proponents of a 'genetic structuralism', stressing historical analysis, structuration and destructuration and, of course, actors' deep-rooted dispositions – labelled habitus (Bourdieu) and 'world vision' (Goldmann). Granted, Goldmann's mentors were Lukács and Piaget, whereas Bourdieu's mentors also included Canguilhem and Bachelard. But profound similarities are nevertheless evident.

Yet time and time again, Bourdieu was to raise as his principal objection to Goldmann the question of the absent cultural *field* as the milieu for specialized skills. Bourdieu shows the ways in which the internal structures of the field are refracted within the literary work.[12] Thus the same basic dispositions can produce

---

11   Williams also justifiably drew attention to the narrow basis for Goldmann's sociology of the literature, which lacks any reference to Shakespearean tragedy and in the novel, to the American as well as British traditions.

12   Bourdieu emphasizes here the chiasmic split between restricted field (eg the avant garde) and large-scale field ('entertainment') as well as the divisions between schools (for example, naturalism and symbolism).

very divergent literary works in relation to the specific region of the literary field that the writer inhabits and the specific historical period in which s/he is writing. Goldmann is challenged for his 'short-circuiting' approach to literature. There is essentially no difference, claims Bourdieu, between Goldmann's early works where he elaborates the homologies between the literary structures, the world-views and social groups' material or political urgencies, and that of his weakest, where these mediations are absent (Bourdieu 1993: 56–7, 180–81).

Now I still hold that Goldmann's *Hidden God* never simply 'short-circuited' the cultural field as Bourdieu claims (Fowler 1997). Why else would theological divisions have such importance in terms of separating or uniting writers, and explaining literary structures? But we can certainly concede that Goldmann largely leaves aside the genesis of semi-autonomous institutional structures in the literary field such as the Académie Française (founded in 1635). He failed to enquire how these and other literary structures affected the ideological dissidence discussed at such length re Jansenism (Viala 1985: 16, 23, 29[13]).

Yet there is something of a paradox about Bourdieu's own position. The abundant critical references to Goldmann suggest a degree of tacit recognition. For Bourdieu *also invokes* Goldmann's key concepts in his own work: this at the very least keeps them part of the sociological imagination, at most suggests a theoretical significance that his overt rejection denied. This debt to Goldmann is strikingly evident in *On Television and Journalism* where Bourdieu refers ironically to audience meters as the 'Hidden God' of the television world, invisibly controlling producers' actions (1998: 25). Note too, Bourdieu's 1990–1991 lectures at the Collège de France, *Sur l'Etat* (2012) which address centrally the role of the noblesse d'Etat in creating a meritocratic legal officier class and the rule of law. Here credit is surely due to Goldmann initially for exploring the tragic and paradoxical vision of the noblesse de robe under French absolutism.[14] Even more importantly, is it purely an accident that 'genetic structuralism' is retained by both sociologists as an approved theoretical approach?

I might note here one of Bourdieu's most well-cited books, *Pascalian Meditations* (2000). Given the explicit homage to Pascal as a sociologist in this work, does it not simultaneously serve as recognition of the celebrated study of

---

13   This point is by no means insignificant – Sapiro (1999) has shown in her illuminating study of French writers in the Second World War how certain positions in the literary field (particularly membership of the Academy and holding of Goncourt prizes) can be correlated with complicity towards the Vichy and occupying Nazi regimes. Just as a single exceptional Academician, François Mauriac, opposed the other celebrated members with his consistently critical, anti-Vichy stance, so Racine, as an earlier Academician, occupied that rare space of insider dissidence. We know from Goldmann that Racine was such an 'internal refugee' but it is certainly true that the impact of such institutional memberships merits more analysis than Goldmann gives it.

14   Despite the congruence of his argument, however, Bourdieu makes no reference to Goldmann in this work (2012).

his predecessor on Pascal and Racine? Indeed many of the positions Bourdieu himself adopts here remind us of Goldmann's Pascal. In this same text, Bourdieu cites Pascal on the object of sociological knowledge being englobed by the observer, who is in turn englobed by the world – a position similar to Goldmann's on the partial identity of subject and object.[15] He ends by referring poignantly to the (Pascalian) paradox of subordinate social groups – their possession of a habitus often accommodated to others' power yet for all that, their incontrovertible possession also of margins of liberty.

Conclusion: Goldmann and Politics: A Radical Humanist

One of Goldmann's greatest achievements was to look back to a 'Pascalian Marx' (MacIntyre) for whom socialism was a risk-laden project in pursuit of authentic values (Goldmann 1964: 300–301, 308–9; MacIntyre 1971: 85, Lovell 1973: 322). MacIntyre is surely right here that what is at stake with Goldmann's work is not simply the question of the hidden God, nor even that of the 'hidden class'. It is, much more profoundly, a gamble on the emancipatory possibility of socialism: a form of society in which the Enlightenment goals of tolerance and liberty are combined with the ending of material deprivation and the achievement of greater equality (Goldmann 1973 and 1977; Cohen 1994: 34–5; Davidson 2014). In this, Kant's vision of a just community might be realized in practice, not, as at present, in the false coin of the West's rhetoric of the international community. The alternative, as noted in World War II by Benjamin, is barbarism; in our time, barbarism via the threat of untrammelled neoliberalism on the one hand or that of absolutist Islam on the other. We need Goldmann to help teach us how to gamble wisely.

References

Anderson, Perry. 1974. *Lineages of the Absolutist State*. London: NLB.
Boltanski, Luc. 2008. *Rendre la Réalité Inacceptable*. Paris: Editions Demopolis.
Bourdieu, Pierre. 1968. 'Structuralism and the Theory of Social Knowledge', *Social Research*, 35(4) (Winter): 681–706.
Bourdieu, Pierre. 1993. *The Field of Cultural Production*. Cambridge: Polity.
Bourdieu, Pierre. 1998 [1996]. *On Television and Journalism*. London: Pluto.
Bourdieu, Pierre. 1996 [1992]. *The Rules of Art*. Cambridge: Polity.
Bourdieu, Pierre. 2000 [1997]. *Pascalian Meditations*. Cambridge: Polity.

---

15   In my view Bourdieu's *Pascalian Meditations* has deepened Goldmann's approach further. But this work similarly elucidates with great realism the remorseless determinants of class power within the present social world whilst also clarifying significant margins for liberty or transformative practices.

Bourdieu, Pierre. 2012. *Sur L'Etat*. Paris: Seuil.
Caute, David. 1971. 'Portrait of the Artist as a Midwife', *Times Literary Supplement*, 26th November.
Cohen, Mitchell. 1994. *The Wager of Lucien Goldmann: Tragedy, Dialectic and a Hidden God*. Princeton: Princeton University Press.
Davidson, Neil. 2014. *Holding Fast to an Image of the Past*. London: Haymarket.
Eagleton, Terry. 1976. *Criticism and Ideology*. London: Verso.
Elias, Norbert. 1996. *The Germans*. Cambridge: Polity.
Elias, Norbert. 2006 [1939]. *The Court Society*. Dublin: University College Dublin Press.
Evans, Mary. 1981. *Lucien Goldmann: An Introduction*. Brighton: Harvester Press.
Fitzpatrick, Sheila. 1970. *The Commissariat of Enlightenment: Soviet Organization of Education and the Arts under Lunacharsky*. Cambridge: Cambridge University Press.
Foucault, Michel. 1970 [1966]. *The Order of Things*. London: Tavistock.
Fowler, Bridget. 1997. *Pierre Bourdieu and Cultural Theory*. London: Sage.
Goldmann, Lucien. 1959. *Recherches Dialectiques*. Paris: Gallimard.
Goldmann, Lucien. 1964 [1956]. *The Hidden God*. London: Routledge and Kegan Paul.
Goldmann, Lucien, et al. 1967. *Littérature et Société*. Brussels: Université Libre de Bruxelles.
Goldmann, Lucien. 1969 [1966]. *The Human Sciences and Philosophy*. London: Jonathan Cape.
Goldmann, Lucien. 1970a. *Marxisme et Sciences Humaines*. Paris: Gallimard.
Goldmann, Lucien. 1970b [1956]. *Racine*. Paris: L'Arche.
Goldmann, Lucien. 1970c. *Sociologie de la Littérature: Recherches Récentes et Discussion*. Brussels: Université Libre de Bruxelles.
Goldmann, Lucien. 1973 [1968]. *The Philosophy of the Enlightenment*. London: Routledge and Kegan Paul.
Goldmann, Lucien. 1974. *Power and Humanism*. Nottingham: Spokesman Books.
Goldmann, Lucien. 1975 [1964]. *Towards a Sociology of the Novel*. London: Tavistock.
Goldmann, Lucien. 1977 [1973]. *Lukács and Heidegger*. London: Routledge and Kegan Paul.
Goldmann, Lucien. 1981. *Method in the Sociology of Literature*. Oxford: Basil Blackwell.
Goldmann, Lucien. 2011 [1945]. *Immanuel Kant*. London: Verso.
Harvey, David. 1989. *The Condition of Postmodernity*. Oxford: Basil Blackwell.
Klaus, Gustav. 1985. *The Literature of Labour*. Brighton: Harvester.
Lovell, Terry. 1973. 'Weber, Goldmann and the Sociology of Beliefs', *Archives Européenes de Sociologie* XIV: 304–23.
Lukács, Gyorgy. 1980. *Soul and Form*. London: Merlin.
Lukács, Gyorgy. 1971 [1923]. *History and Class Consciousness*. London: Merlin.

MacIntyre, Alasdair. 1971. *Against the Self-Images of the Age.* London: Duckworth.

Naïr, Sami and Michael Löwy. 1973. *Lucien Goldmann; ou la dialectique de la totalité.* Paris: Seghers.

Orr, John. 1977. *Tragic Realism and Modern Society.* London: Macmillan.

Piaget, Jean. 1972 [1970]. *The Principles of Genetic Epistemology.* London: Routledge and Kegan Paul.

Piketty, Thomas. 2014. *Capital in the Twenty-First Century*, Harvard, MA: Belknap Press.

Reith, Gerda. 2002. *The Age of Chance.* London: Routledge.

Sapiro, Gisèle. 1999. *La Guerre des Ecrivains.* Paris: Fayard.

Viala, Alain. 1985. *Naissance de l'Ecrivain.* Paris: Minuit.

Virdee, Satnam. 2014. *Racism, Class and the Racialized Outsider.* Basingstoke: Palgrave.

Wikipedia (consulted 10.5.2014) Jansenism.

Wikipedia (consulted 10.5.2014) Jean Racine.

Williams, Raymond. 1971. 'Literature and Sociology: in Memory of Lucien Goldmann', *New Left Review* 67 (May–June): 3–18.

Williams, Raymond. 1977. *Marxism and Literature.* Oxford: Oxford University Press.

Chapter 8

G.D.H. Cole:
Sociology, Politics, Empowerment
and 'How to be Socially Good'

Matt Dawson and Charles Masquelier

In recent years there have been attempts to revisit the history of British sociology. It was often suggested that prior to 1950 'sociology hardly existed in the British Isles as an intellectual enterprise or even a series of pragmatic prescriptions' (Soffer 1982: 768). In particular, the UK was seen as lacking any institutionalized form of sociological study (Anderson 1968); it is only recently that this story has been fully contested. A key topic here has been this 'problem of institutionalization' (Abrams 1968: 4), specifically how the one major institutional event, the appointment of L.T. Hobhouse to the Martin White Professorship in Sociology at the LSE in 1907, denied backing to figures such as Patrick Geddes (Studholme 2008), his collaborator Victor Branford (Scott and Bromley 2013) and H.G. Wells (Levitas 2010). Consequently, scholars have focused on how this meant certain visions of sociology, be they based on biology (Renwick 2012), the environment (Studholme 2008), social reconstruction (Scott and Bromley 2013) or utopianism (Levitas 2010) were lost.

These works have been important and fruitful, however, this history has tended to stop with World War I. British sociology has quickly gained a 'forgotten period' of the years between this and the late 50s/60s when the expansion of university education and the formation of the British Sociological Association provided new impetus to discuss sociology's history (Halsey 2007, Platt 2003). This is despite the fact sociology had a clear presence, and a number of successes, in Britain during these years as a 'floating discipline' (Rocquin 2014).

This chapter considers the work of a scholar active throughout this forgotten period: G.D.H. Cole. Cole is not part of the sociological canon with his name rarely, if ever, occurring in histories of the disciplines or summaries of social theory. There are justifiable reasons for this exclusion, including Cole's own distancing from the discipline (Cole 1957a). However, we will argue a key reason was Cole's era and work; by coming to prominence after these institutionalization battles Cole confronted a form of sociology which was antithetical to his views and goals. Rather than abide by its precepts he sought to combine sociology and politics in a normative theory driven by the idea of individual emancipation. As he put it: '"Social Theory", then, I regard as an essentially normative study, of which the purpose is to tell people how to be socially good, and to aim at social goods and avoid social evils' (Cole 1950: 10).

In what follows we will outline the basis of Cole's sociological outlook. From here we will discuss how Cole linked his sociology to a normatively driven political theory before finally returning to Cole's relation to the sociology of his day. Before that, however, some biographical detail is required.

Who was Cole?

George Douglas Howard Cole was born in 1889 and died in 1959 having been for 14 years the first holder of the Chichele Professorship of Social and Political Theory at the University of Oxford. Throughout his career, running from his first book, *The World of Labour* in 1913 to the posthumous publication of the final volume of his *History of Socialist Thought* in 1960, Cole filled many roles: he was a political theorist, a philosopher, a labour historian,[1] an economist and, as we will suggest, a sociologist. He published incredibly widely across these fields, including over 70 books and numerous articles.

Further to this, Cole held many roles outside academia: he was labour correspondent for the *Manchester Guardian*, a founding member of both the New Fabian Research Bureau and the Society for Socialist Inquiry and Propaganda, twice chairman of the Fabian Society (despite a sometimes frosty relationship with this group), a frequent writer for the New Statesman along with numerous newspapers both national and local,[2] a key player in the Workers Educational Association including its first Director of Tutorial Classes in 1922, a Labour candidate for parliament, director of the UNESCO seminar on workers' education, a writer of socialist ditties and plays, president of the International Socialist Society and a tutor to prominent Labour politicians, such as Hugh Gaitskell and Harold Wilson. He even found time to write 20 detective novels with his wife, Margaret Cole (see Cole 1971 and Carpenter 1973 for detailed biographies of Cole).

During Cole's time, his influence was vast, so much so that a so-called 'Cole Group' formed at Oxford (Gaitskell 1960). Indeed, the period of 1929–1933 has been termed the 'age of Cole' within the Labour party and the wider movement (Riddell 1995) and one obituary canonized him as a 'secular saint' (Martin 1959: 63).

One of Cole's biographies begins with the claim that 'obscurity has never been a threat to G.D.H. Cole' (Houseman 1979: 7) yet we would argue it is a major threat now. The exception to this occurs within socialist theory where his guild, or, as current parlance has it, libertarian, socialism (Cole 1920a) continues

---

1   Having effectively invented this field of study (Owen 1966)

2   The Cole archives in Nuffield College Library, University of Oxford, contain a large selection of such newspaper articles. Their topics are broad, including: contemporary politics, freedom, democracy, economics and capitalism.

to influence a small group of scholars (Schecter 1994; Wyatt 2011; Dawson 2013; Masquelier 2014). His continued influence in this field is perhaps unsurprising given the strongly normative element of Cole's thought, central to his sociology and his conception of what sociology should be.

Cole's Sociology

As we have seen above, Cole had a normative conception of sociological study as telling people 'how to be socially good'. Therefore, his turn to sociology was not due to a positivist desire to know, or an interpretivist will to understand, but rather due to a political drive to change. As he told his students at Oxford: 'that it is desirable to discover [social] regularities (which do exist) in order to know how to act for the best is evident' (Cole n.d.a: 7).[3] Therefore, Cole's fundamental claim that 'the subject-matter of social theory is the action of men [sic, and throughout the chapter] in association' (Cole 1920b: 17) is as much a normative claim concerning the ends of his guild socialism as it is an empirical claim regarding the centrality of function to modernity. Consequently, while in what follows the focus will be in outlining Cole's sociology this, as we shall see in the next section, is intimately tied to his political alternative, with its focus on individual emancipation and political pluralism.

This intimate connection is indicated by the fact that Cole's sociology starts with political theory, namely Rousseau and the general will, as 'the key to any rational social theory must be found in some conception of a General Will' (Cole 1914a: 149–50). However, in turning to Rousseau, Cole in effect 'sociologizes' him, since to understand how the general will is conceived for Cole, we need to begin with the principles which condition the nature of sociality. As Cole puts it:

> non-social man would be neither an egoist nor an altruist in any moral sense: he would be pre-moral. But he would have in him already, as essential parts of his nature, the qualities which under the influence of society would subsequently take on a moral character (Cole 1955a: ix).

Therefore, in drawing upon the trope of 'non-social man', a common hermeneutic device in social theory (Bauman 1990: 5), Cole argues that an 'essential' part of human activity and nature can be found in what he terms the 'associative will' (Cole 1914a: 145). Humans, for Cole, inevitably associate with one another, this is partly expressed through the need for association in 'satisfying common wants' and social action for common purpose (Cole 1920b: 49). Therefore, Cole's sociology is one concerned with association and its expression in *function*; the

---

3 Though undated this lecture, and the other undated references which follow, would have been delivered during the late 1940s or 1950s with perhaps the notes reused throughout this period.

associative will can be found when we have common interests or, as Cole also puts it, 'obligations' or 'loyalties' to others (Cole 1926). While this is primarily work-based loyalties, such as the associative form of production (Cole 1920a), it is also a wider conception, where loyalties are owed to civil bodies, such as Churches, and personal communities, such as the family (Cole 1926).

It is from such associations that morality grows. As has been noted by Lamb (2005) Cole's particular contribution to general will theory is an attempt to understand it as a process of structure and agency, a particularly sociological contribution. To begin with the structural elements, the general will, as the guidelines for moral conduct, grows out of the various associative wills and comes to exert a coercive function upon individuals. As Cole puts it, the general will develops 'a set of fundamental laws and principles that will induce the citizens' to act in line with its precepts (Cole 1955a: xxx). The fundamental precept of the social contract, from which the general will develops, is that a political sovereign exists to allow us to 'realize political liberty by giving up lawlessness and licence' (Cole 1955a: xvii). However, the associative will also drives social action since it is linked to our functional activity, as 'nothing is done without loyalty. Loyalty is the root of the tree of good and evil conduct' (Cole 1926: 156). Therefore, when acting functionally we are not simply acting through self-interest but also through the loyalties and obligations such associative activity engenders. The general will cannot possibly regulate such a diverse society. Consequently:

> As soon as the plurality of loyalties or obligations is admitted, and various groups and associations are seen as the points of focus for these various loyalties, it becomes plain that the individual will or conscience, guided by the consideration of right, is the sole rational arbitrator of such conflicts (Cole 1926: 160).

Therefore, while the general will provides moral precepts for all issues which affect all citizens, roughly speaking, equally and in the same way (Cole 1914a: 152) it is within associational activity that forms of associationally specific and individual morality are developed. However, it would be mistaken to treat these two planes as independent for Cole, since the general will is an *expression* of the desires of associations taken collectively and it is through associational activity that it emerges. As Cole argues: '*there is no General Will unless the people will the good*' (Cole 1955a: xxxvii). In associative action, then, the General Will or common good, i.e., the purpose of the association, becomes an extension of an individual's will, for it is both constituted by, and constitutive of, individual conceptions of the good life.

Consequently, Cole's sociology is fundamentally an *associational* sociology. It takes as its prime unit of analysis the associations formed by individuals, their varying functions and loyalties and how these change over time and space. This includes all the theoretical assumptions such an associational sociology would hold – that we all do form associations, that this is an inevitable part of sociality and that associations have forms of agency, the latter of these is a claim sociologists following Cole have urged the discipline to embrace (Schmitter 1993), though such an embrace has been infrequent. This means Cole's sociology has a clear point of analysis:

> We have to start out, not from the contrasted ideas of the atomized individual and of the State, but from man in all his complex groupings and relations, partially embodied in social institutions of many sorts and kinds, never in balanced equilibrium, but always changing, so that the pattern of loyalties and of social behaviour changes with them (Cole 1950: 15).

Therefore, Cole uses Rousseau's conception of the general will as the basis of his sociology. It was Rousseau's conception of '*pitié*', understood as the most fundamental and natural form of compassion, that particularly appealed to Cole, for it allowed 'sentiment' to become 'a force in the shaping of human affairs' (Cole 1950: 128) and 'rejects whatever leads in society to war or subjection of man' (Cole n.d.b: 8). Cole therefore borrowed from Rousseau the idea that sociality and the moral outlook entailed by the General Will, are grounded in 'human feeling itself' (Cole 1955a: liii) and ought to be construed as a 'primitive social impulse that has been overlaid by bad institutions, but not destroyed' (Cole 1950: 128–9).

It is here that Cole's sociology becomes critical, since he traces these 'bad institutions' back to capitalism and liberal democracy. Capitalism for Cole was the source of the inequality and poverty which blighted society and made equal realization of associative wills impossible due to a difference in resources (Cole 1955a: xxxvii). It also was inhumane in its subordination of individuals to economic requirements and dictates. As Cole put it: 'Socialists have all too often fixed their eyes upon the material misery of the poor without realizing that it rests upon the spiritual degradation of the slave' (Cole 1972: 41). This could especially be seen under contemporary forms of management where 'the worker is treated purely as a raw material of industry' (Cole 1914b: 119). Meanwhile, Cole rejected the fundamental premise of liberal democracy, with its focus on democratic representation on the arbitrary principle of location, rather than the socially lived differentiation of function (Cole 1920a). As we shall see, both of these were confronted in Cole's political alternative of guild socialism.

Before turning to that, however, it is important to note that Cole differentiated himself from two figures that seem similar to him, Marx and Durkheim. His relationship to the former is somewhat complex, for although he did not identify as a Marxist, he was keen to acknowledge his debt to Marxism (Cole 2010). This was unlike most sociologists of the period, in whom Marxism generated a fearful and conservative reaction (Rocquin 2014: 198). Cole in fact devoted an entire book – *The Meaning of Marxism* – to the task of re-assessing this school of thought in the light of empirical conditions and as a response to the vast array of (mis) interpretations of Marx's work. Here Cole attempts to recover 'the constructive influence of the minds of men' (Cole 2010: 17) in historical change, which some of the precepts of scientific Marxism had effectively obscured. Cole, therefore, not so much wished to reject the materialist conception of history as to praise Marx's recognition of the constantly changing nature of 'all living things' (Cole 2010: 3), even with the challenge posed by a newly emerging middle class to radical social change and scientific Marxism's 'profound error to contribute to "classes" … any reality distinct from that of the individuals which compose them' (Cole 2010: 1). Here one finds another explanation for Cole's fervour for the General Will's capacity to treat the 'reality' of the common good and the 'reality' of individual conceptions of the good life as co-constitutive.

Cole's similarities to Durkheim are notable and wide (see Dawson 2013) and indeed Cole read Durkheim and appreciated much of his work. He crowned him, reflecting the canon at the time, 'the most important French sociologist after Comte and LePlay' and praised his insistence on the 'functional character of diversity' (Cole 1952: 125). However, he had two key criticisms. Firstly, he argued that while Durkheim's discovery of coercive social facts was central he didn't fully discuss *why* societies develop their particular value structures (Cole n.d.c: 4). Secondly, he criticizes Durkheim for rejecting the notion of class struggle which reflects his nature as a 'conservative social thinker', who 'emphasizes the danger of new social tendencies coming into conflict with the existing moral order of a society, and so leading to its disruption' (Cole 1952: 127). Both of these points are united in Cole's focus on the demands of capital as both giving society certain value structures and in making class struggle central.

Therefore, Cole took up a unique position in the emerging sociological canon of his day, distancing himself from key figures and placing himself in the tradition of Rousseau.[4] In doing so, he had a key grounding for a critical and normative sociology, in which he opposed the perversion of a 'primitive social impulse' by 'bad [liberal capitalist] institutions' to the actualization of the General Will within a socialist alternative. In the following section we will look further at how Cole linked his sociology and politics.

Cole's Politics and Alternative

While we have noted above that Cole had an associational sociology, his normative focus was always driven by individual freedom and empowerment. He shared with Durkheim a belief that contemporary societies were marked by a regime of moral individualism (Cole 1950: 151–6) and put his own valuing of this into religious language with the claim that 'my Zeus is man' (Cole 1950: 16). Indeed, it was due to this belief in individual empowerment that Cole turned to associations since each individual was realized or 'made particular' by engaging in associational activity (Cole 1920b: 19–20). Therefore, this drove Cole's alternative: guild socialism.

---

4   Of course an irony here is that, unbeknown to Cole, Durkheim had also lectured approvingly on Rousseau from a sociological perspective (Durkheim 1970).

Guild socialism, in Cole's hands, was based on the two critiques which, as noted above, emerged from his critical sociology. Firstly, capital not only exacerbated poverty but also reduced the individual autonomy and freedom found in work. Cole refused to accept that people could not 'suffer deeply from spending their lives in tasks in which they find no pleasure' (Cole 1957b: 17) and, drawing his inspiration from William Morris (Cole 1957b), identified the source of this lack of pleasure with a lack of autonomy in a form of production subjected to the rule of the capitalist market. We have no evidence that Cole read Marx's *Economic and Philosophical Manuscripts*, but had he done so, he would have surely been impressed by its critique of the wage system, the division of labour and its concern for the role of work in the individual's 'open revelation of human faculties' (Marx 2000: 102). However, Cole did not limit the scope to a critique of labour and was keen to emphasize the fact that the 'good life is a blend of satisfactions achieved from consumption and satisfactions achieved from successful creation' (Cole 1950: 97). As such, he recognized the need to restore control in both spheres, for even the consumer failed to experience true autonomy on a marketplace dominated by 'commercial agencies' (Cole 1972: 107). Such a concern for self-realization of individuals *qua* producers and consumers led him to advocate the replacement of the capitalist system of allocation via the market with dialogical coordination between producers and consumers organized into democratic associations. Additionally, since a key tenet of guild socialism was that 'economic power precedes political power' (Cole 1920a: 180), ruling class power was seen to permeate political institutions, meaning that the state assumed 'more nakedly and obviously the shape of an instrument of class domination' (Cole 1920a: 22).

The second critique concerns the nature of representative democracy, since assuming that one person can represent each individual in all their functional activity 'flagrantly violates the fundamental principles of democracy' (Cole 1920a: 31), instead:

> The essentials of democratic representation, positively stated, are, first, that the represented shall have free choice of, constant contact with, and considerable control over, his representative. The second is that he should be called upon, not to choose someone to represent him as a man or as a citizen in all the aspects of citizenship, but only to choose someone to represent his point of view in relation to some particular purpose or group of purposes, in other words, some particular function. All true and democratic representation is therefore functional representation ... Brown, Jones and Robinson must therefore have, not one vote each, but as many different functional votes as there are different questions calling for associative action in which they are interested (Cole 1920a: 32–3).

Both of these critiques lead Cole to develop a system based upon associations, the guilds, representing individuals in their three fields of production, consumption and 'civic activities'. Each guild then has executive authority over its particular field (Cole 1920a). Importantly for Cole, this would be a highly devolved system so that the main activity of guilds happens at the level of 'the factory, or place of work' (Cole 1920a: 48). Guilds would be representative bodies where workers vote on issues of procedure as well as related concerns such as wages, appointment of managers and workplace regulations and would be in dialogue with consumers regarding the allocation of resources. This recognizes the value of political and moral individualism and how this is 'made particular' by functional activity while also removing the power of private capital by placing control in hands of the producers and consumers alike.

Within such a system the state, refashioned as the 'commune', has its field of activity greatly limited to co-ordination between guilds that negotiate their common interests and desires. While this commune body still has some executive activities (foreign affairs, 'coercive' functions, taxation) the principle of functional representation makes sovereignty multiple and connected to associative wills (Cole 1920a: 139–40). Furthermore, since 'the good State must be a State based on equality – on the equal participation of all its citizens' (Cole 1955a: xxxvii), the guilds ensure that all citizens get functional democratic voices in socialized corporations and, by removing the market mechanisms in favour of negotiation, lessen advantages of income while guaranteeing dialogical coordination.

These are the broad outlines of the guild socialist system which we don't have the space to explore further (see Dawson 2013: 62–72, 106–9; Masquelier 2014: 143–68). Instead, what is important for our discussion here is that Cole's guild socialism rests upon his sociological viewpoint and critique. Only by conceiving of the general will as emerging in a process of interaction between associative and general wills, with the goal of equal participation from all, can the justification for guild socialism be realized.

Reflecting Cole's wider interests and his turn to sociology, he also used guild socialism as an inspiration for practice, where 'willing the good' in this case was based upon the gradualist concept of 'encroaching control', i.e., actions 'directed to wrestling bit by bit from the hands of the possessing classes the economic power which they now exercise' (Cole 1920a: 196). Unsurprisingly, this required an association, the trade unions, to be active in advancing control and the gaining of economic power. Therefore, not only was Cole's sociology linked to an alternative, but also a way of realizing this alternative. It is this focus on means *and* ends – what later writers would term Cole's attempt to become the labour movement's *eminence grise* (Riddell 1995: 947) – which gave his sociology a unique position in its day.

Cole and British Sociology

Above we outlined what we termed Cole's 'sociology'; however, nowhere does Cole use that term to describe his work. Indeed, as we shall see below, Cole rejected the label of 'sociologist'. This is despite the fact Cole had some early and important connections to the world of British sociology. For example he published in the *British Journal of Sociology* (Cole 1957a), the *Sociological Review* (Cole 1914b) and the *American Journal of Sociology* (Cole 1946). He was also one of the sponsors on a letter which called for the formation of what would become the British Sociological Association (Platt 2003: 18–20), reviewed many of the key sociological books of his day, such as Lockwood's *Blackcoated Worker* (Cole 1959) and was acquainted with many of the early sociologists in the UK, including Barbara Wootton via the Workers' Educational Association (Oakley 2011: 96) and Michael Young who worked under him during Cole's brief period at the Ministry of Labour during World War II (Cole 1971: 231). Furthermore, his 1955 *Studies in Class Structure* has been claimed as one of the first sociological monograph on class in the UK (Abraham 1973: 626); its discussion of the emergence of a new 'technical' middle class and changes in forms of social mobility with the emergence of new occupations prefigured much sociological debate on class in the second half of the twentieth century.

Cole also contributed towards the further institutionalization of sociology in Britain. Upon returning to Oxford – as a Reader in Economics in 1925, during the war as the leader of the Nuffield Social Reconstruction Survey and later as the Chichele Professor – Cole agitated for greater inclusion of the social sciences at the University (Worswick 1960). For Carpenter it was largely due to Cole's advocacy on University committees that lectureships in sociology were established and that 'Oxford finally came to accept sociology' (Carpenter 1973: 219). Indeed, throughout his time in the Chichele professorship Cole was certainly one of the few, and perhaps the only, lecturer at Oxford to teach the theories of sociologists, including Durkheim, Comte, Turgot, LePlay, Ginsberg, Weber, T.H. Marshall and Parsons (Cole 1952).

It also seems that at the time, and for some time after, Cole was thought of as a sociologist. As part of a torrid attack by the writer St. John Ervine in 1934 on Cole as 'the greatest enemy of freedom alive in this land' compared to whom 'Sir Oswald Mosely is a devout lover of liberty' (Ervine 1934a) Ervine claimed that 'I have no doubt whatever of his authority or his influence among a large number of ardent politicians and sociologists' (Ervine 1934b). From a more sympathetic position, Houseman spoke of how Cole's desire to write accessible texts on social matters made him an early advocate of 'popular sociology' (Houseman 1979: 94), while Scott argues that Cole's ideas 'became influential elements in the emerging mainstream' of British sociology textbooks (Scott 2014: 214). Cole was also enthusiastic about one element of the emergence of sociology. In the UK, political and economic theory had largely been separated as disciplines. However, due to the growth of sociology in continental Europe, including the work of Durkheim, this divorce 'has not been anything like so complete' (Cole 1934: 3). This, for Cole, was to the great credit of sociology since economics and politics cannot be divorced in theory or practice, reflecting his desire to overcome such boundaries, condemning the '*isolation* of specialized studies from the general study of Society as a whole' (Cole 1950: 29).

Yet Cole rejected the label of sociologist. To understand why, it is easiest to quote him at length.

> Because I hold strong subjective views on these and other social questions, and have always taken part and interest in social investigation primarily for the purpose of furthering causes in which I believe, I have always rejected the appellation of "social scientist" and have been reluctant to accept that of "sociologist" for fear of being expected to restrict my conclusions to what can be inductively demonstrated on the basis of purely factual studies. This does not mean that I reject, or seek to minimize, the importance of studying as impartially as possible all the relevant "social facts" on the presence of which any effective action for change must needs rest to a very great extent. I want certain things because I believe them to be worth wanting, not because they are actually wanted (Cole 1957a: 167).

Therefore, as Cole put it,

> I am not a "social scientist", but a social idealist who tries to make use of the factual verdicts of scientific investigators, but not to be ruled by them, except in excluding the impracticable from my field of aspiration (Cole 1957a: 168).

We have seen above how Cole operated as a 'social idealist' in his attempt to link ideal conditions of existence to a normative project. The more pressing issue for this section is what led Cole to paint this picture of sociology and then differentiate himself from the discipline. To understand this, we must return to the question of the state of British sociology during this 'forgotten period' of its history.

The pre-WWI period of British sociology, the time of the 'problem of institutionalization', would have been a congenial environment for Cole. It is easy to imagine him engaging with Geddes' idea of sociology as applied civics given his own inspiration from William Morris and the ideas contained in his *A Factory as it May Be* (cf. Geddes 1904; Cole 1957b). He also would have been in agreement with the key argument of Wells that sociology is the 'creation of Utopias – and their exhaustive criticism' (Wells 1906: 367) given his own focus on using social theory to assist in willing the 'good society' (Cole 1950: 1–16). Alas, Cole was born too late for such debates. Therefore, when Cole speaks of sociology in this period having an 'outlaw' status (Cole 1950: 23) he was referring to its second quest, following institutionalization: the one for scientific recognition. As Renwick notes, after the battles for the Martin White Professorship, the task of establishing sociology as an autonomous science began (Renwick 2012: 170–77). In doing so, two distinct paths emerged, traced by Cole (1952: 117–18). One path, which Cole linked to the LSE, turned to evolution and the philosophy of history. Since this was influenced by the work of Max Weber it also tended to adopt the concept of value-free study. The second field, influenced by Durkheim, tended to move into the field of cultural anthropology through its use of the comparative method. Once again, this method tended to value objectivity in its desire to make value-free comparisons. In order to achieve such objectivity Cole argued sociology had become an increasingly 'statistical' discipline with only a few acolytes of theorizing left. These few had, in turn, become non-empirical and akin to philosophers rather than sociologists (Cole 1950: 26–7).

All of these elements, as we have seen, clashed with Cole's conception of intellectual study. Firstly, he was strongly opposed to intellectual specialization, which he saw as especially prominent in the greater use of statistical techniques. Secondly, while always valuing the role of theory, he consistently sought to connect this to material conditions, saying the social theorist is constantly concerned with finding 'data' (Cole 1950: 12). Thirdly, it contrasted with Cole's belief in sociology and social theory as the study of how to be 'socially good'. However, what counts as *good*, and the ends we should be seeking, is fundamentally, for Cole, a moral judgement (Cole 1950: 249) and, as he also argued, 'you can't *prove* anything to be good' (Cole n.d.d: 4). While Weber used a similar distinction between 'facts' and morals in his defence of value-freedom Cole goes in the opposite direction, arguing:

> It is often suggested that the sociologist will be endangering his objectivity if he identifies himself with the advocacy of any specific social policy, and that he ought in his investigations to set aside his personal beliefs and values and confine himself to a coldly impartial survey of facts. But what nonsense this is! ... the investigator who remains coldly aloof will never discover some of the most essential facts – especially the facts about the value-judgments of the persons whose conditions and mutual relations he is setting out to study. His duty as a sociologist is to remain aware of his bias, and to correct it in arriving at his conclusions: his duty cannot be not to have a bias, for it is often his having one that is his strongest inducement to undertake his investigations (Cole 1957a: 170–71).

Therefore, since moral positions lead us to certain topics and to appreciating the position of those we study, it is inevitable that morals, and biases, become part of sociological analysis. The fact that for Cole so many sociologists had attempted to ignore this, in effect creating a divide between a 'pure sociologist' who simply collects facts and a 'policy maker' who can decide ends, was the key problem with the sociology he encountered (Cole 1957a: 171). It is notable how close this view is to that of Howard Becker in his classic *Whose Side are we On?* (1967). Therefore, not only was Cole born too late for debates on the utopian elements of sociology, he was also born too early for debates on its values and normative ends.

There are undoubtedly other reasons Cole didn't make it into the sociological canon. His aversion towards specialization in favour of generalism is shared by other 'failed' sociologists, such as Geddes (Law 2012). Moreover, given the importance of books in canon building (DaSilva and Vieira 2011), Cole lacked that one truly great text which could be put on reading lists as a systemization of his thought, reflecting Cole's desire to write broadly and quickly, rather than carefully and in-depth (Carpenter 1973: 217–27). *Guild Socialism Restated* and *Social Theory* were close – the latter of which Scott (2014: 213) places as one of four 'pioneer' British sociology textbooks – but these were shaped by the aforementioned normative view, making them unsuitable for sociology's emerging quest for scientific recognition. But, to truly understand why Cole is not placed within the history of British sociology, it is central to understand the conditions of institutionalized sociology during his time. Cole simply did not 'fit' within the discipline's quest for scientific recognition and therefore was left to work within and across other disciplines. As we have suggested, had Cole been born later or earlier this may have been different, but sociology had the unfortunate luck of Cole working in the forgotten period of the discipline while also being alienated from it.[5]

Conclusion

As this chapter has hopefully shown Cole was a unique intellectual, yet he also confronted many of the issues which our discipline still confronts today; for example, what it means to be a 'sociologist' but also be 'public' and 'political'. He had his share of successes and continued to feel pride in the idea that his guild socialist work may have 'left a strong impression behind' on much of the Labour movement (Cole 1932: 66). But, Cole never lost his fundamentally optimistic, utopian urges. Despite his advocacy of a link between sociology and policy he could never be what Burawoy later termed a 'policy sociologist', required to craft policy with the ends decided by someone else (Burawoy 2005); Cole would always want to decide the ends too, hence why he defined policy broadly as 'what *ought* to be done' (Cole 1957a: 158). He held strong to the view that 'one could set out to be scientific *and* moral'; to decide both means and ends (Cole 1950: 249). This assured that Cole had a troubled relationship with leading lights in the Labour party who not only felt they had the authority to decide the ends but would flinch at Cole's utopianism. Indeed, when Clement Attlee would have Cole to visit he

---

5   It is striking how similar Cole's position is to someone else alienated from British sociology in this period: Karl Mannheim. Having arrived at the LSE in 1933, Mannheim instantly, and famously, clashed with Ginsberg and what he saw as the 'untheoretical empiricism' of British sociology (Kettler et al. 1984: 120). Such a breach became even more pronounced when Mannheim turned his hand to normative prescriptions and the construction of his 'Third Way' (Mannheim 1943). He was eventually forced to give up on sociology, spending the last year of his life in education research. Therefore, Mannheim and Cole confronted a form of sociology totally unaccommodating of their utopian and theoretical leanings. Indeed, Cole provided a lengthy review of one of Ginsberg's books where, rarely mentioning Ginsberg, he makes clear his belief in the need for both empirically driven theoretical enquiry and an orientation towards how actors can produce social change (Cole 1953). While Mannheim had already 'made his name' as a sociologist before coming to Britain, Cole had no such opportunity to be removed from British sociology.

would welcome him by saying 'give me a pair of starry eyes Douglas and I will do what you say' (Foot 1968: 53).

So Cole was a dreamer but there was another part of his personality we haven't covered. While many speak of his kindness and humility (see Martin 1959) he was also, by all reckoning, a bit lacking in humour and very much your stereotypical 'aloof intellectual' (Brown 1960). Cole was, in perhaps his most lasting public contribution, the inspiration for the character of Professor Yaffle in *Bagpuss*. Oliver Postgate, Cole's nephew by marriage and creator of the show, justified his choice by saying he wanted a character who 'had no sense of humour and wasn't a bit ridiculous' but who also was a 'distinguished academic personage who would claim to know everything and would go *"nerp, nerp, nerp"* in a birdy way' (Postgate 2010: 296). Recognizing these two parts of Cole character, the dreamer convinced by the value of associational forms of socialism and the dry academic puts us in mind of how Cole concluded his biography of another humourless dreamer, Robert Owen. The final words Cole used to defend Owen can apply equally to himself: 'Well, "non-sensical notions", as well as bores, are oftentimes the salt of the earth' (Cole 1930: 322).

Acknowledgements

Matt Dawson would like to thank the Warden and Fellows of Nuffield College, University of Oxford for kindly granting permission to reproduce material from the G.D.H. Cole archive, and the library staff at the college for facilitating access to the papers. Thanks also to the sociology subject area, University of Glasgow, for funding a trip to the archives.

References

Abraham, J.H. 1973. *Origins and Growth of British Sociology.* London: Penguin.
Abrams, P. 1968. *The Origins of British Sociology 1834–1914.* Chicago: University of Chicago Press.
Anderson, P. 1968. 'Components of the National Culture', in R. Blackburn and P. Anderson (eds), *Student Power.* Harmondsworth: Penguin, pp. 214–84.
Bauman, Z. 1990. 'Effacing the Face: On the Social Management of Moral Proximity', *Theory, Culture and Society* 7(1): 5–38.
Becker, H. 1967. 'Whose Side are We On?', *Social Problems* 14(3): 239–47.
Brown, I. 1960. 'G.D.H. Cole as an Undergraduate', in A. Briggs and J. Saville (eds), *Essays in Labour History: In Memory of G.D.H. Cole.* London: Macmillan and Co. Ltd, pp. 3–5.
Burawoy, M. 2005. 'For Public Sociology', *American Sociological Review* 70(1): 4–28.

Carpenter, L.P. 1973. *G.D.H. Cole: An Intellectual Biography*. Cambridge: Cambridge University Press.

Cole, G.D.H. 1914a. 'Conflicting Social Obligations', *Proceedings of the Aristotelian Society* 15 (1914–1915): 140–59.

Cole, G.D.H. 1914b. 'Discussion on Scientific Management', *Sociological Review* 7(2): 119–20.

Cole, G.D.H. 1920a. *Guild Socialism Re-stated*. London: Parsons.

Cole, G.D.H. 1920b. *Social Theory*. London: Methuen & Co.

Cole, G.D.H. 1926. 'Loyalties', *Proceedings of the Aristotelian Society* 26 (1925–1926): 151–70.

Cole, G.D.H. 1930. *The Life of Robert Owen*. London: Macmillan & Co.

Cole, G.D.H. 1932. *Modern Theories and Forms of Industrial Organization*. London: Victor Gollancz Ltd.

Cole, G.D.H. 1934. *Some Relations between Political and Economic Theory*. London: Macmillan & Co.

Cole, G.D.H. 1946. 'The Study of Social Facts', *American Journal of Sociology* 52(2): 147–9.

Cole, G.D.H. 1950. *Essays in Social Theory*. London: Macmillan.

Cole, G.D.H. 1952. *Politico-Economic Theories Part II (1850-)*. Lecture, Cole Collection, Nuffield College, University of Oxford. Box 55, Document E3/13/1/1-172.

Cole, G.D.H. 1953. 'The Idea of Progress: Review article of *The Idea of Progress: A Revaluation* by Morris Ginsberg', *British Journal of Sociology* 4(3): 266–85.

Cole, G.D.H. 1955a. 'Introduction', in J.J. Rousseau (1968) *The Social Contract and Discourses*. London: Everyman's Library, J.M. Dent and Sons, pp. v–xxxviii.

Cole, G.D.H. 1955b. *Studies in Class Structure*. London: Routledge.

Cole, G.D.H. 1957a. 'Sociology and Social Policy', *British Journal of Sociology* 8(2): 158–71.

Cole, G.D.H. 1957b. *William Morris as a Socialist: A Lecture*. London: William Morris Society.

Cole, G.D.H. 1959. 'Review of: The Blackcoated Worker, A Study in Class Consciousness by David Lockwood', *British Journal of Sociology* 10(1): 71–3.

Cole, G.D.H. 1972. *Self-Government in Industry*. London: Hutchinson.

Cole, G.D.H. 2010. *The Meaning of Marxism*. London: Routledge.

Cole, G.D.H. N.d.a. *Is There a Science of Politics?* Lecture on Introduction to Social and Political Theory course, Cole Collection, Nuffield College, University of Oxford. Box 53, Document E3/2/3/1-7.

Cole, G.D.H. N.d.b. *Nature and the Natural Man*. Lecture on Rousseau's Politics course, Cole Collection, Nuffield College, University of Oxford. Box 55, Document E3/18/2/1-8.

Cole, G.D.H. N.d.c. *Sociology and Psychology in Relation to Political Theory*. Lecture on Introduction to Social and Political Theory course, Cole Collection, Nuffield College, University of Oxford. Box 53, Document E3/2/4/1-7.

Cole, G.D.H. N.d.d. *Concepts of Freedom and Democracy.* Lecture on Introduction to Social and Political Theory course, Cole Collection, Nuffield College, University of Oxford. Box 53, Document E3/2/5/1-7.

Cole, M. 1971. *The Life of G.D.H. Cole.* London: Macmillan Press.

DaSilva, F.C. and M.B. Vieira 2011. 'Books and Canon Building in Sociology: The Case of *Mind, Self and Society*', *Journal of Classical Sociology* 11(4): 356–77.

Dawson, M. 2013. *Late Modernity, Individualization and Socialism: An Associational Critique of Neoliberalism.* Basingstoke: Palgrave Macmillan.

Durkheim, E. 1970. *Montesquieu and Rousseau: Forerunners of Sociology.* Michigan: University of Michigan Press.

Ervine, S.J. 1934a. 'Notes on the Way', *Time and Tide*, 24 November, Cole Collection, Nuffield College, University of Oxford. Box 6, Document A1/36/6/3-4.

Ervine, S.J. 1934b. 'Ervine's Response', *Time and Tide*, 22 December, Cole Collection, Nuffield College, University of Oxford. Box 6, Document A1/36/6/6.

Foot, P. 1968. *The Politics of Harold Wilson.* Harmondsworth: Penguin.

Gaitskell, H. 1960. 'At Oxford in the Twenties', in A. Briggs and J. Saville (eds), *Essays in Labour History: In Memory of G.D.H. Cole.* London: Macmillan and Co. Ltd, pp. 6–19.

Geddes, P. 1904. 'Civics as Applied Sociology', in Sociological Society, *Sociological Papers 1904.* London: Macmillan, pp. 103–18.

Halsey, A.H. 2004. *A History of Sociology in Britain.* Oxford: Oxford University Press.

Houseman, G. 1979. *G.D.H. Cole.* Boston, MA: Twayne Publishers.

Kettler, D., V. Meja and N. Stehr. 1984. *Karl Mannheim.* Chichester: Ellis Horwood.

Lamb, P. 2005. 'G.D.H. Cole on the General Will: A Socialist Reflects on Rousseau', *European Journal of Political Theory* 4(3): 283–300.

Law, A. 2012. 'Scholastic Ambivalence and Patrick Geddes: A Sociology of Failed Sociology', *Journal of Scottish Thought* 5: 41–71.

Levitas, R. 2010. 'Back to the Future: Wells, Sociology, Utopia and Method', *Sociological Review* 58(4): 530–47.

Mannheim, K. 1943. *Diagnosis of our Time: Wartime Essays of a Sociologist.* London: Routledge.

Martin, K. 1959. 'G.D.H. Cole', *New Statesman*, 17 January, 63.

Marx, K. 2000. 'Economic and Philosophical Manuscripts', in D. McLellan (ed.), *Karl Marx: Selected Writings.* Oxford: Oxford University Press.

Masquelier, C. 2014. *Critical Theory and Libertarian Socialism: Realizing the Political Potential of Critical Social Theory.* London: Bloomsbury.

Oakley, A. 2011. *A Critical Woman: Barbara Wootton, Social Science and Public Policy in the Twentieth Century.* London: Bloomsbury.

Owen, G. 1966. 'G.D.H. Cole's Historical Writings', *International Review of Social History* 11(2): 169–96.

Platt, J. 2003. *The British Sociological Association: A Sociological History.* Durham: sociologypress.

Postgate, O. 2010. *Seeing Things: A Memoir.* London: Canongate Books.

Renwick, C. 2012. *British Sociology's Lost Biological Roots: A History of Futures Past.* Basingstoke: Palgrave Macmillan.

Riddell, N. 1995. '"The Age of Cole?" G.D.H. Cole and the British Labour Movement, 1929–33', *The Historical Journal* 38(4): 933–57.

Rocquin, B. 2014. 'British Sociology in the Inter-War Years', in J. Holmwood and J. Scott (eds), *Palgrave Handbook of Sociology in Britain.* Basingstoke: Palgrave Macmillan, pp. 189–210.

Schecter, D. 1994. *Radical Theories: Paths Beyond Marxism and Social Democracy.* Manchester: University of Manchester Press.

Schmitter, P. 1993. 'Organizations as (Secondary) Citizens', in W.J. Wilson (ed.), *Sociology and the Public Agenda.* London: Sage, pp. 143–63.

Scott, J. 2014. 'Building a Textbook Tradition: Sociology in Britain, 1900–68', in J. Holmwood and J. Scott (eds), *Palgrave Handbook of Sociology in Britain.* Basingstoke: Palgrave Macmillan, pp. 211–35.

Scott, J. and R. Bromley. 2013. *Envisioning Sociology: Victor Branford, Patrick Geddes, and the Quest for Social Reconstruction.* New York: State University of New York Press.

Studholme, M. 2008. 'Patrick Geddes and the History of Environmental Sociology in Britain: A Cautionary Tale', *Journal of Classical Sociology* 8(3): 367–91.

Soffer, R. 1982. 'Why do Disciplines Fail? The Strange Case of British Sociology', *The English Historical Review* 97(385): 767–802.

Wells, H.G. 1906. 'The So-Called Science of Sociology', in Sociological Society, *Sociological Papers 1906.* London: Macmillan, pp. 357–69.

Worswick, G.D.N. 1960. 'Cole and Oxford, 1938–1958', in A. Briggs and J. Saville (eds), *Essays in Labour History: In Memory of G.D.H. Cole.* London: Macmillan and Co. Ltd, pp. 25–40.

Wyatt, C. 2011. *Defetishized Society: New Economic Democracy as an Alternative to Capitalism.* London: Continuum.

Chapter 9

Social Monads, Not Social Facts: Gabriel Tarde's Tool for Sociological Analysis

Álvaro Santana-Acuña

Standard accounts of the history of sociology often present the rise of the discipline in a linear fashion. From the cradle of the Scottish and French enlightenments, sociology benefitted from Comte's and Spencer's pioneering efforts and decades later from Durkheim's and Weber's early structural enterprises (Collins 1994; Eriksson 1993; Ritzer 2010). Yet, as most contributors to this volume point out, the evolution of the discipline is neither teleological (for it suggests an arrow) nor even ramified (for it suggests a common trunk), but rather messy and multiplex. In its early days there were numerous alternatives to draw the boundaries and contents of sociology. My particular contribution to this exercise in avoiding sociological amnesia and in expanding the horizon of alternative sociologies is the study of Gabriel Tarde's monads. Why Tarde? And why monads? My contention is that, in the late 19th century, the production of sociological knowledge about society could have been concerned not with the analysis of social facts but with that of social monads. In 1893, one year before Durkheim launched his programmatic call for the study of social facts in *The Rules of Sociological Method* ([1894] 1973), Tarde – one of his rivals – advanced his own programmatic call for sociological enquiry: the transformation of monads into *social* monads. I argue that Tarde's effort was truly groundbreaking. Writing on monads, that is, on single, simple, and independent units, can be traced back to the Pythagoreans (5th century BC). In the 17th century, the German mathematician and philosopher Gottfried Leibniz renewed their study. However, Tarde criticized Leibniz for conceiving of monads as closed atoms and offered a new definition: monads were interactive units. For Tarde, this turned monads into social atoms and thus into an object of sociological research. He advanced his contribution in *Monadology and Sociology* (*Monadologie et sociologie* [(1893) 1999]), a work that remains peripheral to the sociological canon.

In analysing Tarde's transformation of monads into social units, this chapter suggests that the social monad could have become a foundational tool of the nascent discipline of sociology. This chapter does so by comparing Tarde's social monads to Durkheim's social facts. With that comparison, this chapter seeks two additional and larger goals. First, it reflects upon the idea of the sociological canon (Alexander 1988; Connell 1997; Ritzer 2010) and, second, it offers some insights on why Tardian sociology has attracted international attention in recent years.

Building on this second goal, the chapter suggests that, rather than treating them as 'curiosities', engaging with works outside the structuralist tradition can provide researchers with an alternative arena for sociological innovation. This is the case of Tarde's non-structuralist tool of the monad in *Monadology and Sociology*.

The chapter proceeds in the following way. The first two sections introduce the figure of Gabriel Tarde and the concept of the monad. The next three sections analyse Tarde's neo-monadology and specifically how he turned monads into social monads and why his neo-monadology cannot be described as individualistic but rather as unitarian, that is, not as being concerned with agentic individuals, but rather with socialized and interactive units. The last two sections compare Tarde's social monads and Durkheim's social facts.

Tarde: The Sociologist, His Work, and His Disciplinary Standing

Gabriel Tarde (1843–1904) was a sociologist, criminologist, and social psychologist. A native of the Dordogne (southwestern France), he served there as a magistrate until 1894, when he was appointed director of the criminal statistics bureau at the Ministry of Justice in Paris. Thanks primarily to his path-breaking work in criminology, in 1900 he was named professor of modern philosophy at the Collège de France, to this day one of the nation's most prestigious higher education and research establishments (Clark 1973).

Tarde's major works include *La Criminalité comparée* (1890), *La Philosophie pénale* (1890), *Les Lois de l'imitation* (1890), *Les Transformations du droit. Étude sociologique* (1891), *Monadologie et sociologie* (1893), *La Logique sociale* (1895), *Fragment d'histoire future* (1896), *L'Opposition universelle. Essai d'une théorie des contraires* (1897), *Écrits de psychologie sociale* (1898), *Les Lois sociales. Esquisse d'une sociologie* (1898), *L'Opinion et la foule* (1901), and *La Psychologie économique* (1902).[1] Their translation into English has been irregular and sporadic. Translations comprise his work in criminology, *Penal Philosophy*; in sociology, *The Laws of Imitation* and *Social Laws: An Outline of Sociology*; and even his science fiction utopia *Underground Man* (H.G. Wells wrote the preface for the English edition). The most recent addition is *Monadology and Sociology*, available since 2012.[2]

Accordingly, Tarde's influence has mostly been limited to criminology and to a lesser extent to sociology. In France, social psychologist Serge Moscovici (1976, 1981) studied social movements, minorities, and masses, as well as the role of innovation in social change drawing upon Tarde's works. More recently, at the onset of the poststructuralist turn in the human and social sciences, philosopher

---

1   An online list of his complete works, including his fiction writings, is available on the French Ministry of Justice website. http://www.enap.justice.fr/ressources/index. php?rubrique=15. Retrieved July 26, 2014.

2   Tarde, Gabriel. [1893] 2012. *Monadology and Sociology*. Melbourne, Australia: re.press.

Gilles Deleuze (1968) and sociologist and anthropologist Bruno Latour (2002, 2008) have contributed to bring Tardian sociology back in. In the United States, scholars, especially those related to the Chicago School of Sociology, took up Tarde's theories on innovation, imitation, and diffusion (e.g., Rogers [1962] 2003). In 1969 the University of Chicago Press dedicated to his work a volume of selected writings entitled *On Communication and Social Influence*, which is part of the seminal 'The Heritage of Sociology' series that features the work of canonical (e.g., Durkheim and Weber) and non-canonical but influential sociologists (e.g., Max Scheler and Pitirim Sorokin). As another sign of the growing interest in Tarde's sociology, the volume was reissued in 2010.

Yet, for almost a century, Tarde has also been regarded as an esoteric sociologist (Clark 1973; Latour 2002). This characterization is mostly due to his call for an understanding of social life as made out of monads, as he presented it in *Monadology and Sociology*. Yet as this chapter seeks to show, in 1893 the call for a sociology anchored in monadological analysis was far from esoteric. Writings on monads punctuate the history of Western philosophy since the Pythagoreans to Leibniz (more on this below). To put it differently, in the late 19th century, the call for a sociology of monads was no less arcane than a sociology of social facts or social structures, since the latter had not yet emerged as dominant sociological tools. Hence, if Tarde's monads became a difficult idea to grasp in the 20th century, it is partly due to the historical process by which structuralist understandings of social life (e.g., Durkheim's collective representations, Weber's ideal types, Lévi-Strauss's structures, and Parsons's systems) took preeminence over less or non-structuralist understandings (such as Tarde's or his contemporary, Simmel).

It remains to be seen whether the interest in post- or non-structuralist understandings of social life (Bauman 2000; Giddens 1990; Latour 2005) would make Tarde a more canonical author. Since the early 21st century new contributions not only make him less of an esoteric sociologist but also they reveal the existence of alternative ways of thinking about sociology during its formative decades. At least in France, some of these alternatives were eclipsed by the success of Durkheimian sociology (Lukes 1985; Riley, Miller, and Pickering 2013). One such alternative was 'the monad'.

Monads: More a Way of Framing Reality than a Thing

The monad is primarily a philosophical concept. In its most basic definition, it refers to a way of framing reality characterized by the idea of unity. Beyond this definition, the monad can be formulated in multiple ways, from metaphysics to materialism. Hence, the monad can encompass from the perfect or supreme unity (that is, the monad becomes something similar to the idea of the One, First Being, or God) to the minimal unity (e.g., the atom). The monad can also be regarded as a microcosm containing within it the totality of possible beings. The origins of monadic thought are customarily linked to the Pythagoreans (5th century BC), especially Philolaus, Archytas, and Pythagoras himself. They regarded the monad as the first existing thing or original unity. It was, as Diogenes Laertius (1853: 8.19) put it, 'the beginning of everything'. Then, according to the Pythagoreans, from the original monad emerged the dyad, from the dyad the numbers, from the numbers the signs, from the signs the lines, from the lines the plain figures, from the plain figures the solid figures, from the solid figures the sensible bodies, which are four: fire, water, earth, and air.

The idea of the monad as a foundational 'unit' of reality made its way into Platonic and Neoplatonic philosophy (e.g., Syrianus, Nicomachus, and Iamblichus). Centuries later, via Neoplatonism, the monad entered medieval Christian theology mainly as a reference to God (e.g., Thierry of Chartres, Dominicus Gundissalinus, and Nicholas of Cusa) and, during the late Renaissance and the Scientific Revolution, it was taken up by Giordano Bruno, Henry More, and Gottfried Leibniz. In *De triplici minimo et mensura* (1591) and *De monade, numero et figura* (1591), Bruno (1548–1600), a Dominican friar and philosopher, reaffirmed the connection between the divine and the monad. God, in short, was the supreme monad. But also it continued to be an indivisible unit that constituted the minimal element of spiritual and material things. Like Bruno, in his early writings Henry More (1614–1687), a philosopher of the Cambridge Platonist School, equated the monad to God, which he called 'Nature Monadicall' and 'unmoved Monad' (Reid 2012: 51). However, in his late writings, More shifted towards a more materialistic (and arguably secular) definition, which was closer to the idea of the atom: 'By physical monads, I understand particles so minute that they cannot be further divided or dispersed into parts' (ibid.).

In the 1690s the German philosopher and mathematician Gottfried Leibniz, who had access to More's late writings, took up this *atomic* understanding of the monad. He laid out such an understanding in *La Monadologie* (1998)[3] a work originally written in French in 1714 and conceived as a treatise on the science of unity. This work not only continues to be regarded as the most influential contribution to modern monadic thought, but also it was Leibniz's alternative to the Cartesian dualism between mind and body. He offered a metaphysical system of monads that eliminated dualisms. He defined the monad as a simple substance, which was indivisible, autarchic and without extensions, parts, or shape. The universe consisted of monads; they were the first element of every composed thing, possessed actions and passions (§49), and were endowed with the power of perception (§15). The monads with higher perception power were 'souls', while the rest were formed by the perceiving mind into aggregates that constituted material objects. When it came to creating or suppressing monads, God was the only one capable of doing so.

Thus, for Leibniz the monad was an irreducible force, containing in itself the source of all its actions. This was a critical point of his monadology. As he famously put it: 'the monads have *no windows* through which something can enter or leave'

---

3   References to this work will appear as parenthetical section citations.

(§7 – my emphasis). This meant that he believed no monad exerted its influence over another, since each was an individuality defined by the ensemble of its intrinsic characteristics (§9). His autarchic view of the monad had important implications for the way in which change could occur (an aspect criticized by Tarde). For Leibniz, change could never happen due to reciprocal influence among monads. Instead, each monad was equipped with an internal principle of change (§10–11) and everything was regulated by a pre-established harmony (§78–79). As I will explain below, Tarde believed the opposite: monads were constantly interacting. Yet, from Leibniz, Tarde retained the goal of offering an anti-Cartesian way of thinking, that is, an anti-dualist system that did not distinguish by default between, in Tarde's case, the individual and society. Rather, monadic thought permitted Tarde to present them as part of the same continuum of reality.

After Leibniz, especially during the 19th century, monadic thought experienced two significant changes. First, the atomic (materialistic) understanding of the monad rose to prominence (as opposed to the spiritual or providential understanding; that is, the emphasis on God as a monad); and second, the idea of the unity of the monad was equated to the idea of the unity of the natural and social realms. These two changes made it possible that the monad could be increasingly referred to, in the natural sciences, as a 'single-celled organism' and, in the human and social sciences, as the 'individual human subject', especially if separated from society.[4] In short, these changes confirmed a semantic shift by means of which the monad was used not to point out to God, but to individual natural and social elements. This was the context of modern materialism and individualism in which Tarde formulated his call for neo-monadology. He did so, not by endorsing the individuality of the monad (as in Leibniz), but rather by showing that they were social units, interacting with each other. In so doing, Tarde's revision of classical monadology led to the invention of *social* monads.

Neo-Monadology: A Manifesto for a New Sociological Way of Seeing

Monadology and Sociology (hereafter *MS*)[5] can be divided into two parts. In the first one, Tarde sought to convince readers about the existence and appropriateness of thinking about the world from a modern scientific viewpoint in terms of monads. As he claimed, 'science tends to pulverize the universe, to multiply beings indefinitely' (43); an avalanche of new discoveries in biology, astronomy, physics, etc., he argued, demonstrated that monads really existed. But 'we have just seen that science, after pulverizing the universe, necessarily spiritualizes its dust' (55).

---

4   'monad, n.' OED. 2014. http://www.oed.com.ezp-prod1.hul.harvard.edu/view/Entry/121054?redirectedFrom=monad. Retrieved July 26, 2014.

5   References to this work will appear as page citations. All translations are mine.

In other words, he criticized the divorce that separated empirical findings and the theories underlying them from the overarching logic that should govern science.

The reunification of both (theory/empirical evidence and scientific logic) was the objective of the second part of *MS*, in which Tarde analysed the objections sociology faced in order to become a disciplinary analytical viewpoint. He argued that 'the affirmation of monads' (55) in scientific discourse was a crucial step in that direction and he sought to convince his readers by also employing common sense arguments; for instance, by acknowledging the intelligence of small things, such as monads, versus big things (53).

MS was thus a real manifesto, in which Tarde attempted to prove empirically that a major change in the perception of reality had been taking place in the human, social, and natural sciences in recent decades:

> All this may seem strange, but in the end, all this it is no more than a commonly accepted way of seeing, commonly accepted until now by scientists and philosophers, and which the universal sociological viewpoint must have the logical effect of delivering it to us (67).

What was previously seen and conceptualized as homogeneous (e.g., human cells, the cosmic nebulous, the life of nations, the structure of atoms, the functioning of illnesses, etc. (34 & 72)) had become increasingly more and more nuanced, detailed, and multiform. In short, the world, he argued, was moving towards the infinitesimal:

> We see where this trend leads us if pushed to the limit: to monads that fulfill the wish of the boldest Leibnizian spiritualism. Whereas the vital principle, disease, another entity treated as a person by ancient doctors, is pulverized into infinitesimal disorders of histological elements, and, moreover, largely due to the discoveries of Pasteur, the parasitic theory of disease, which explains these disorders by internal conflicts of tiny organisms, is spreading every day and even with an excess that must be called a reaction. But parasites also have their parasites. And so on. Again the infinitesimal! (35)

For Tarde, what laid beneath this major change in perception were monads. Although scientists and ordinary people had not yet observed them, he insisted that they ought to believe in them:

> Before the telescope, which has revealed us the multiformity of nebulae, stellar types, double and variable stars, did not we dream universally, beyond the known sky, beyond immutable and incorruptible heavens? And in the infinitely small, which remained, even more than the infinitely large, inaccessible to our observations, do not we dream also about the philosopher's stone in a thousand forms, the identical atom of chemists, the supposedly homogeneous protoplasm of naturalists? (72)

By collapsing both areas, the empirical (namely, reality was much smaller than previously believed) and the theoretical (monads were an even smaller part of the reality that science was beginning to see empirically), Tarde pursued a critical enterprise in *MS*: to establish a robust connection between progress and groundbreaking discoveries in all sciences and his own scientific agenda of making a case for the material existence of monads. The book's opening left no doubt of his triumphalism:

> Leibniz's monads have come a long way since their father. By various independent channels they now enter, according to the opinion of scientists themselves, the heart of modern science. It is remarkable that all secondary hypotheses involved in this great event ... are being established scientifically (33).

Tarde nevertheless knew that his own age was quite 'mechanistic', which deprived people from believing in monads (52), and he also condemned a common prejudice: the unknown was considered less intelligible (54).

Inventing Social Monads

To compensate for these shortcomings, Tarde revised classical monadology to translate monads into sociological language. His path-breaking revision of Leibniz was twofold: first, he made monads *social*, that is, he transformed them into a suitable concept to refer to human affairs as social and, second, he conceived of monads as a theoretical tool to overcome the duality of the world, especially society versus the individual.

It could then be argued that Tarde's call for a change in the perception of reality was in fact dual: via monads and the social. Their coupling confirms that Tarde was as committed as other leading intellectuals at the time (such as Durkheim) to create and shape the limits of sociology as a true discipline of the social. Indeed, as seen above, the use of monadology as a foundation of his sociological agenda was far from being an esoteric enterprise. By choosing Leibniz's monadology, Tarde tried to overcome the pervasive dualism (especially in its Cartesian version) between body and mind and, more generally, between matter and spirit. He criticized that, while science was reducing the scale of observation, it still did not go beyond this dualism. He realized that a similar dualism – the individual versus society – permeated the young discipline of sociology. So, a critical improvement of the Leibnizian theory of monads, which he called neo-monadology, was his alternative to overcome such dualism.

In Leibniz, monads were indivisible, closed, and immaterial. They acted as spiritual forces and also differed from each other. Unlike Tarde, Leibniz believed that monads were simple substances, without smaller parts; in other words, they were true closed atoms that formed the universe but could not communicate among them for they lacked external windows. Nevertheless, Leibnizian monads condensed and reflected the totality, and were ordered by the law of pre-established harmony that governed their interaction. Tarde decisively departed from Leibniz's paradigm in opposing the idea of closed monads:

> Many characters, many mysteries perplex the philosopher in particular. Can we hope to solve them by designing open monads that inter-penetrate each other instead of being external to each other? I believe, and I observe that, on this side again, the progress of science, I mean not only contemporary but modern, promotes the emergence of a renewed monadology. The discovery of Newtonian attraction, of action at a distance and at any distance, of material elements on each other, shows the attention that one must pay to their impenetrability. Each of them, once regarded as a point, becomes a sphere of action extended indefinitely (since the analogy suggests that gravity, like all other physical forces, spreads itself sequentially), and all these interpenetrating spheres are specific domains to each element, perhaps as specific domains that, although mixed, we falsely take them for a single space (56–57 – my emphasis).

For Tarde, seeking to transform monads into a foundation of sociology (as a science of interpenetrating realms), the Leibnizian universe of closed monads was a dead-end. Monads, on the contrary, were open, had contacts among them, and interacted in an open universe. Monads met and cooperated in order to create the world. In short, they were social:

> Left to itself, therefore, a monad can do nothing. That is the central fact, and it immediately explains another, *the tendency of monads to get together* (66 – original emphasis).

It could be argued that Tarde's epistemological recognition of monads' interactive nature developed out of the historical context of late nineteenth-century Europe, when the 'social question' became an everyday concern for scholars, activists, and politicians, and out of the institutional need to create a science that could make sense of reality's growing sociality (Donzelot 1984, Procacci 1993). Yet Tarde's neo-monadology was not a call in favor of social holism. On the contrary, he recognized that certain dimensions of reality were non-social and aspired to demonstrate that monads behaved socially and shaped society.

Since human beings were also social ('the strong instinct of sociability that provokes in men the desire to agglomerate' (61)), Tarde's groundbreaking move was to equate the social life of monads to the social life of human beings. For him, the society of monads resembled the society of humans:

> In a society no individual can act socially or be in any way without the collaboration of a large number of other individuals, mostly ignored by the first. Obscure workers who, through the accumulation of small facts, prepare the development of a large scientific theory formulated by a Newton, a Cuvier, a Darwin, form

somehow a kind of organism whose genius is the soul, and their work is the cerebral vibrations of which this theory is the conscience ... We observe also that the obscure workers I just mentioned can have as much merit, erudition, strength of mind, as the glorious beneficiaries of their work. This is incidentally the way to address the prejudice that leads us to judge as inferior to us all external monads. If the self (*le moi*) is no more than a leading monad among myriads of accompanying monads in the same brain, why do we believe in their inferiority? Is a monarch necessarily more intelligent than his ministers or his subjects? (66).

For Tarde the social entailed cooperation or interaction among individuals, which consequently led to the formation of a larger universe: society. Yet, another departure from Leibniz's paradigm was necessary to transfer monadology to the social world. It was necessary that complex entities could be monads too. When applied to the social world, this meant that an individual could be a monad of society:

> If we look at the social world, the only one known to us from *within*, we see officers, men, more differentiated, more individually characterized, richer in continual variations than the machinery of government, the laws and systems beliefs, dictionaries and grammars themselves (69).

A social-shaped-by-individuals did not mean that Tarde favored ontological individualism (or social holism). On the contrary, by claiming that individuals could be understood as monads he actually sought to do away with the dualism of the individual versus society. That dualism was sterile because for him monads showed no duality in nature. In other words, Tarde's monadological individuals were a monistic unit. Society emerged as a result of the interaction of individuals, but of individuals that behave like social monads. That is, they behave openly, interactively, never completely isolated, and as part of the entire universe. As Tarde put it:

> It is really surprising to see men of science, so engaged in repeating about everything that *nothing is created* (*rien ne se crée*), implicitly admitting as something obvious that *simple reports of various beings can themselves become new beings added numerically to the first*. Yet this is what we admit, perhaps without realizing it, when, the hypothesis of monads being rejected, we attempt by means of another thing and notably by the game of atoms, to explain these two capital appearances, a new living individual and a new me (67 – original emphasis).

Consequently, when applied to the social, neo-monadology could not simply be reduced to the search for the smallest *material* atom. Since an individual (who was not, materially speaking, the smallest part) acted as a monad within a larger society, Tarde's neo-monadology ultimately became a metaphor of the social world, a game of analytical scales. This distinction is central since Tardian sociology has been incorrectly labeled as individualistic (Durkheim 1972, Latour 2002, Scott 2007, Tarde [1969] 2010).

Unitarianism, or Why Tarde's Neo-Monadology is Not Individualistic

Presenting Tarde's approach to monads as further confirmation of his 'individualistic' sociology is, I would argue, inadequate because, first it fails to understand the theory and history of monadology as well as its philosophical context; second it misinterprets the scope and ontology behind Tardian neo-monadology; and third it is greatly influenced by the tendency to oppose Durkheim and Tarde as if they neatly incarnated in scientific writing the dualism of society versus the individual. Instead, my claim is that Tarde was a theorist of what I call 'unitarianism' (Santana-Acuña 2015). Drawing on his neo-monadology, he theorized society not as governed by agentic individuals, but rather by socialized and interactive units. His analytical distinction between individuals and units is absolutely crucial because, for Tarde, interactive units could encompass everything, from entire nations to individuals. As mentioned above, Tarde equated the social life of monads to the social life of human beings. For him, no individual (like no monad) could act socially without collaborating with a larger number of other individuals. Furthermore, Tarde rejected ontological individualism by arguing that individual consciousness was activated via monads, which were involved in thought processes:

> In this ultra-gaseous world, for example, the beam does not always walk in a straight line; the more we get closer to the individual element, the more the variability in the observed phenomena ... Thus, as society, as life, chemistry seems to bear witness to the need for universal difference, the principle and the end of all hierarchies and all developments (77–78).

Rather than falling under the label of ontological individualism (arguably a conceptual shortcut we still owe to the institutional triumph of Durkheimian structuralism), Tardian neo-monadology seems closer to Adam Smith's and other Scottish thinkers' (such as Thomas Reid and Adam Ferguson) understanding of the social as the result of interaction among individuals, that is, as *beings-in-association* (Santana-Acuña 2015). In Smith's *The Theory of Moral Sentiments* (1759), the social was neither about fully rational but moral (that is, sentimental) individuals nor about an impersonal force that constrained and structured individuals' lives. For Smith, humans' exchange of sentiments was the basis of sociality. Similarly, in Tarde, 'we can define [society] in our opinion [as] the reciprocal possession, under extremely varied forms, of all by each' (85). Society then entailed human interdependence among different human beings and, like nature, it was continuously changing and being replaced:

> In any development sufficiently long, we observe a succession and interlacement of phenomenal layers (*couches phénoménales*), alternately remarkable in their regularity and caprice, permanence and transience of the reports they present to us. The example of societies is very adequate to grasp this great fact and to suggest at the same time its true meaning (73).

Therefore, contingency (fugacity, caprice, variability, difference, etc.), as it also occurs in nature (77), embodied in Tarde one of the constitutive components of the social:

> Men who speak all different accents, intonations, voice tones, gestures: that is the social element, real chaos of discordant heterogeneities. Yet in the long run, out of this confusing Babel emerge general patterns of language, formulated in grammatical laws (74).

The real question then was: how did ordered patterns (e.g., language and grammar) emerge from heterogeneous rather than homogeneous conditions (e.g., millions of people speaking with different accents)? His answer was that human capacity to fill out the space of difference constituted also the space for the emergence of the social. Again, he saw no actual dualism between the individual and society, but rather a continuum. In consequence, for Tarde, the social was *a contingent regularity in human interdependence across time and space*, and social evolution and forms were guided by permanent change and diversity:

> [H]ere, in social change and social aggregations, to which we belong and where we have the advantage of holding the two extremes of the chain ... we see clearly that order and simplicity are simple terms, stills (*alambics*) where deposits somehow the elementary diversity powerfully transformed ... Diversity, and not unity, is at the heart of things: this conclusion can be inferred from the general remark that a simple glance at the world and science allows us to do. Everywhere an exuberant wealth of unheard variations and modulations burst of these permanent themes called living species, stellar systems, balances of any kind, and eventually it kills them and renews them entirely (76 & 78).

This constituted Tarde's final departure from Leibniz's monadology. While the German philosopher conceived of monads operating according to a pre-established harmony, the French sociologist defined them as components of a diverse and messy reality, constantly in the making, being assembled and reassembled.

Durkheim's Alternative: Social Facts

As a baffled Charles Dickens wrote in the opening paragraph of *Hard Times* ([1854] 1869: 7), 'Facts alone are wanted in life' and 'nothing but Facts' should be taught to boys and girls at school. By the mid-19th century the study of 'facts' had become a remarkably novel phenomenon. Dickens' opening precisely captured the growing reputation of a new unit of knowledge: 'the modern fact' (Poovey 1998). The fabrication of modern facts aimed to produce systematic knowledge from descriptions of observed particulars, mainly as a result of the popularity of numerical representation as the privileged means for gathering and presenting facts. In the second half of the 19th century, a particular type of modern fact attracted increasing attention: the 'social fact' (Cabrera and Santana-Acuña 2006, Poovey 2002, Procacci 1993). A key problem of the social fact was how to define its empirical contents, so that it could be used to study society methodically and scientifically. This was Durkheim's main concern in *The Rules of Sociological Method* ([1894] 1973), in which he offered his own definition of the social fact. Along with it, he advanced alternative tools, such as 'social currents' and 'social substratum' (*le substrat social*), which, like Tarde's monads, did not become part of mainstream sociological discourse (Terrier 2011). Only the tool of 'social facts' became foundational to the discipline and stuck in the long term.

Yet in the 1890s, Durkheim's call for a sociology based on the study of social facts was arguably more arcane than Tarde's revision of the monads as social. Durkheim argued that the social fact was a thing-in-itself and it had a life of its own, which was independent of and different from the individual consciousness of its carrier. That thing, the social fact, could not be seen in its purest form because it was distinct from its individual manifestations. And yet, according to Durkheim, the social fact was a real objective force; it had enough 'constraining power' to structure the actions of individuals even against their own will (e.g., an individual who abandons himself to the behavior of a crowd). Their constraining power became more apparent when individuals broke rules and laws. Hence, social facts were primarily 'coercive', which was the main characteristic to recognize them: their power of 'external coercion ... over individuals' (Durkheim [1894] 1973: 21). However, he obviated that the implementation of a punishment for breaking a rule or law would not be carried out by the thing-in-itself (the social fact) but by actual individuals. Tarde ([1890] 1993), who referred to social facts in dealing with units, argued that 'the individual facts that [Durkheim calls] social are not the elements of a social fact, they are only the manifestation of it' (Vargas et al. 2008: 764).

Durkheim, in short, opted for emphasizing the coercive dimension in the making of social relations, while Tarde ([1890] 1993) favored imitation. For Durkheim, the best example of coercion as a foundation of the human being's socialization was the education of children. Curiously enough, education is inextricably linked to imitation, a Tardian theme (Vargas et al. 2008).

Tardian versus Durkheimian Sociology: Competing Discourses on the Social

The image of society Durkheim had in mind was not one of interaction, namely, of a universe of interacting units. This image was closer to Tarde's; society was the material evidence of humans' spontaneous order and grouping. For Durkheim, on the contrary, society became a being that existed in itself, 'une réalité *sui generis*'.[6] While for Durkheim society was already present (as if its existence somehow

---

6   'Society is a reality *sui generis*. It has its own characteristics that cannot be found, or cannot be found in the same form, in the rest of the universe. Therefore, the representations that express it have a different content than purely individual representations and one can

predated that of the individual), Tarde did not take society completely for granted. In fact, he was aware of its increasing pervasiveness in scientific and everyday lexicon:

> It is remarkable that science tends strangely to generalize the notion of society by a logical addition to its previous trends. [Science] talks about animal societies ... cellular companies, why not atomic societies? Did I mention the societies of planets, solar and stellar systems? All sciences seem destined to become branches of sociology ... Then why not the molecule, for instance, could be a society like the plant or the animal? (58 & 59).

Tarde ultimately understood society as a natural phenomenon (for him the social and the organic did not become entirely isolated spheres) and more importantly as a material object in search of its place inside the nascent discipline of sociology (like Durkheim). But Durkheim sought to isolate the social from the organic sphere. Despite these clear differences, it is worth emphasizing that research on the Tarde-Durkheim divide (a) has focused markedly on the institutional dimension and (b) has overlooked crucial similarities between the two authors.

(a) Institutional dimension. Although it cannot be denied that there was an evident institutional divide between Tarde and Durkheim,[7] in my analysis of *MS* I sought to demonstrate that it was more the outcome of a real epistemological divide: their irreconcilable conceptions of the social. While in Durkheim the social was a true objective force that structured individual action and society became a being that existed in itself and, consequently, could not be reduced to an aggregate of individuals, Tarde emphasized the individual (or unitarian) dimension in the making of society via social interaction (or interpenetration of units):

> [A] serious obstacle arises when we come to human societies. In this case we are at home, it is we who are the real components of these coherent systems of people called cities or states, regiments or congregations ... But no matter how intimate, deep, harmonious a social group is, we never see to flow *ex abrupto* in the middle of surprised associates (*associés surpris*) a real and not just

---

be assured in advance that the first ones add something else to the second ones' (Durkheim [1912] 1968: intro, sec. II).

7   Whereas Tarde was an influential intellectual at the time and in 1900 reached the summit of the French academic system by obtaining a chair at the Collège de France, Durkheim, who fought for a long time to gain an important academic position in Paris, obtained the chair of education at the Sorbonne shortly after, in 1902. The institutional factor continues to be meaningful; the Collège de France remains mainly a research institution, while Durkheim occupied a position that provided him with power over the training of secondary school teachers. However, it is unclear how Durkheimian sociology triumphed at the institutional level, since the generation of students he trained were drafted to serve in the army (and many died) during World War I (Lukes 1985; Terrier 2011). Only throughout the 1920s, Durkheimians arguably won the institutional war and Tardian sociology became a marginal trend.

metaphorically *collective self*; a wonderful result if the conditions were given. No doubt there is always an associate that represents and personifies the whole group or a small number of associates (the ministers of a government) who, each in a particular aspect, individualize them no less fully (68).

(b) Similarities. By focusing on the causes underlying the Tarde-Durkheim divide, research has overlooked a central similarity, which paradoxically serves as a major cause for the conflict: their disciplinary commitment. Having different agendas in mind, both Tarde and Durkheim sought forcefully to institute sociology in France as a science of the social. By transforming suicide into a true social phenomenon, Durkheim sought to rescue it from psychological explanations. And Tarde in his studies on criminology transformed crime into a social phenomenon. Opposing in particular the theories of Cesare Lombroso, who defended the biological origins of criminality, Tarde argued that the origins of crime were social. Another and even more striking similarity is that both did not understand the social as a holistic reality. Rather, reality was formed by non-social and extra-social dimensions that did not interest sociologists but other disciplines (e.g., psychology).[8] Hence, Tarde and Durkheim shared a common and critical enterprise: to enlarge, fix, standardize, and institutionalize the disciplinary boundaries of sociology. They did so by advancing competing definitions of the social.

On Tarde's Return. The Representation of Society: From the Table to the Network

Why has Tarde's sociology gained currency in the last two decades? It could be argued that the spread of post-structuralism (Bauman 2000, Giddens 1990), the epistemological rehabilitation of human agency (e.g., via Actor-Network Theory) (Latour 2005), and the late 20th-century crisis of the social (Cabrera and Santana-Acuña 2006) set new intellectual conditions that oriented research interest towards a sociology such as Tarde's, which is non-structural, attentive to questions of agency, and critical of the taken-for-grantedness of the social. These conditions have led to an international attempt (especially in France and the United States) to unearth Tardian sociology and to apply it empirically.[9]

---

8   'At the same time we are English or French, we are mammals, and accordingly we carry in our blood not only germs of social instincts that predispose us to imitate our neighbors, to believe what they believe, to want what they want, but also the seeds of non-social instincts, among whom are the antisocial ones. Certainly, if society had made us entirely, it would have made us only sociable beings' (81). See also *MS*, 76, 80, 90, and 96. In Durkheim, see e.g., *Le Suicide* (1897), especially book I, on the extra-social factors of suicide.

9   See Anonymous (2001), the special issue of *Economy and Society* on Tarde (Anonymous 2007), Latour (2002, 2008), and Vargas et al. (2008).

Beyond the abovementioned conditions, I want to advance a more visual and tangible reason for the renewed interest in Tardian sociology. Such interest coincides with ongoing changes in the visual representation of the social. Unlike Tarde, who claimed in 1893 that monads have not yet been seen, Durkheim claimed a year later that statistics permitted observation of social facts in their pure form. Fast-forwarding to the present, methodological developments in social network analysis and Actor-Network Theory (ANT) over the last three decades have offered an alternative understanding of social forces. These developments represent social forces not as numerical graphs and tabulated statistical numbers (as in Durkheim). Rather, they visualize social forces as single units or nodes (from individuals to nations) connected by constantly changing social ties (the latter could encompass from the spread of happiness through a network of individuals to the flows of global trade relations among nations). This image of society as a dynamic network of ties among single units rather than as a still statistical table, that is, the image of society as single units connected by multiple and constantly changing ties is arguably closer to the universe of interacting social monads Tarde had in mind when he wrote *Monadology and Sociology*. Hence, it could be argued that Tarde's way of framing reality as social monads now offers a more fluid and less structural understanding of social relations that matches recent and new ways of visually representing society and social bonds as networked and dynamic.

In addition, without diminishing the importance of the previously discussed institutional factors involved in promoting Durkheimian versus Tardian sociology, it is worth taking into consideration a supplementary and less explored technical reason. In the 1890s the lack of suitable means of representing a networked society of single units (as it has now become pervasive thanks to network analysis and computers) could have contributed to make Tardian sociology more daunting technically and less appealing empirically than Durkheim's tabulated reality of statistical social facts, as epitomized by his classic study *Suicide*.

Yet to explain Tarde's decline and Durkheim's success, it has become standard to argue (Durkheim 1972, Scott 2007, Tarde [1969] 2010) that Tarde was a theorist of individualism at a time when individualism was under attack and, hence, his return could be associated with a parallel return of individualism in the last three decades. However, as this chapter sought to show, Tarde's neo-monadology was neither anchored in the notion of methodological individualism nor in that of social holism. Instead, Tarde sought to question this and other sterile dichotomies via what I call unitarianism – his view of society as composed of socialized and interactive units; and not of agentic individuals. This is why Tarde's ideas have attracted more attention among ANT scholars than among partisans of methodological individualism. Key features of the ANT 'sensibility', as John Law and Vicky Singleton (2013) put it, are (1) the concern with social flows and ties rather than structures and (2) the task of avoiding easy dichotomies and taken-for-granted concepts such as society and the individual (Latour 2005). This chapter contended that, in Tarde's neo-monadology, one can found elements of the ANT sensibility: an understanding of social affairs as the result of interactive, interpenetrating monads, in which the dualism between the individual and society does not work by default. Likewise, Tarde's neo-monadology did not locate causality in structural forces, but rather in interdependence and interaction. The social units he referred to as monads played such a role. They facilitated an understanding of the social as a non-individualistic and autonomous space, full of permanent interaction and contingency; in other words, they functioned as an extra-individual dimension that could not be entirely governed by human beings. This unitarian approach was different from the structuralist and constraining understanding of social facts embraced by Durkheim and different from the individualistic understanding of society.

Finally, by showing how Tarde turned monads into social monads, this chapter sought to reflect upon the idea of the sociological canon by analysing how the non-structuralist tool of the monad departs from the canonical (namely, structuralist) understanding of the social. Tardian social monads functioned ultimately as an analytical tool that placed the source of individual action outside the self. Durkheim pursued a similar strategy with his tool of social facts. Unlike Durkheim, Tarde did not locate causality in supra-human structural forces, but rather in people's interdependence and interaction. Hence, this chapter suggested that engaging with works outside the structuralist tradition is not only important for learning about the discipline's history but more meaningfully because they can provide researchers (as in the case of ANT and social network analysis) with a different arena for sociological innovation.

References

Alexander, Jeffrey. 1988. 'The Centrality of the Classics', in A. Giddens and J.H. Turner (eds), *Social Theory Today*. Palo Alto: Stanford University Press, pp. 11–57.

Anonymous. 2001. 'Mineure: Tarde intempestif', *Multitudes* 7. Online (http://multitudes.samizdat.net/spip.php?page=rubrique&id_rubrique=10).

Anonymous. 2007. 'Special Issue: Gabriel Tarde', *Economy and Society* 36(4): 509–643.

Bauman, Zygmunt. 2000. *Liquid Modernity*. Cambridge and Malden, MA: Polity Press and Blackwell.

Cabrera, Miguel and Álvaro Santana-Acuña. 2006. 'De la historia social a la historia de lo social', *Ayer: Revista de Historia Contemporánea* 62: 165–92.

Clark, Terry. 1973. *Prophets and Patrons: The French University and the Emergence of the Social Sciences*. Cambridge, MA: Harvard University Press.

Collins, Randall. 1994. *Four Sociological Traditions*. New York: Oxford University Press.

Connell, R.W. 1997. 'Why Is Classical Theory Classical?', *American Journal of Sociology* 102(6): 1511–57.

Deleuze, Gilles. 1968. *Différence et répétition*. Paris: Presses Universitaires de France.

Dickens, Charles. [1854] 1869. *Hard Times for These Times*. New York: Hurd and Houghton.

Donzelot, Jacques. 1984. *L'Invention du social: essai sur le déclin des passions politiques*. Paris: Fayard.

Durkheim, Émile. 1897. *Le Suicide: étude de sociologie*. Paris: F. Alcan.

Durkheim, Émile. [1912] 1968. *Les Formes élémentaires de la vie religieuse, le système totémique en Australie*. Paris: Presses Universitaires de France.

Durkheim, Émile. 1972. *Émile Durkheim: Selected Writings*. Cambridge, UK and New York: Cambridge University Press.

Durkheim, Émile. [1894] 1973. *Les Règles de la méthode sociologique*. Paris: Presses Universitaires de France.

Eriksson, Björn. 1993. 'The First Formulation of Sociology: A Discursive Innovation of the 18th Century', *Archives Éuropéennes de Sociologie* 34: 251–76.

Giddens, Anthony. 1990. *The Consequences of Modernity*. Cambridge: Polity.

Laertius, Diogenes. 1853. *The Lives and Opinions of Eminent Philosophers*. London: H.G. Bohn.

Latour, Bruno. 2002. 'Gabriel Tarde and the End of the Social', in P. Joyce (ed.), *The Social in Question: New Bearings in History and the Social Sciences*. London and New York: Routledge, pp. 117–32.

Latour, Bruno. 2005. *Reassembling the Social: An Introduction to Actor-Network-Theory*. Oxford and New York: Oxford University Press.

Latour, Bruno. 2008. 'L'Économie, science des intérêts passionnés. Préface à la republication partielle de Psychologie économique', in G. Tarde, *Psychologie économique*. Paris: Les Empêcheurs, pp. 2–10.

Law, John and Vicky Singleton. 2013. 'ANT and Politics: Working in and on the World', *Qualitative Sociology* 36(4): 485–502.

Leibniz, Gottfried Wilhelm. [1714] 1998. *Monadologie: Französisch/Deutsch*. Stuttgart: P. Reclam.

Lukes, Steven. 1985. *Emile Durkheim, His Life and Work: A Historical and Critical Study*. Stanford, CA: Stanford University Press.

Moscovici, Serge. 1976. *Society against Nature: The Emergence of Human Societies*. Atlantic Highlands, NJ: Humanities Press.

Moscovici, Serge. 1981. *L'Âge des foules: un traité historique de psychologie des masses*. Paris: Fayard.

Poovey, Mary. 1998. *A History of the Modern Fact: Problems of Knowledge in the Sciences of Wealth and Society*. Chicago: University of Chicago Press.

Poovey, Mary. 2002. 'The Liberal Civil Subject and the Social in Eighteenth-Century British Moral Philosophy', *Public Culture* 14(1): 125.

Procacci, Giovanna. 1993. *Gouverner la misère: la question sociale en France, 1789–1848*. Paris: Seuil.

Reid, Jasper. 2012. *The Metaphysics of Henry More*. Dordrecht: Springer.

Riley, Alexander, William Watts Miller and W.S.F. Pickering (eds). 2013. *Durkheim, the Durkheimians, and the Arts*. New York and Oxford: Berghahn Books.

Ritzer, George. 2010. *Classical Sociological Theory*. New York: McGraw-Hill Education.

Rogers, Everett. [1962] 2003. *Diffusion of Innovations*. New York: Free Press.

Santana-Acuña, Álvaro. 2015. 'Outside Structures: Smithian Sentiments and Tardian Monads', *The American Sociologist* 46(2).

Scott, John. 2007. 'Gabriel Tarde', in J. Scott (ed.), *Fifty Key Sociologists: The Formative Theorists*. London: Routledge, pp. 174–7.

Tarde, Gabriel. [1890] 1993. *Les Lois de l'imitation*. Paris: Kimé Éditeur.

Tarde, Gabriel. [1893] 1999. *Monadologie et sociologie*. Le Plessis-Robinson, France: Institut Synthélabo.

Tarde, Gabriel. [1969] 2010. *On Communication and Social Influence. Selected Papers*. Chicago: University of Chicago Press.

Terrier, Jean. 2011. *Visions of the Social: Society as a Political Project in France, 1750–1950*. Leiden and Boston: Brill.

Toews, David. 2003. 'The New Tarde: Sociology after the End of the Social', *Theory, Culture & Society* 20(5): 81–98.

Vargas, Viana, Bruno Latour, Bruno Karsenti, Frédérique Aït-Touati, and Louise Salmon. 2008. 'The Debate between Tarde and Durkheim', *Environment and Planning D: Society and Space* 26(5): 761–77.

Chapter 10

Alasdair MacIntyre's Lost Sociology

Neil Davidson

Introduction

Alasdair MacIntyre is perhaps the most admired moral philosopher in the English-speaking world today. And, as one might expect, for most of his professional life he has been employed by institutions of higher education to perform precisely this role. Yet for a brief period in his career, a few years which encompassed the upheavals of 1968, MacIntyre was employed as a Professor of Sociology at the University of Essex at Colchester. The exceptional nature of this entry in his CV is not, however, an aberration, but the institutional aspect of a phase in his intellectual development which saw Macintyre interrogate and deploy the methods and categories of sociology, and of the social sciences more generally, with a level of sympathy unexpected in the light of his previous positions.

In his earliest publications, MacIntyre attempted to establish the inner connections and similarities between Christianity and Marxism. His first major work, *Marxism: an Interpretation*, famously argued that 'the two most relevant books in the modern world are St. Mark's Gospel and Marx's *National Economy and Philosophy*, but they must be read together' (MacIntyre 1953: 109). During this phase of his thought MacIntyre had very little to say about sociology except – as we shall see – to argue that Marx was not a sociologist. Around 1958, when MacIntyre temporarily abandoned religious belief, he began to describe himself as a Marxist and this self-identification lasted for approximately ten years. He also began to discuss sociology in ways which were often highly critical, although usually respectful towards the founding fathers Weber and – especially – Durkheim (see, e.g., MacIntyre 1961 and MacIntyre 1965). Nevertheless, there was a clear difference in the attitude he displayed towards sociology in his 'political' writings for the socialist press and his 'professional' writings for academic journals: in the latter it was taken with much greater seriousness.

From his public disavowal of Marxism and revolutionary politics in 1968, however, sociology moved from being a subordinate element in his thinking to the standpoint from which he now assessed both Christianity and Marxism as ideologies. But by 1973, in a further dramatic reversal, MacIntyre had come to regard sociology itself as essentially ideological and its practitioners at least as complicit in undemocratic practices as the Marxist revolutionaries from whom he now distanced himself. MacIntyre's conversion to Roman Catholicism and adoption of Aristotelianism in its Thomist form in the early 1980s coincided with the publication of *After Virtue*, the work which both consolidated his global reputation and extended his critique of sociology still further. Weberianism in particular was now indicted, not only as an ideological barrier to comprehending society, but as an actual *programme* for bureaucratic domination over it.

MacIntyre's engagement with sociology has been as 'lost' as was, until recently, his engagement with Marxism, although the former is in fact inseparable from the latter. Both critics and admirers relentlessly fixate on *After Virtue* and its sequels, and consequently tend to relegate his earlier work to mere sketches for them. Yet an understanding of those books, and in particular the extremity of their anti-Weberianism, can only be achieved by examining MacIntyre's work over a longer timescale, starting with his Marxist phase.

The Unhappy Relationship of Marxism and Sociology

MacIntyre's original position was in many respects a conventional one among Marxists. The concept of 'Marxist sociology' is now very familiar, but a cohort of Marxist sociologists within Western colleges and universities only emerged during the 1970s. Prior to that point there was a small minority of mainly North American *radical* sociologists, of whom Wright Mills and Gouldner were the best-known; but *Marxist* sociologists were extremely rare. In the UK during the 1950s and 1960s, sociologists, even left-wing sociologists, tended to be suspicious of Marxism. As one leading British sociologist, A.H. Halsey, wrote of his colleagues at the London School of Economics, 'they were committed to a socialism that had no need of Marxism and no need for communism precisely because it was so deeply rooted in working-class provincialism' (Halsey 2004: 84). Stuart Hall ploughed a lonely furrow in the emergent field of cultural studies while John Westergaard, more closely concerned with central questions of class, only published his substantial work in the mid-1970s; and they were rare exceptions. If other Marxists were employed as sociologists then their theoretical views found expression through political activism rather than their academic work. Why was the discipline so forbidding for total critiques of capitalist society?

As some Nanterre students explained during the French explosion of 1968, the reason trainee sociologists like themselves were in the vanguard of the revolt was not because their discipline encouraged them to question the existing order, but for precisely the opposite reason: it was integrated into the structures of capitalist power. They were rebelling against sociology as part of their rebellion against the larger system which sociology helped to uphold (Cohn-Bendit, Dutiel, Gerard and Granautier 1968). This is not to make the absurd suggestion that all sociology has been intrinsically counter-revolutionary or supportive of capitalism, although figures such as Spencer and Parsons clearly were; but the tendency is clear and can be traced back to the founders themselves. Take their immersion in nationalism: MacIntyre once noted of Durkheim and Weber: 'In 1914 when the barbarism of bourgeois civilization erupted in World War I, each identified his own nation as being enlisted in the cause of civilization and his nation's opponents as being enlisted in that of barbarism' (MacIntyre 1974: 25).

At the end of the revolutionary period in the mid-1970s, Tom Bottomore, another of the very few British Marxist sociologists, produced a short book called *Marxist Sociology*. In it, he treated virtually everything Marxists had written as illustrative of his title, although intellectual honesty led him to call a key section 'Marxists *against* sociology' (Bottomore 1975: 31–48). This accurately reflected the attitude of the Classical Marxist tradition, which had always been unremitting hostile, from Marx's own intemperate dismissal ('this shitty positivism') of Comte's pseudo-encyclopaedic posturing onwards (Marx 1987: 292). Only Bukharin's attempt to redefine Marxism as 'a system of sociology' in 1921 stands out from the consensus (Bukharin 1925). But the mechanical formulations for which this work is notorious indicate the problems involved in assimilating one to the other. Bukharin was heavily criticized by Lukács (1972) and even more severely by Gramsci, who understood that sociology was in effect an *alternative* to Marxism, not only incompatible with, but opposed to it: 'Has not sociology tried to do something similar to the philosophy of praxis?' In his view Bukharin had effectively embraced 'the philosophy of non-philosophers': 'Vulgar evolutionism is at the root of sociology, and sociology cannot know the dialectical principle with its passage from quantity to quality' (Gramsci 1971b: 426, Q11§26). In some respects this blanket rejection was unfair and can partly be explained by the intensity of contemporary class conflicts which tended to militate against more discriminating judgements. If we were to only select works from the two decade before the First World War, Simmel's essay on the effects of urbanism on modern consciousness, or Weber's on the reasons for the decline of Roman civilization are scarcely minor or nugatory contributions to social thought (Simmel 1971; Weber 1998). Beyond the politics of that particular conjuncture, Marxist distrust of sociology was not because it was completely unable to produce any insights, but rather because the methods it employed were designed to prevent overall comprehension of the social world.

In *After Virtue* MacIntyre praises the Scottish Enlightenment figure Adam Ferguson for seeing 'the institution of modern commercial society as endangering at least some traditional virtues': 'It is Ferguson's type of sociology which ... seeks to lay bare the empirical, causal connection between virtues, practices and institutions' (MacIntyre 1985: 195–6). MacIntyre is a undoubtedly right to admire Ferguson; but contrary to these claims the latter was not a 'sociologist', any more than his colleague Adam Smith was an 'economist', popular though these classification are. Take, for example the effusions of Arthur Herman:

> The Scottish Enlightenment embarked on nothing less than a massive reordering of human knowledge. It sought to transform every branch of learning – literature and the arts; the social sciences; biology, chemistry, geology, and the other physical and natural sciences – into a series of organized disciplines that could be taught and passed on to posterity (Herman 2001: 54).

But to claim that the Scottish Enlightenment created these specialisms is to invert the truth: academic specialization presents a world of fragments, something which would have been alien to Smith and his contemporaries, who still required scientific knowledge of the world as a whole. The subjects which Herman lists were merely different ways of approaching human social development and their boundaries co-existed and often overlapped, to say the least and extended to the natural sciences. In the late 1780s Dugald Stewart wrote in a letter that he was 'now employed in premeditating two Lectures – the one on the Air-Pump, and the other on the Immortality of the Soul' (Veitch 1854: lvi, note). Not only did Sir John Dalrymple write *An Essay towards a History of Feudal Property in Great Britain* (1757), he was also a chemist who invented a process for manufacturing soap out of herrings (Ridpath 1922: 165–6, note 1). Strict disciplinary categories did not exist during the lifetime of these thinkers, and their establishment, between the 1830s and 1870s, was one indication that the Enlightenment had ended as an intellectual movement expressive of the heroic phase of the bourgeois ascendancy. The birth of the disciplines saw the end of totality as a characteristic of mainstream theory. The most obvious example, Smith's *The Wealth of Nations* (1776), illustrates what was lost. We can find in this work elements which would now be allocated to 'economics', 'sociology' and 'psychology', but also to 'history' and 'moral philosophy'; but to read these categories backwards into it is to commit a teleological error. Nor was Smith an early exemplar of 'interdisciplinarity'; he saw the world as a whole, and drew on the modes of thought – some as yet untitled – necessary to understand it. As John Dwyer comments:

> Writing during a period before psychology, economics, politics and sociology had been hived off into separate disciplines, they were constantly confronted with the need to make their findings square with a more comprehensive human reality. Only with considerable difficulty could they assume an isolated individual, an ideal market, a political model or social laws (Dwyer 1998: 197).

Interestingly, it is in MacIntyre's recent thought that he makes this argument most clearly: 'The established scheme of human knowledge in the Scottish seventeenth and eighteenth centuries was – and to some limited degree this persisted into the nineteenth century – a unitary and more or less integrated scheme, the articulated disciplinary parts of which involved continual reference to one another.' MacIntyre notes that this had implications for 'the professors', who 'had to be widely knowledgeable outside their own special discipline' (MacIntyre 1988: 250). Although written specifically about Scotland, which MacIntyre claims as the site of a particular 'tradition', he in effect sees 'integration' as characteristic of Enlightenment thought as a whole, compared with that of the present. Today, instead of 'practically effective social thought' he argues that we have 'a set of small-scale academic publics within each of which rational discourse is carried on, but whose discourse is of such a kind as to no practical effect on the conduct of social life' (MacIntyre 2006: 185). The birth of the 'social sciences' involved the dismemberment of the master-category of Political Economy and the fragmentation of knowledge about the social world into a series of discrete subjects, each dealing with a particular aspect of social life. Why?

Weber himself argued that inescapable aspects of capitalist modernity were the conjoined drives toward specialization and its accompaniment, professionalization, in the academy as much as in the organization of the state or business enterprise. From this perspective sociology is simply a specific example of a general process. At one point Weber felt it necessary to apologize for straying outside his own discipline, even though he regarded that as unavoidable:

> ... however objectionable it may be, such trespassing on other special fields cannot be avoided in comparative work. But one must take the consequences by resigning oneself to considerable doubts concerning the degree of one's success. Fashion and the zeal of the *literati* would have us think that the specialist can to-day be spared, or degraded to a position subordinate to that of the seer. Almost all sciences owe something to dilettantes, often very valuable view-points. But dilettantism as a leading principle would be the end of science (Weber 1976: 29).

Weber's argument here is disingenuous, as the necessity for a serious and scholarly approach to intellectual work is quite separable from the validity or otherwise of the disciplinary fields within which such work is undertaken.

But disciplinary fragmentation was not simply a product of the specialization internal to capitalist production it was also consequent on the changed position of the bourgeoisie in relation to the other social classes. Knowledge of the world as a whole was necessary for a bourgeoisie still struggling for power; once in power, clarity was reserved for those mechanisms necessary to maintain the functioning of the system. Although overstated, Lukács nevertheless identified an important aspect of the bourgeois world-view: 'The survival of the bourgeoisie rests on the assumption that it never obtains a clear insight into social preconditions of its own existence' (Lukács 1971: 225). Sociology was a response to the strains of industrialization and the threat of working class revolution; but also specifically conceived as an alternative to the Marxism which was associated with working class politics (Anderson 1992: 56–60; Therborn 1976: 135–44). Sociology held a special place in the new disciplinary firmament since it was the one which came closest to reproducing the lost wholeness of Enlightenment thought, but in a radically impoverished way.

Marxism, however, did retain the Enlightenment notion of totality. Marxist analysis may focus on specific aspects of social life – Marx's *Capital* is one of the most sustained examples of such an analysis – but it has to do so without succumbing to the notion that 'the economic' can be abstracted from 'the social' or 'the political': analysis of any particular aspect is only a moment in the whole. In short, there is no Marxist sociology or Marxist economics or Marxist anything else; there is just Marxism, although it will necessarily intersect with the subject matter of these disciplines (Harvey 2001: 77–8; Ollman 2003: 139–40). This does not mean that Marxism is a 'theory of everything'; it is rather an attempt to explain how historical change has taken place in the past and how human beings can make history in the present, under conditions which the past has bequeathed to them (Eagleton 1997: 34–5; Eagleton 2003: 33–4). Other theories or methods, often on the borderline of social and natural science such as those associated with Darwin or Freud, are necessary to explain aspects of existence for which Marxism has no locus. Both evolutionary biology and psychoanalysis were compatible with Marxism, but they were distinct from it.

The final difference between Marxism and sociology concerned the distinction between is and ought or, more precisely, their respective attitudes towards science (and 'facts') on the one hand and politics (and 'values') on the other. Weber famously argued that the intrusion of the latter into the realm of the former was a matter of scandal (Weber 1948: 145–7). But the adoption of any set of political values involved a necessarily arbitrary choice (Weber 2004: 355). Interestingly, there is a strand in Marxist thought which takes a similar position, starting with Engels:

> When one is an economist, a "man of science", one does not have an ideal. One elaborates scientific results, and when one is, to boot, a party man, one struggles to put them into practice. But when one has an ideal, one cannot be a man of science, having, as one then does, preconceived ideas (Engels 1995: 183).

This is one of the – actually quite rare – occasions where Engels was being genuinely undialectical. The dualism expressed here was, however, entirely typical of the dominant neo-Kantian tendency of the Second International and expressed most clearly by Hilferding in his 1911 claim that Marxism was 'only a theory of the laws of motion of society', with no necessary consequences for action: 'For it is one thing to acknowledge a necessity, and quite another thing to work for that necessity' (Hilferding 1981: 23–4). Equally typical was the opposition of the Hegelian Marxist current which emerged during the First World War in solidarity with the Russian Revolution, but Karl Korsch act here as a surrogate for them this tendency. He noted, against Hilferding, that historical materialism 'is incompatible with separate branches of knowledge that are isolated and autonomous, and with purely theoretical investigations that are scientifically objective in dissociation from revolutionary practice'. If 'the fluid methodology of Marx's materialist dialectic' was simply transformed 'into a number of theoretical formulations about the causal interconnection of historical phenomena in different areas of society' the consequence could only be 'a general systematic sociology' (Korsch 1970: 60, 62). He did not regard this outcome as desirable.

The overall position was perhaps most clearly stated by Lucien Goldmann in 1957, in a critique of Maximilien Rubel's claim that Marx had failed to resolve a tension between revolutionary ethics and scientific investigation: 'Statements and evaluations being indissolubly linked in Marx's work … the value judgment is never autonomous and independent of the analysis of facts, and thereby is *not ethical*, while the statements are never objective and free from any particular standpoint, and thereby are *not sociological*' (Goldmann 1968: 20). Rubel had also received similar criticism the previous year, for a collection of Marx's writings co-edited with Bottomore. And here we can rejoin our main subject, for the reviewer was MacIntyre himself, prefiguring Goldmann's position: 'The attempt to present Marx as a scientific sociologist in the modern sense is like presenting *Hamlet* as a play about Rosencrantz and Guildenstern' (MacIntyre 1956: 266). Yet, curiously, the period of his adherence to Marxism, which began shortly afterwards saw him modify his position.

MacIntyre's Initial Critique of Social Science

'MacIntyre's first major paper on social science itself was "A Mistake about Causality in Social Science", published in 1962', writes Stephen Turner (2003: 75). In fact, his first discussion of social science in general and sociology in particular appeared two years earlier in a directly political intervention for the New Left, two years into his Marxist phase. 'Breaking the Chains of Reason' made the case for Marxism as a method by defending it against the criticisms of Karl Popper, who had claimed that Marxism was deficient on three main grounds, all of which supposedly tended towards totalitarianism on the Russian model. MacIntyre briefly dismantles these positions, which were at the time treated as incontestable, not only within orthodox social science, but also on the right-wing of the Labour Party.

First, Popper claimed Marxism was historicist, meaning that it claimed to have discovered the underlying trends of historical development and could therefore predict future patterns of events. But Marx did not believe that he had discovered the inevitable course of human history, but a potential outcome made possible by developments within capitalism:

> Knowledge of the trends that are dominant is for Marx an instrument for changing them. So his belief that he has uncovered 'the economic law of motion of capitalist society' is not a belief in an absolute trend, but a trend whose continuance is contingent on a variety of factors including our activity (MacIntyre 2008b: 150).

There are two issues here, both of which MacIntyre was to address in greater detail over the next half-decade.

One is the identification of social trends. 'So, "all history is the history of class struggle" ... is not a generalization built up from instances, so much as a framework without which we should not be able to identify our instances; yet also a framework which could not be elaborated without detailed empirical study' (MacIntyre 2008b: 151; Marx and Engels 1973: 67). MacIntyre had evidently read the *Grundrisse* by the mid-1960s, before it had been translated into English (MacIntyre 2008d: 322–3). He was therefore aware that the general method of Political Economy described by Marx there as 'obviously ... scientifically correct' begins with an abstract conception, proceeds by moving back and forth between it and concrete examples in a process that deepens the original concept and eventually arrives at a view of the concrete as 'a rich totality of many determinations and relations' (Marx 1973: 100–102). MacIntyre himself wrote 'the knowledge of man himself depends on grasping the individual as part of a totality':

> Yet we cannot grasp the totality except insofar as we understand the individuals who comprise it. Marx wrote: "A loom is a machine used for weaving. It is only under certain conditions that it becomes *capital*; isolated from these conditions it is as far from being capital as gold, in its natural state, is from being coin of the realm." What are these conditions? They include both the existence of a whole system of economic activity and the informing of human activities and intentions by concepts which express the relationships characteristic of the system. We identify a loom as capital or gold as coin only when we have grasped a whole system of activities as a capitalist or monetary system. The individual object or action is identifiable only in the context of the totality; the totality is only identifiable as a set of relationships between individuals. Hence we must move from parts to whole and back from whole to parts (MacIntyre 2008e: 313; Marx 1977: 211).

The other issue is in relation to human self-activity. Shortly before 'Breaking the Chains of Reason' appeared in print, MacIntyre wrote, in a directly political context, of how the social world cannot be treated as subject to objective and insurmountable laws:

> The Marxist standpoint starts from the view that this question is not a question about a system outside us, but about a system of which we are a part. What happens to it is not a matter of natural growth or mechanical change which we cannot affect. We do not have to sit and wait for the right objective conditions for revolutionary action. Unless we act now such conditions will never arise (MacIntyre 2008a: 102).

As it stands this passage is susceptible to voluntarist interpretation, but four years later MacIntyre refined his position, drawing explicitly on Goldmann's work on the similarities between tragic and dialectical thought:

> Both know that one cannot first understand the world and only then act in it. How one understands the world will depend in part on the decision implicit in one's already taken actions. The wager of action is unavoidable (MacIntyre 2008e: 314. See also, e.g., Goldmann 1968: 18).

This aspect of MacIntyre's thought clearly has affinities with that of Antonio Gramsci: 'In reality one can "foresee" to the extent that one acts, to the extent that one applies a voluntary effort and therefore contributes concretely to creating the result "foreseen"' (Gramsci 1971b: 438, Q11§15).

The second of Popper's claims was that Marxism ascribed views and actions to collective social actors, particularly classes, whereas in reality only individuals could be said to possess these qualities. MacIntyre however argued that, as an alternative to dealing with collectives, 'methodological individualism' was incoherent:

> You cannot characterize an army by referring to the soldiers who belong to it. For to do that you have to identify them as soldiers; and to do that is already to bring in the concept of an army. For a soldier just is an individual who belongs to an army. Thus we see that the characterization of individuals and of classes has to go together. Essentially these are not two separate tasks (MacIntyre 2008b: 152).

The third of Popper's claims was that Marxism was partisan, seeking not to discover partial scientific understanding, but to justify positions to which it was already committed because of its historicism. MacIntyre argued that Popper is wrong to demand objectivity, or as he puts it, a concern for means rather than ends. On the one hand, means and ends cannot be separated in this way. On the other, his claim is 'self-refuting':

> For to assert that our concern can only be with the means and to add that the result of that concern can only be limited and particular statements of social correlation is already to be partisan. An example of what Popper takes to be a genuine discovery of the social sciences is that "You cannot have full employment without inflation" (the rider "in our type of economy" is not added). If such limited discoveries are all that we can hope for from the social sciences, it follows that we cannot hope to transform society as such; all that we can hope to change are particular features of social life. To adopt this view of the means available for social change is to commit oneself to the view that the only feasible ends of social policy are limited reformist ones, and that revolutionary ends are never feasible. To be committed to this is to be partisan in the most radical way (Macintyre 2008b, 152–3).

These arguments relate to social science methodology in general terms, but 'Breaking the Chains of Reason' also involved made a central criticism of sociology in particular. All versions of the discipline, he argued, whether of the right like Parsons or of the left like Wright Mills, shared a fundamental determinism. Indeed, he was in some senses more critical of the latter – who was of course deeply critical of both the Grand Theory and what he called the Abstracted Empiricism characteristic of the discipline – because his elitism, his refusal to ground his socialism in proletarian self-activity, tended to negate the otherwise important critique of modern capitalism contained in his work (MacIntyre 2008b: 154–6; MacIntyre 2008c: 242–4). In the incandescent final paragraphs of 'Breaking' MacIntyre takes Keynes and Trotsky as great representative figures exemplifying the contrast between bourgeois social science and revolutionary Marxism, suggesting that intellectuals had to choose between them, including, of course, himself.

The Sociological Turn

Against a general underlying positivism which, from Weber on, had assumed that society could be analysed in the same way as nature, 'Breaking' had asserted the need for totality – in this context, that society and nature do indeed have to be understood in the same way, but historically and dialectically in both cases. Yet, in relation to question of methodology, there was an ambiguity in MacIntyre's own position which emerged in the 1962 paper which Turner mistakenly argued was his first major intervention in social science debates. Here MacIntyre took seriously the theme of Winch's *Idea of a Social Science* (1958). In examining the motives for action by particular groups, Winch argued, social science had to restrict itself to elucidating their 'reasons' adduced by the groups themselves, rather than seeking underlying 'causes' external to their own conceptual schemas. This was useful to MacIntyre in that it allowed him to criticize Weber's explanation for the emergence of the Protestant work ethic, the details of which need not concern us here (but see MacIntyre 1962: 55). MacIntyre did not accept the full extremity of Winch's position, which would have relegated social science to a branch of philosophy concerned with conceptual analysis, or his implicit relativism; what is nevertheless of note is that this type of conception could co-exist with his Marxism. Over the next 3–4 years, however, the former would impinge ever more strongly on the latter's terrain, although MacIntyre would develop specific criticisms of Winch's own work (MacIntyre 1971a: 229). MacIntyre's 'professional' work as a philosopher in particular begins to display a kind of dualism – possibly influenced by his reading of the early Lukács – in which positivism is deemed appropriate for the natural sciences, but not for the social sciences.

   It is clear that he had entertained doubts about the continuing validity of Marxism from around 1965 (Davidson 2014: 161–8). McMylor argues that MacIntyre had made his 'sociological turn' roughly between this point and 1968, particularly in his work on secularization and atheism (McMylor 1994: 31–8). In the course of one of these discussions about secularization, MacIntyre noted: 'Within sociology at the moment there is a dispute between those who want to stress that the analysis of a society and the explanation of its forms should be in terms of its basic norms and values, and those, ranging from David Reisman at one end of the scale and the Marxists at the other, who want to argue that either technological or economic or demographic relationships are more fundamental.'

MacIntyre then affirmed that his own position was both 'largely on the Marxist side of the argument' and 'incompatible with certain parts of classical Marxism':

> It turns out ... to be false that, as Marx put it, "The ruling ideas are always the ideas of the ruling class." For ... the key ideas of British society, the ideas typified by the secondary virtues, are ideas of the necessity of class compromise and class co-operation, and that if the ruling class had tried, and when the ruling class did try, to impose their own virtues and values on other groups, when for instance they tried to use religion as a class weapon, they failed to make these ideas the ideas of the community as a whole (MacIntyre 1967: 35; Marx and Engels 1976: 59).

These formulations were not new in MacIntyre's writings. 'All sorts of facts may limit social consciousness', he wrote in *International Socialism* the year before these lectures were delivered: 'But false consciousness is essentially a matter of partial and limited insight rather than of simple mistake' (MacIntyre 2008d: 252–3). But Marx' and Engels' early formulations on the 'ruling ideas' – redolent as they are of a residual Enlightenment elitism – were not the last word of Classical Marxism on the subject. Here, as is the case in a number of areas, MacIntyre's non-engagement with Gramsci, in this case in relation to his writings on 'contradictory consciousness', forces him to look for explanatory frameworks outwith Marxism which can in fact be found within it (e.g., Gramsci 1971a: 333–4, Q11§12).

What seems to have occurred is that MacIntyre, from a position of accepting a dualist approach to the social and natural sciences in which positivism was appropriate to the latter, moved to one in which it was also appropriate to the former – the very position he had originally rejected. In effect this was the methodological expression of his lack of confidence in the explanatory power of Marxism and abandonment of the category of totality. More significantly, however, MacIntyre still drew on Marxist positions to argue for the essential historicity of certain concepts, meaning that they become incomprehensible after the conditions which gave rise to them have disappeared (MacIntyre 1971b; see also MacIntyre 1966: 1–8). In his critique of Baruch Knei-Paz's book on Trotsky, he wrote, 'there is no way to do the history of ideas adequately without doing genuine history and, more particularly, that the treatment of social and political ideas in abstraction from those contexts from which they derive life is doomed to failure, something which Trotsky knew very well' (MacIntyre 1979: 114). The irony, however, that he used this approach to explain what he regarded as the inadequacy of Marxism itself.

MacIntyre's version of the Pascalian 'wager' depended on the possibility of the working class performing a revolutionary role, but he now no longer believed that this was possible. Ironically, given his earlier critique of Popper, he seems to have treated this failure in Popperian terms as an empirical refutation of the theory of proletarian revolution. MacIntyre argued that hitherto Marxists had explained away the failure of Marx's predictions either by claiming that time scale was simply longer than had hitherto been supposed, or by a series of 'supplementary hypotheses' including those of the labour aristocracy and 'doctrinal corruption', but these were ways of avoiding two painful facts: 'The first of these was that the working class – not just its leadership – was either reformist or unpolitical except in the most exceptional of circumstances, not so much because of the inadequacies of its trade union and political leadership as because of its whole habit of life' (MacIntyre 1968a: 90–91). MacIntyre adopted this version of the argument as the sixties drew to a close:

> It would be inconsistent with Marxism itself to view Marxism in any other way: in particular, what we cannot do is judge and understand Marxist theory as it has really existed with all its vicissitudes in the light of some ideal version of Marxism. It follows that by the present time to be faithful to Marxism we have to cease to be Marxists; and whoever now remains a Marxist has thereby discarded Marxism' (MacIntyre 1970: 61).

The point therefore, was not that Marxism had never been true, but that it no longer was:

> [Marx] envisages the concentration of workers in large factory units and the limits set upon the growth of wages as necessary conditions for the growth of [political] consciousness; but he says nothing about how or why the workers will learn and assimilate the truths which Marxism seeks to bring to them. ... Indeed, one might write the history of the age which Marxism illuminated so much more clearly than any other doctrine did, the period from 1848 to 1929, as one in which Marx's view of the progress of capitalism was substantially correct, but at the end of which the Marxist script for the world drama required the emergence of the European working-class as the agent of historical change, the working-class turned out to be quiescent and helpless (MacIntyre 1970: 42–3).

There is, however, a second irony here, which MacIntyre believed explained the failure of the working class and consequently of Marxism. MacIntyre's previously insistence on the capacity of human self-activity to transform the world had mainly been in relation to the working class and one of his grounds for distinguishing between the social and natural sciences (MacIntyre 2008d: 260–61). He now argued that the capitalist class itself was in a position to effectively regulate the economy and thus prevent the recurrence of crisis, reducing the possibility of working class dissatisfaction and contributing to the 'quiescence' especially after 1945, when 'the ability of capitalism to innovate in order to maintain its equilibrium and its expansion was of a radically new kind. Consequently, not only has the future crisis of capitalism had – for those who wished to retain the substance of the classical Marxist view – to be delayed, there had to be additional explanations why, in the new situation, capitalism is still liable to crisis in the same sense as before' (MacIntyre 1968: 105). He did not find these explanations convincing.

It is interesting, however, to examine one of the explanations he rejects. MacIntyre's argument against Marcuse was in part because the latter too easily accepted the claims of US social and political scientists like Bell and Lipset about a West in which class consensus reigned on the basis of apparently endless growth, providing previously unimagined levels of welfare and mass consumption, presided over by competing political elites. Not only did Marcuse share the conventional view that fundamental conflicts had been resolved, except at the margins of capitalist society; if anything he exaggerated the extent of supposed social control even further, by imbuing it with a technological-determinist character in which human aspirations were not merely suppressed, but actually created. As MacIntyre pointed out, the problem with this was not merely the elitist overtones – why was Marcuse able to escape the domination to which the vast majority of people were apparently subject? – but that he was, in all relevant ways, insufficient 'sociological' in a positive sense: failing to distinguish between liberal democratic and totalitarian regimes, especially in their fascist form, and blind to the actual contradictions to which modern capitalist societies gave rise among their working class populations – nor least by creating needs which they are incapable of meeting (MacIntyre 1970: 62–73). But perhaps the ferocity of MacIntyre's rage at Marcuse is also partly symptomatic of the fact that he too had decided that the working class was incapable of liberating itself.

In 'Breaking the Chains of Reason' he had concluded by quoting the eleventh thesis on Feuerbach: 'The philosophers have hitherto only interpreted the world, the point remains to change it' (MacIntyre 2008b: 166; Marx 1975: 423). A decade later he concluded an essay on rationality be quoting them again, in a rather different context: 'Happily or unhappily, the philosophers cannot be restricted merely to interpreting the social sciences; the point of their activity is to change them' (MacIntyre 1971c: 259). The level of ambition here is somewhat reduced, to say the least, but was this simply MacIntyre's inner Keynes triumphing over his inner Trotsky, as many of his critics in effect claimed (Binns 1972: 41–2)? In fact, even after making his shift towards sociology, MacIntyre could never completely commit to it as an alternative to Marxism. For one thing, he could never completely accept the very boundaries between aspects of social life enshrined in the disciplines:

> ... any given economic system, with its corresponding bodies of theory, always involves a delimitation of 'the economic' as contrasted with, say, the political or the moral. But the concept of what belongs to the economic is indeed essentially contestable (MacIntyre 1973b: 9).

As he notes, the boundaries of 'the economic' constitute the essential difference between bourgeois and Marxist economics; what he cannot bring himself to recognize is Marxism rejects the very concept of the 'economic'.

The tensions within his thought at this time are caught in a passage where he clearly outlines the differences between Marx and Weber on the fundamental issue of is and ought:

> What Weber feared would result from the fusion of Is and Ought Marx believed resulted from their separation. … Yet in their different and incompatible ways Marx and Weber are nonetheless alike in one crucial respect. Both see sociology as not only the discovery of the facts about the social world, and even as the ordering of those facts within a theoretical framework which will enable us to understand and predict, but also and above all providing us with the kind of grasp of social reality which will remove the hold on us of our own society's characteristic forms of self-justification (MacIntyre 1968b: 400).

It is however intellectually incoherent simply to state that the standpoint adopted by these thinkers can both provide insights: that may be true, but the positions are antithetical to each other and cannot be maintained in tandem. MacIntyre resolved this tension by discovering that Weberianism (and social science) and Marxism (and revolutionary socialism) had more in common than was commonly supposed.

The Theory and Practice of Bureaucratic Domination

This discovery ensured that MacIntyre's dalliance with sociology and the social sciences more generally was relatively brief. In particular, around 1973 he began to find in professional social science a parallel to the undemocratic practices which he had earlier come to believe were intrinsic to contemporary revolutionary organization, albeit from the other side of the barricades. The former constituted a cohort of 'experts' which drew up 'taxonomies' and made 'predictions': 'his taxonomic ordering represents a set of structures that determine the form of social life in ways that ordinary agents do not perceive; and his predictions represent the determinativeness of a future not available to ordinary agents'. And, in a return to the argument linking Parsons and Wright Mills, MacIntyre now claimed that the concept of 'the expert' 'does not appear merely in the work of the orthodox political and social scientists; it is equally present in the work of their radical opponents', not merely Lipset, but Gouldner also (MacIntyre 1973a: 337–40).

But if radical sociology was complicit in the ideology of 'expertise', revolutionaries themselves occupied the same prophetic or priestly role as the fully orthodox. According to MacIntyre, they were likely to have five main characteristics. First, an 'all-or-nothing existence', whose activities allow them, second, to 'sustain a plausible social existence'. Third, they must believe that their activities have 'world-historical significance', justification for his revolutionary beliefs, despite their apparent lack of significance in the world: 'In this way miniscule Trotskyist groups can represent their faction fights as a repetition of the great quarrels of the Bolshevik party.' Fourth, the tension between activity and aspiration give their lives life an inevitable precariousness: 'Joseph Conrad understood this; so did Henry James; so, in his own way, did Trotsky.' Fifth, and finally, revolutionaries must feel their activities are justified by both history and their own activity, but both are refutable by counter-examples: 'This requirement is in obvious tension, however, with the revolutionary's commitment to make the predictions derived from his theory come true' (MacIntyre 1973a: 337–41).

The professional social scientist claims to understand what is required to maintain social stability; the professional revolutionary, what is required to overthrow it; but both tend to be products of the same social class, united by a common elitism. Both were also linked to a third group, the industrial managers:

> The expert, whether professional social scientist, industrial manager, or revolutionary, claims a special right to be consulted and a special right to be maintained in a position where he is available to be consulted. The ideology of expertise embodies a claim to privilege with respect to power (MacIntyre 1973a: 342).

For MacIntyre, revolutionaries were a Quixotic, dying breed. But the other two groups were not, and they were closely linked, not as types, but as components in a system of power. Few would disagree with the proposition that sociologists cannot stand outside of the societies they seek to understand, but MacIntyre now argued that, in certain respects at least, their work actually provided programmatic material for state and industrial managers, whose activity they theorize: 'Molecules do not read chemistry books; but managers do read books of organization theory' (MacIntyre 1998a: 64). These claims did of course lend further weight to his argument concerning the difference between the natural and social sciences; but methodology was not MacIntyre's main concern at this stage in his argument, which climaxed in the pages of *After Virtue*.

Here MacIntyre writes of particular social roles which are not merely occupations, but recognizable *characters*, compelled to exhibit certain behaviours in a way that say, a dentist, does not. Like the characters in Japanese Noh drama or Medieval Mystery plays, we know what to expect from these characters because their roles do not merely set limits on their action, but in a strong sense determines it. Macintyre argues that the existence of these characters functions to legitimate the societies of which they are a part, by which he does not mean that they necessarily receive universal acceptance, but that even those who oppose their social function have frame their opposition in relation to them. In this context, MacIntyre refers, among other characters, to the Aesthete, the Therapist and, of course, the Manager (MacIntyre 1985: 23–31). This was not the first time that the pages of MacIntyre's work had been populated by characters embodying certain positions. In 'Notes from the Moral Wilderness', written very early in his Marxist career (1958–1959), MacIntyre wrote about *the* Stalinist, *the* Moral Critic of Stalinism, *the* Liberal, *the* Marxist even; but these were characters defined by their political choices rather than social positioning. Ironically, the

MacIntyre of *After Virtue* is in some ways closer to Marx's own approach in *Capital* Volume 1, where he discusses the ways in which the Capitalist acts as the social embodiment of capital, regardless of his personal wishes – or rather, the Capitalists do so, since the basis of capitalism in competitive accumulation means that capitals always exist in the plural.

Under capitalist modernity, the type of bureaucracy represented by the Manager is characteristic, not merely of the institutions of the capitalist state, but also of capitals themselves, most obviously in the great multinational corporations; in both cases managers claim to possess a special form of expertise:

> Civil servants and managers alike justify themselves and their claims to authority, power and money by invoking their own competence as scientific managers of social change. Thus there emerges an ideology which finds its classic expression in a pre-existing social science theory: Weber's account of bureaucracy. ... the rationality of adjusting means to ends in the most economical and efficient way is the central task of the bureaucrat and that therefore the appropriate mode of justification of his activity by the bureaucrat lies in his (or later her) ability to deploy a body of scientific and above all social scientific knowledge, organized in terms of and understood as comprising a set of universal law-like generalizations (MacIntyre 1985: 86).

MacIntyre argues that although Weber's account was drawn from analysis of the organic, unplanned development of bureaucracy, above all in the classic form displayed by the Prussian civil service, it was sufficiently accurate as a theorization that it has been recognized as such, not only by sociologists, but by the bureaucrats themselves, as expressed in the managerial and business textbooks which almost universally employ this framework. In this sense then, Weber is, as Eric Olin Wright presents him, a bourgeois Lenin, codifying but also extending the practice of his class – or at any rate the class he associated himself with – in theory (Wright 1978: 182–3). Weberianism was not only an analysis of bureaucracy, it was a programme for establishing it. By this point, the most damning thing MacIntyre could think to say about Marxists was this:

> ... as Marxists organize and move towards power they always do and have become Weberians in substance, even if they remain Marxists in rhetoric; for in our culture we know of no organized movement towards power which is not bureaucratic and managerial in mode and we know of no justifications for authority which are not Weberian in form. And if this is true of Marxism when it is on the road to power, who much more so when it arrives. ... When Marxism does not become Weberian social democracy or crude tyranny, it tends to become Nietzschean fantasy. (MacIntyre 1985: 109, 262).

As this suggests, MacIntyre believe that people who are opposed to capitalism or at least want it to be radically reformed share essentially the same social role.

Those who without abandoning the standpoint of civil society take themselves to know in advance what needs to be done to effect needed change are those who take themselves to be therefore entitled to manage that change. Others are to be the passive recipients of what they as managers effect. This hierarchical division between managers and managed is thus legitimated by the superior knowledge imputed to themselves by the managing reformers, who have cast themselves in the role of educator.

In this context MacIntyre refers to reformers like Owen and the Webbs, but also ('at least on occasion') to Lenin, suggesting that these characters include not merely reformers but also revolutionaries (MacIntyre 1998b: 231).

Conclusion

MacIntyre's embrace of what Knight calls 'revolutionary Aristotelianism' in *After Virtue* – a position which the former later embraced – allowed him to escape from the paradox of seeking an alternative to Marxism in a body of sociological thought and procedure which he came to identify with capitalist bureaucracies, and this way actually moved in some respects back towards a notion of totality closer to his original Marxist position (Knight 1996; Knight 2011; MacIntyre 1998c). Even though he has written of the need for 'practice-based local participatory community' to 'understand and learn from both Christianity and Marxism', he has not extended this to sociology (MacIntyre 2008g: 425).

MacIntyre originally embraced sociology as a substitute for the Christian and Marxist perspectives which he came to believe could no longer explain the world to his satisfaction, but found that it could not do so either: partly because there is no single sociological theory which could provide that kind of coherence; partly because in order to make any critical point, sociology has to incorporate insights from other disciplines, which tends to call into question the validity of the category of 'society' detached from geography, economy, polity or culture; partly because he found sociology *as a practice* to be as oppressive as the traditions he had earlier embraced. These are certainly problems for MacIntyre, but perhaps even more so for sociology.

References

Anderson, Perry. 1992 [1968]. 'Components of the National Culture', in *English Questions*. London: Verso.

Binns, Peter. 1972. 'Review of *Against the Self-Images of the Age*', *International Socialism*, second series, 50 (January/February): 41–2.

Bottomore, Tom. 1975. *Marxist Sociology*. London: Macmillan.

Bukharin, Nikolai I. 1925 [1921]. *Historical Materialism: A System of Sociology.* New York: International Publishers.

Cohn-Bendit, Daniel, Jean-Pierre Dutiel, Bertrand Gerard and Bernard Granautier. 1968. 'Why Sociologists?', in Alexander Cockburn and Perry Anderson (eds), *Student Power: Problems, Diagnosis, Action.* Harmondsworth: Penguin Books.

Davidson, Neil. 2014 [2007–2011]. 'Alasdair MacIntyre as a Marxist', in *Holding Fast to an Image of the Past: Explorations in the Marxist Tradition.* Chicago: Haymarket Books.

Dwyer, John. 1998. *The Age of the Passions: An Interpretation of Adam Smith and Scottish Enlightenment Culture.* East Linton: Tuckwell.

Eagleton, Terry. 1997. *Marx and Freedom.* London: Phoenix.

Eagleton, Terry. 2003. *After Theory.* London: Allen Lane.

Engels, Friedrich. 1995 [1884]. Engels to Paul Lafargue, c. 11 August 1884, in *Collected Works*, vol. 47, London: Lawrence and Wishart.

Gramsci, Antonio. 1971. *Selections from the Prison Notebooks*, Quintin Hoare and Geoffrey Nowell Smith (eds). London: Lawrence and Wishart.

Gramsci, Antonio. 1971a [1929–1934]. 'The Study of Philosophy', in Gramsci 1971.

Gramsci, Antonio. 1971b [1929–1934]. 'Problems of Marxism', in Gramsci 1971.

Goldmann, Lucien. 1968 [1957]. 'Is There a Marxist Sociology?', *International Socialism*, first series, 34 (Autumn): 13–20.

Halsey, A.H. 2004, *A History of Sociology in Britain: Science, Literature and Society.* Oxford: Oxford University Press.

Harvey, David. 2001 [1978]. 'On Countering the Marxist Myth – Chicago Style', in *Spaces of Capital: Towards a Critical Geography.* Edinburgh: Edinburgh University Press.

Herman, Arthur. 2001. *The Scottish Enlightenment: The Scot's Invention of the Modern World.* London: Fourth Estate.

Hilferding, Rudolf. 1981 [1910]. *Finance Capital: A Study in the Latest Phase of Capitalist Development*, Tom Bottomore (ed.). London: Routledge and Kegan Paul.

Knight, Kelvin. 1996. 'Revolutionary Aristotelianism', in Ian Hampsher-Monk and Jeffrey Stanyer (eds), *Contemporary Political Studies*, vol. 2. Nottingham: Political Studies Association of the United Kingdom.

Knight, Kelvin. 2011, 'Revolutionary Aristotelianism', in Paul Blackledge and Kelvin Knight (eds), *Virtue and Politics: Alasdair MacIntyre's Revolutionary Aristotelianism.* Notre Dame, IN: University of Notre Dame Press.

Korsch, Karl. 1970 [1923]. 'Marxism and Philosophy', in *Marxism and Philosophy.* New York: Monthly Review Press.

Lukács, Georg. 1971 [1923]. 'Reification and the Consciousness of the Proletariat', in *History and Class Consciousness: Studies in Marxist Dialectics.* London: Merlin Press.

Lukács, Georg. 1972 [1925]. 'N. Bukharin, *Historical Materialism*', in *Tactics and Ethics: Political Writings, 1919–1919.* London: New Left Books.

MacIntyre, Alasdair. 1953. *Marxism: An Interpretation*. London: Student Christian Movement Press.

MacIntyre, Alasdair. 1956. 'Review of T.B. Bottomore and M. Rubel, *Karl Marx: Selected Works on Sociology and Social Philosophy* and P. Laslett, ed., *Philosophy, Politics and Society*', *Sociological Review*, 4(2) (December): 265–6.

MacIntyre, Alasdair. 1961. 'Beyond Max Weber', *New Statesman* (3 February): 181–2.

MacIntyre, Alasdair. 1962. 'A Mistake About Causality in the Social Sciences', in Peter Laslett and W.G. Runciman (eds), *Philosophy, Politics and Society: a Collection*. Second Series. Oxford: Blackwell.

MacIntyre, Alasdair. 1965. 'Weber at his Weakest', *Encounter* 25(1) (July 1965): 85–7.

MacIntyre, Alasdair. 1966. *A Short History of Ethics*. New York: Macmillan.

MacIntyre, Alasdair. 1967 [1964]. *Secularization and Moral Change: The Riddell Memorial Lectures*. Oxford: Oxford University Press.

MacIntyre, Alasdair. 1968a. *Marxism and Christianity*. New York: Schocken Books, 1968.

MacIntyre, Alasdair. 1968b. 'Living or Dead?', *New Statesman* (27 September): 400–401.

MacIntyre, Alasdair. 1970. *Marcuse*. London: Fontana.

MacIntyre, Alasdair. 1971. *Against the Self-Images of the Age: Essays on Ideology and Philosophy*. London: Duckworth.

MacIntyre, Alasdair. 1971a [1967]. 'The Idea of a Social Science', in MacIntyre 1971.

MacIntyre, Alasdair. 1971b. '"Ought"', in Macintyre 1971.

MacIntyre, Alasdair. 1971c. 'Rationality and the Explanation of Action', in MacIntyre 1971.

MacIntyre, Alasdair. 1973a. 'Ideology, Social Science and Revolution', *Comparative Politics* 5(2) (April): 321–42.

MacIntyre, Alasdair. 1973b. 'The Essential Contestability of Some Social Concepts', *Ethics* 84(1) (October): 1–9.

MacIntyre, Alasdair. 1974. 'Durkheim's Call to Order', *New York Review of Books* (7 March): 25–6.

MacIntyre, Alasdair. 1979. 'Review of Baruch Knei-Paz', *The Social and Political Thought of Leon Trotsky*', *American Historical Review* 84(1) (February): 113–14.

MacIntyre, Alasdair. 1985 [1981]. *After Virtue: A Study in Moral Theory*. 2nd edn. London: Duckworth.

Macintyre, Alasdair. 1988. *Whose Justice? Which Rationality?* London: Duckworth.

MacIntyre, Alasdair. 1998. *The MacIntyre Reader*, Kelvin Knight (ed.). Cambridge: Polity Press.

MacIntyre, Alasdair. 1998a [1979]. 'Social Science Methodology as the Ideology of Bureaucratic Authority', in MacIntyre 1998.

MacIntyre, Alasdair. 1998b [1994]. 'The *Theses on Feuerbach*: A Road not Taken', in MacIntyre 1998.

MacIntyre, Alasdair. 1998c [1997]. 'Politics, Philosophy and the Common Good', in MacIntyre 1998.

Macintyre, Alasdair. 2006 [1995]. 'Some Enlightenment Projects Reconsidered', in *Ethics and Politics: Selected Essays*, vol. 2. Cambridge: Cambridge University Press.

MacIntyre, Alasdair. 2008. *Alasdair MacIntyre's Engagement with Marxism: Selected Writings, 1953–1974*, Paul Blackledge and Neil Davidson (eds). Leiden: E.J. Brill.

MacIntyre, Alasdair. 2008a [1960]. 'What is Marxist Theory for?', in MacIntyre 2008.

MacIntyre, Alasdair. 2008b [1960]. 'Breaking the Chains of Reason', in MacIntyre 2008.

MacIntyre, Alasdair. 2008c [1962]. 'C. Wright Mills', in MacIntyre 2008.

MacIntyre, Alasdair. 2008d [1963]. 'Prediction and Politics', in MacIntyre 2008.

MacIntyre, Alasdair. 2008e [1964]. 'Pascal and Marx: On Lucien Goldmann's *Hidden God*', in MacIntyre 2008.

MacIntyre, Alasdair. 2008f [1965]. 'Marxist Mask and Romantic Face: Lukács on Thomas Mann', in MacIntyre 2008.

MacIntyre, Alasdair. 2008g [1995]. '1953, 1968, 1995: Three Perspectives', in MacIntyre 2008.

Marx, Karl. 1973 [1857–1858]. *Grundrisse: Foundations of the Critique of Political Economy (Rough Draft)*. Harmondsworth: Penguin Books/New Left Review.

Marx, Karl. 1975 [1845]. 'Concerning Feuerbach', in *Early Writings*. Harmondsworth: Penguin Books/New Left Review.

Marx, Karl. 1977 [1847/9]. 'Wage Labour and Capital', in *Collected Works*, vol. 9. London: Lawrence and Wishart.

Marx, Karl. 1987 [1866]. Marx to Engels, 7 July 1866, in *Collected Works*, vol. 42. London: Lawrence and Wishart.

Marx, Karl and Frederick Engels. 1976 [1845–1846]. *The German Ideology: Critique of Modern German Philosophy According to Its Representatives Feuerbach, B. Bauer and Stirner, and of German Socialism According to Its Various Prophets*, in *Collected Works*, vol. 5. London: Lawrence and Wishart.

Marx, Karl and Frederick Engels. 1973 [1848]. 'Manifesto of the Communist Party', in *The Revolutions of 1848*, David Fernbach (ed.). Harmondsworth: Penguin Books/New Left Review.

McMylor, Peter. 1994. *Alasdair MacIntyre: Critic of Modernity*. London: Routledge.

Ollman, Bertell. 2003 [1979]. 'Marxism and Political Science: Prolegomenon to a Debate on Marx's Method', in *Dance of the Dialectic: Steps in Marx's Method*. Urbana: University of Illinois.

Ridpath, George. 1922. *Diary of George Ridpath: Minister of Stichel, 1755–1761,* J. Balfor Paul (ed.). Edinburgh: Scottish History Society.

Simmel, Georg. 1971 [1903]. 'The Metropolis and Mental Life', in *On Individuality and Social Forms,* Donald I. Levine (ed.). Chicago: University of Chicago Press.

Therborn, Goran. 1976. *Science, Class and Society: On the Formation of Sociology and Historical Materialism.* London: New Left Books.

Turner, Stephen P. 2003. 'MacIntyre in the Province of the Philosophy of the Social Sciences', in Mark C. Murphy (ed.), *Alasdair MacIntyre.* Cambridge: Cambridge University Press.

Veitch, John. 1854. 'Memoir of Dugald Stewart', in W. Hamilton (ed.), *Dugald Stewart, Collected Works,* vol. 10. Edinburgh: Thomas Constable.

Weber, Max. 1948 [1918/1919]. 'Science as a Vocation', in Hans H. Gerth and C. Wright Mills (eds), *From Max Weber: Essays in Sociology.* London: Routledge and Kegan Paul.

Weber, Max. 1976 [1904–1905]. *The Protestant Ethic and the Spirit of Capitalism.* London: George Allen and Unwin.

Weber, Max. 1994 [1919/1920]. 'The Profession and Vocation of Politics', in Peter Lassman and Ronald Speirs (eds), *Political Writings.* Cambridge: Cambridge University Press.

Weber, Max. 1998 [1896]. 'The Social Causes of the Decline of Ancient Civilization', in *The Agrarian Sociology of Ancient Civilizations.* London: Verso.

Winch, Peter. 1958. *The Idea of A Social Science and Its Relation to Philosophy.* London: Routledge and Kegan Paul.

Wright, Eric Olin. 1978 [1974]. 'Bureaucracy and the State', in *Class, Crisis and the State.* London: Verso.

Chapter 11

Castoriadis and Social Theory: From Marginalization to Canonization to Re-radicalization

Christos Memos

Introduction

Koestler's (2005: 144) point that 'the most productive times for revolutionary philosophy had always been the time of exile' encapsulates well the state of social thought in the years before and immediately after World War II. Over this period, drastic changes took place around the globe and every aspect of social life was influenced: economy, politics, standards of living, culture. Against this background, many types of migration emerged, causing considerable impact on societies and cultures. Amongst these, the migration of intellectuals grew in volume and changed in character, particularly after the Nazi's seizure of power in Germany. The majority of the intellectual émigrés moved from Hitler's Europe to the United States and a smaller group fled to the United Kingdom. Although the Germans' influence and relatively large numbers was distinctive, this wave of intellectual refugees included intellectuals from several European countries. A large number of these illustrious intellectuals, who were forced to migrate prior to 1940, were related to the social sciences: amongst so many others, economists such as Joseph Shumpeter, Ludwig von Mises, Wassily Leontief, Paul Baran, Oscar Lange, Karl Polanyi and Franco Modigliani, as well as sociologists, political scientists and philosophers such as Max Horkheimer, Otto Kirchheimer, Leo Lowenthel, Herbert Marcuse, Theodor Adorno, Hannah Arendt, C.N. Friedrich, Leo Strauss, Rudolf Carnap.

This forced expatriation concerned not only highly developed European countries. In many developing countries scholars emigrated or were forced to move from their countries to France, England or the United States. A typical example of the latter was provided by Greece. During the period of the Second World War some Greek intellectuals left the country, but the Greek migration directed mostly to America was 'the smallest of all and entirely musical' (Fermi 1971: 135). A considerable intellectual exodus from Greece to France took place after the end of the Second World War, when Greece became one of the centres of antagonism between the Soviet Union on the one hand and Great Britain and the United States on the other. Due to Anglo-American intervention and the agreement among the Great Powers, Greece was denied the right to freely decide upon its own political and social system, thus remaining by force under the capitalist rule. The British imperialist armed intervention and the conflict with the Greek popular democratic movement resulted in the armed conflict of December 1944 (known as 'Dekembriana'), which was the prelude to the outbreak of the Greek civil war (1946–1949). The military defeat of the left and resistance movement led to the 'Varkiza Agreement', a peace agreement in name only. Instead of reconciliation, non-violence and socio-political stability, the treaty signalled a new phase of violence known as the 'White Terror' period (1945–1946). Brutal right wing violence, purges, rapes and atrocities were committed against the most progressive and radical part of the Greek population. Thousands of people were prosecuted, jailed and murdered and basic human rights and civil liberties were banned. Right wing terrorism expanded into every aspect of Greek society and was coupled with cultural decay and intellectual, scientific regression. Under these circumstances, thousands of the poorest citizens fled to the mountains to survive. On the other hand, some young Greeks, many of them of bourgeois origins, were given a privileged way out from this tragic and critical situation.

In December 1945, approximately 220 young Greek intellectuals travelled on a ship called 'Mataroa' from Piraeus to France thanks to a scholarship provided by the French government. This exodus could be viewed as the last part of the intellectual migration that took place in Europe from 1933 to 1945. Among the young immigrants were future leading Greek intellectuals, including the prominent figure of Cornelius Castoriadis (1922–1997). Living and writing in post-war France, Castoriadis contributed significantly to the flourishing of social and critical theory. This chapter examines Castoriadis's trajectory from obscurity and the margins of post-war French intellectual and political milieu to the misappropriation and canonization of his thought after the 1970s and argues for a re-radicalization of his thought. First, it considers his formative experience in Greece and examines how the post-war French political, economic and ideological conditions and the group and journal *Socialisme ou Barbarie* contributed to Castoriadis's radicalization, thus consigning him, at the same time, to obscurity and marginalization. The chapter goes on to investigate some reasons for the rising interest in the social and political thought of Cornelius Castoriadis, expressed in both academic and political circles after the 1970s and has led not only to his international recognition but also to a triple diversion of the political and radical meaning of his theorizing. In the first place, his work was nihilistically defamed, rejected and dismissed by the largest part of the Marxist and radical Left. After the 1970s, Castoriadis's radical and left critique of Totalitarianism, Marx and Marxism was misconstrued and misused by the 'new philosophers'. Over the last twenty years, his ideas have mostly been praised and utilized in ways that deprived them of their original critical and radical meaning or political significance. Castoriadis's project has been subjected to a continuing canonization expressed through the construction of a 'new jargon'. The chapter concludes by arguing for a need to restore to Castoriadis's work its proper political and radical problematic.

Castoriadis and *Socialisme ou Barbarie*: Critical Theory in the Shadows

'I was 30, came from America, and was searching in the ashes of 1946 for the Phoenix' egg, you were 20, came from Greece, from the uprising, from jail ... You were Kostas Papaioannou, a universal Greek from Paris' (Paz 1988: 537, 539). Octavio Paz, the Nobel prize-winning Mexican poet, wrote these verses after the death of his friend philosopher Kostas Papaioannou, who was a friend of Castoriadis and fellow-traveller on the 'Mataroa'. Paz's poem also captures succinctly the early years in Greece and the formative experience of Cornelius Castoriadis. He was born on 11 March 1922 in Constantinople (Istanbul), and grew up in Greece during the interwar period, where he received a first-rate multilingual education, appropriate to his bourgeois background. From his early years as a high school student, Castoriadis expressed a profound interest in ancient Greek and Marxist philosophy. His intellectual inquiries led him to political engagement, which was expressed through his participation in the Greek communist movement. It was a period of intense political and ideological conflicts that deeply influenced Castoriadis's later theoretical and political orbit. The young Castoriadis experienced the Greek fascist regime of Metaxas (1936–1941) and the Nazi occupation of Greece. Later on, he decided to abandon the Greek Communist Youth as soon as he realized that his efforts to alter the 'chauvinistic policy', centralism and bureaucratization of the Greek communist party (K.K.E.) were in vain.

He thus joined the Trotskyists and in particular, the anti-chauvinist group led by Agis Stinas (1900–1987). Stinas was a leading member of the Greek Communist Party, but later on he espoused Trotskyism and led several Trotskyist groups that resulted from the fragmentation and numerous splits of the Trotskyist Greek movement. Trotskyism and Stinas's ideas had a strong and enduring impact on Castoriadis's intellectual trajectory and determined his theoretical problematic over the first twenty years of his life in France: the degeneration of the Russian Revolution and the bureaucratization of the working class movement, the role played by Lenin and Bolshevism and Trotsky's unsatisfactory analysis of the class character of the USSR. Because of their action, Castoriadis and his Trotskyist comrades were persecuted by the Germans, the Greek Stalinists and later on by the British army and the right-wing Greek government. In this respect, in his formative years in Greece, Castoriadis became familiar with the actual political function of both Stalinism and Trotskyism, and got a very strong taste of the dogmatism and authoritarianism of the orthodox Marxism of the Greek communist movement. More importantly, as a Trotskyist during the occupation years, he ran the risk of being arrested and murdered by the Greek Stalinists, inducing obsessions or traumas, which were to be mirrored in his later critique of Marx and Marxism. Also and while Castoriadis was still living in Greece, he expressed a strong interest in the phenomenon of bureaucracy by studying and writing on the thought of Max Weber (Καστοριάδης 1988). Later on in France, the efforts he made to explicate the class nature of the USSR and interpret Soviet society were determinedly influenced by Weber's views. Castoriadis constructed two 'ideal types' that belonged to the same system of 'bureaucratic capitalism', describing the USSR as 'total bureaucratic capitalism' and the western societies as 'fragmented bureaucratic capitalism'.

Castoriadis's exodus to France in 1945 not only saved his life but also provided him with the opportunity to continue his studies, combining his personal experience in Greece with new theoretical concerns and influences. Based on this formative experience, Castoriadis pursued his political commitment and remained active in the Trotskyist movement by joining the French section of the Fourth international (International Communist Party). It was there that he met Claude Lefort and along with some other members of the party formed a small oppositional group. Lefort very characteristically remembered his first encounter with Castoriadis:

> I first heard him lecture to the Party on the USSR in preparation for the Third Congress. His analysis overwhelmed me. I was convinced by him before he even reached his conclusion. I would have never been able to articulate the economic foundation that he provided for his conclusion. Castoriadis's arguments seemed to me worthy of the best Marx, but the Trotskyists deemed them heresy (Lefort 1976–1977: 174).

In 1948, however, they left the French Trotskyist party, basically rejecting the Trotskyist explication of the Stalinist phenomenon. One year later, Castoriadis and Lefort founded a radical independent political and theoretical group and published the first issue of the journal *Socialisme Ou Barbarie* in March 1949. This means that, from his very first years in France, Castoriadis chose to pass through the Scylla of the orthodox Marxists and the Charybdis of the liberal intellectuals and viewed himself as a radical and independent scholar and, concomitantly, as a leftist opposition to the Left. Going against the tide he successfully resisted both the pressure from the ideological dominance of the French Communist Party and the 'marketization' of intellectuals. It is important to stress here that the French Communist Party reached the peak of its influence and won five million votes in 1945 and by 1947 it consisted of 900,000 members. Needless to say, the French communist intellectuals remained anchored in their traditional Soviet-type Marxist interpretations of the world. Against this background, Castoriadis's political and theoretical stance posited a strong continuity with Max Horkheimer's premise that 'the real social function of philosophy lies in its criticism of what is prevalent' (1972: 264). In pursuing this end, he challenged what was prevalent in the Marxist theoretical tradition in his time: the orthodox Marxism of the second and third international. Based on Marx's thought he attacked 'orthodox Marxism', Leninism, Trotskyism and Stalinism. He also resisted the reduction of Marxian thought to ideology and attempted an uncompromising critique of the Soviet Union, when the vast majority of the so-called 'leftist intellectuals' did not dare challenge the dominance of the orthodoxy of the Communist Parties. It was, as Papaioannou would characterize this struggle, *'les idées contre l'ideologie'* (Papaioannou, 1969: 46).

For Castoriadis, the crisis and contradictions in orthodox Marxist thought could not be overcome separately from the social reality of orthodox Marxism. He launched his immanent critique of Marxism in an attempt at defending Marx from the orthodoxy. The critical confrontation with Trotsky's thought revealed his inconsistencies and brought to the surface his claim that it was necessary to re-examine the question of the class nature of the USSR. For Castoriadis, more specifically, Trotsky was responsible for 'theoretical monstrosities' and his blindness to Stalinism 'was a blindness of its own origins: of the bureaucratic tendencies organically incorporated into the Bolshevik party from the start' (Castoriadis 1988a: 8). These bureaucratic tendencies were clear both in the analysis of the USSR and the structure of the Trotskyist parties. In Lefort's words, 'little by little the Trotskyist party appeared to me to be a microcosm, which at its heart reproduced the models of behavior and social relations typical of bureaucratic organization' (Lefort 1976–1977: 175). Thus, instead of analysing the nature of Stalinism and the bureaucracy and their implications, Trotsky reiterated and reproduced conventional Leninist practices and theoretical schemata. Similar to Leninism, Trotskyism disregarded the idea of the autonomous action of the working class and its self-government and proved to be a serious obstacle to a radical critique of the traditional revolutionary organizations.

Drawing much of his inspiration from Russia (1917–1918), Spain (1936) and Hungary (1956) Castoriadis argued that 'the content of the socialist reorganization of society is first of all *workers' management* of production' (Castoriadis 1988b: 95). In this sense, Castoriadis determinedly castigated the Leninist notion of the Party, making the claim that 'the true creator of totalitarianism is Lenin' since 'it was Lenin himself who created the institution without which totalitarianism is inconceivable and which is today falling into ruin: the totalitarian party' (Castoriadis 1997a: 65). Castoriadis brought to our attention the fact that one of the focal points for a critical understanding of the decline of the Russian Revolution was the struggle between the *Workers' Opposition* and the Bolshevik leadership. 'Contrary to the prevailing mythology', for Castoriadis, 'it was not in 1927, or in 1923, or even in 1921 that the game was played and lost, but much earlier, during the period from 1918 to 1920' (Castoriadis 1993a: 98). This struggle mirrored the two contradictory elements of Marxism: the *Workers' Opposition* represented the most radical and subversive elements of the Marxist tradition, emphasizing and privileging the self-organization, self-determination and self-emancipation of the working class. Conversely, the Leninist position reflected Marxism's positivism, as well as its own economistic and developmental logic, and played an instrumental role in shaping the character and nature of the former Soviet Union. 'Union of Soviet Socialist Republics, USSR: Four Letters, Four Lies' (Morin 1998: 3). This claim summarizes Castoriadis's views regarding the actual character of the Soviet regime in a nutshell. Nevertheless, he firmly believed that the 'Russian question was and remains the touchstone of the theoretical and practical attitudes that call for revolution, and this question was also the richest vein, the royal road to the comprehension of the most important problems of contemporary society' (Castoriadis 1988a: 7).

Castoriadis endeavored to develop a rich and in-depth analysis of the Soviet regime, not of course without inconsistencies and imitations. In these theoretical elaborations, he underwent a number of conceptual turns that were depicted in the different terms he used in order to conceptualize the peculiarity of the Soviet regime: 'a new historical formation', 'a third historical solution', 'bureaucratic society', 'total bureaucratic capitalism', 'total and totalitarian bureaucratic capitalism' and 'stratocracy'. What could be considered as the lynch-pin that linked all the above-mentioned designations is Castoriadis's persistence in critically re-evaluating the USSR by stressing its distinctiveness as a new social and historical formation. Working within Marxism, he contrasted Marx's thought with the several modalities of Marxism claiming to incarnate it. This juxtaposition and his critical confrontation with the historical and political facts (e.g., the Hungarian Uprising of 1956) led him to make an effort to elucidate and explore the stagnation and crisis of Marxism. Yet, in his numerous attempts to make sense of the theory and practice of the 'Russian enigma', he came to the point of realizing not only the discontinuity between Marx and orthodox Marxism, but he was also led to argue that the problems and obstacles which existed in the theory and practice of Marxism could be traced back to Marx's own thought. In other words, dealing with the intractable issue of the nature of the Soviet regime and indicating how Marx's meaning was misconstrued by Trotsky and Lenin, Castoriadis worked within Marxism and moved from Marx to Marxism and vice versa. Hence, he emphatically noted that '*Capital* is to be read in the light of Russia, not Russia in the light of *Capital*' (Castoriadis 1997b: 228).

Seeking to identify Marx's responsibility for the metamorphosis of orthodox Marxism to 'state ideology' and 'reformist practice', Castoriadis raised penetrating questions with regard to Marx's writings with a view to tracing the metaphysical presuppositions and positivistic elements of his thought. His critique was premised on two basic pillars: first, he recognized that Marx's deification of the concept of technique determined Marx's theory of history and his analysis of capitalism; and second, he argued that Marx was deeply immersed in the values of Western humanism and in capitalist imaginary significations. Castoriadis articulated a radical critique of Marxism and Marx during the 1950s and 1960s and was automatically pushed by the Stalinist intellectuals and the French Communist Party to the margins of intellectual debate. As Khilnani has pointed out,

> after the defeat of fascism, in an atmosphere thick with accusations of collaboration and betrayal, anti-Fascism was most easily displayed by support for the Soviet Union. In this context, the anti-Soviet and revolutionary critique made by those such as Castoriadis and Lefort could not gain much force (Khilnani 1993: 135).

Castoriadis had great difficulties in taking French citizenship and was only granted full French citizenship in 1970. Over this period, Castoriadis wrote using pseudonyms such as Paul Cardan, Pierre Chaulieu, Jean Delvaux and Jean-Marc Coudray, 'for fear of endangering his émigré status in France' (Khilnani 1993: 130). As a group, *Socialisme Ou Barbarie* had a very restricted influence and Castoriadis very eloquently described this marginalization: 'We were absolutely isolated. There was a period when, after the outbreak of the Korean war, we were less than a dozen in the group. And the audience was extremely limited, residual ultra-leftist groups' (Castoriadis 1990: 36). Later on, the situation started to change and the political events and changes that took place after the death of Stalin gave a new vigour to *Socialisme Ou Barbarie*. In Castoriadis's words:

> After 1953 with Stalin dead, the Berlin revolt, the Czechoslovakian strikes in '54, then Hungary and Poland in '56, the atmosphere started changing, and the review gained some audience-never very important. At the time we were selling about 1,000 copies of the magazine, which were read around. Then came the Algerian war, and the stand we took against the Algerian war. There was a kind of renaissance amongst the student youth at that time. People started coming and the group grew. Some time in 1958/59, in the whole of France, including the provinces, we were about 100. By '62, '63, '64 we could hold public meetings in Paris with, say, 300 or 400 people. But all of this, as you see, was extremely, limited (Castoriadis 1990: 36–7).

Yet, despite the isolation of the group, according to Hirsh, the journal

> proved significant as the only vehicle for a systematic gauchiste critique of the communist movement during the height of the Cold War. While many leftist intellectuals (with Sartre in the lead) buried their qualms and sided with the Soviet Union against the capitalist West, *Socialisme Ou Barbarie* continued a critique of both sides (Hirsch 1981: 113).

Forty issues of the journal were published before 1965, when the cessation of publication was announced, and the group ceased to exist in 1967. The *Socialisme Ou Barbarie* group developed close relationships with the 'Johnson-Forest Tendency' (C.L.R. James and Raya Dunayevskaya) in the U.S.A and the British group and journal *Solidarity* (Maurice Brinton). The critical endeavour of the group also included a parallel effort to analyse and explicate the crisis and dynamic of modern capitalist societies in order to re-invigorate the revolutionary project. Their work was indisputably uncomfortable and annoying, notably for the leftist and Communist parties. The Soviet regime's attempt to impose its political and ideological dominance, based on its official dogma of 'Marxism-Leninism' and the Stalinist policy of the Communist parties in Western societies, had created a context which marginalized and excluded every independent and 'unorthodox' radical thinker from public debate. As Primo Levi very forcefully put it, 'uncomfortable truths travel with difficulty' (Levi 1989: 129).

The Diversionists: From 'Marginalization' to 'Totalitarianism' to the Construction of a 'New Jargon'

In their *Communist Manifesto*, Marx and Engels envisioned the growth of the rapidly rising working class movement as 'the self-conscious, independent movement of the immense majority, in the interest of the immense majority' (Marx and Engels 1991: 44), whose constant quantitative and qualitative development will rely 'solely and exclusively upon the intellectual development of the working class, as it necessarily had to ensue from united action and discussion' (Marx and Engels 1991: 33). Autonomous and self-determining action, intellectual growth and united action should constitute the core of the radical and subversive movement in its social struggles to negate capitalist social relations and create a different system of life and an alternative society. And all these fundamental elements should be informed by free and independent critical thinking. Luxemburg captured this point implicitly and categorically: 'Freedom is always and exclusively freedom for the one who thinks differently' (Luxemburg 1970: 389). Unfortunately, the tradition of the anti-capitalist movement throughout the last century not only flies in the face of Luxemburg's dictum, but appeared to confirm one of Lukács's, final verdicts: 'we are all still Stalinists' (Lukács 1972: 56). Lukacs's statement could describe the state of intolerance, exclusiveness and hatred that marked a large part of the post-world Left in France. Any open theoretical and political criticism of the Soviet regime, Marxism or Marx was taboo and repressed. A distinctive theoretical contribution was easily accused of being 'reactionary' and often misused and distorted not only by the 'right', but also by 'left' parties and intellectuals. As Albert and Hahnel have noted,

> In a world where most who attack the orthodoxy do so from the right, it is easier
> for leftists to line up in its defence. It is common as well for all critics to be
> immediately labelled "anticommunist", "bourgeois", "reactionary", or worse as
> the case may be. Such sectarian name-calling is very potent. Lumping all critics
> of the orthodoxy with those whose purposes are indeed reactionary this reverse
> baiting effectively intimidates most leftist critics. It asserts that there can be
> no justifiable criticism, only ill-motivated anti-communism, so that those that
> venture critical analysis run the risk of simultaneously losing all 'revolution
> credibility'. The orthodoxy is sacrosanct and disbelievers are heretics, beholden,
> one way or another, to the capitalist devil (Albert and Hahnel 1978: 7).

In post-war France under the political and ideological dominance of the French Communist Party it was inconceivable for someone to criticize Stalin, let alone Lenin. Intellectuals such as Sartre and Aragon did not dare criticize Stalin and usually expressed their admiration for him. The party had managed to capitalize on its own role in the Resistance and the fact that it was seen by the new generations as being the only French political power that symbolized the heroic and glorious victory of the USSR against Nazi Germany. As a result, a critical attitude towards the USSR could be easily rejected, marginalized and designated as reactionary and counterrevolutionary. As described by Khilnani, this situation was particularly the case in France:

> Contrary to the situation in Britain, where the much more immediately (and differently) felt effect of writers like Koestler and Orwell made it perfectly reasonable, if by no means mandatory, to reject the Soviet Union as a political model and yet continue to remain on the Left, in France it was not until the 1970s that such a position became intellectually and politically sustainable (Khilnani 1993: 129)

In most cases, the Marxist or radical Left approach to Castoriadis was a nihilistic, ill-equipped and dogmatic denunciation and repudiation of his theorizing. Having settled for decades 'for the role of revolutionary-by-proxy', 'cuckolded and defeated as revolutionaries sans revolution' (Vaneigem 1983: 215), traditional Leftists and Marxists seem to have perceived nothing new as they had seen and known it all before (Viénet 1992: 105). They decisively constituted a catalytic factor in the marginalization of his thought, at least in the period before the collapse of the Soviet regime. Castoriadis's contribution remained unknown and was unwisely and crudely seen as 'reactionary'. This development was facilitated by Castoriadis's theoretical limitations, political contradictions and erroneous judgments. In particular, Castoriadis's later unfortunate and unsound position that the former USSR was a military and stratocratic society (see Castoriadis 1981 and Castoriadis 1980–1981) in its own way, opened the door for the distortion of his views and theoretical contributions. Leftists and Marxists not only defamed his whole political and intellectual history, but also his flawed analyses came under severe criticism, which placed 'Castoriadis's demonstration among the crudest speculations of an obsolete Kremlinology having more to do with the demonology of centuries past than with the modern study of social and political phenomena' (Rittesporn 1982: 22).

On the other hand, and given the historical and political context of the 1970s and 1980s, Castoriadis's views gained a wider audience and at the same time were distorted by the 'new philosophers' (Bernard-Henri Levy, André Glucksmann, etc.) and the 'Stalinists of anti-communism' who emerged in France throughout this period (Dews 1980; and Dews 1979). These 'Stalinists of anti-communism' consisted of 'an intelligentsia which was, almost by definition, considered to be on the left' that 'has packed up its bags and gone over to the other side. It now addresses its criticisms, not to French society, but to those who dare to think of transforming it' (Delwit and Dewaele 1984: 324). More specifically, during the 1970s an attempt was made by the 'new philosophers' to misuse and misappropriate Castoriadis's critique of the Soviet system, Marxism and Marx. The 'new philosophers' revived interest in the term 'totalitarianism', but they attributed to it a completely different meaning than the Greek intellectual used. In the name of democracy and human rights they attacked and ridiculed any radical anti-capitalist voice, identifying it with totalitarianism and 'red fascism', regardless of the fact that Castoriadis held that the defence of the Soviet Union was actually anti-revolutionary and his critique was 'launched from the Left, in the name of authentic revolution' (Khilnani 1993: 129). For them, any attempt to overthrow capitalism and transform capitalist social relations would inevitably lead to 'red terror', blind violence and deification of state power. Having placed the notion of totalitarianism at the centre of their elaborations, and drawing upon thinkers such as Castoriadis, Arendt or Popper, they put particular stress on the dissemination of their anti-statist, anti-radical and anti-Soviet ideas. Likewise, Castoriadis's critique of Marx and Marxism was also read and construed as being akin to the post-modernist view that rejects grand narratives and advocates western forms of liberal and representative democracy.

Castoriadis not only rejected the 'new wave of diversionists' (Castoriadis 1993b: 275), as he called the 'new philosophers' approach to his work, but he also reacted against the misuse and the distortion of his own ideas. For Castoriadis, it is explicit that the function of the 'new philosophers' 'fully plays into the interests of the apparatuses' (Castoriadis 1993b: 277) with a view to 'covering over in advance the true questions by "answers" *which have for their effect and their function to stop dead in its tracks the movement of reflection* and to take the edge off the political and revolutionary critique of totalitarianism on the one hand, of Marxism on the other' (Castoriadis 1993b: 275). And Castoriadis goes on with his forceful critique:

> The new wave of diversionists does not ask: How is totalitarianism *actually* engendered? Shamelessly pillaging through what a few of us have been working out for the past thirty years, it hastily lifts from this work a few elements whose meaning it distorts in order to say: Totalitarianism *is* Marx, *is* Hegel, *is* Fichte, *is* Plato. It understands neither what thinking means nor the *unfathomable* relationship historical thought and historical reality entertain. Diverting the critique of Marx that we had made from a political, praxical, revolutionary perspective – a critique that was bringing out precisely the capitalist, Western, metaphysical heritage of which Marx had remained prisoner, to discover *thereby* what in Marx remained *on the hither side* of a revolutionary aim – it tries to draw from this critique the following absurd conclusion: it is *precisely as* a revolutionary that Marx would have engendered the Gulag (Castoriadis 1993: p. 276).

Amongst other things, what is at stake here is the manner in which Castoriadis has been received, read and used by both the critical, radical and anti-capitalist tradition and the existing social and theoretical order, the 'intellectual establishment'. After the '*nouveau philosophes*', and more particularly, the years following the demise of the former USSR, the work of Castoriadis was subjected to a ruthless and peculiar academization and canonization. Over the last twenty five years, the vast majority of Castoriadis's interpretations have focused almost exclusively on Castoriadis's later psychoanalytical-philosophical writings, thus unreasonably diverting attention from Castoriadis's political writings and the radical content of his thought, which marked his whole theoretical itinerary. It seems that, as was the case with numerous academics and intellectuals after the movements of the sixties, the demise of the regimes in Eastern Europe provided scholars 'with a minimum of ideological justification' or a 'legitimation' both for the profound disregard of radical ideas and practices that followed the collapse and 'for their own incipient privatization while also retaining some sort of "radical sensibility"' (Castoriadis 1997c: 53, 54). The philosophical writings of the later Castoriadis, as happened with specific aspects of the work of Gramsci or the members of the Frankfurt School, were convenient for 'a retrospective legitimation of withdrawal, renunciation, noncommitment, or of a punctilious and measured commitment' (Castoriadis 1997c: 53). Indisputably, Castoriadis left himself open to this treatment both because of the direction and content of a large part of his later theoretical elaborations and due to the fact that he unfortunately did very little to clarify that he aimed at a 'political and revolutionary' (Castoriadis 1993b: 275) critique of totalitarianism, Marxism and Marx, from a 'political, praxical, revolutionary perspective' (Castoriadis 1993b: 276). Inherent contradictions and limits of his thought were pushed to the more conservative and apolitical extreme by the academic and intellectual apparatuses. Castoriadis responded by challenging the distortion of his critical project, though belatedly and unsuccessfully, and endeavored to champion the radicalism of his theoretical endeavor. As he vigorously reminds us,

> The workers' movement began well *before* Marx, and it had nothing to do with Fichte or with Hegel ... The question posed is not how to 'replace Marxism' but how to create a new relationship between thinking and doing, how to elucidate things in terms of a practical project without falling back either into the system or into doing just anything (Castoriadis 1993b: 276).

Unfortunately, once again after the 1970s, Castoriadis's political and revolutionary critique of Totalitarianism, Marxism and Marx has been misconstrued by 'the new wave of diversionists' and new Stalinists of anti-Marx, anti-Marxism and anti-communism are produced among Castoriadis's adherents. This new diversion has led to a distorted and misleading reception of Castoriadis's theorizing. One of the main vehicles for this new diversion has been the construction of a new jargon. Through this metamorphosis of Castoriadis, his thought ceased to be a moment of critical reason and anti-capitalist struggles. It was reduced to a jargon, a new world of magical words, technical terms and mechanical expressions. Castoriadis's later philosophical language has been transformed into a mystification and has been reified, thus making it being devoid of content, let alone political and radical content. In many academic circles, for example, Castoriadis is known, read and used as a psychoanalyst or his work has been standardized into reified and abstract key concepts such as creative imagination, social imaginary significations, chaos, creation *ex nihilo*, monad, self, body, psyche, magma, tragedy, ensemblistic-identitary logic, legein and teukhein, Anlehnung, the living being, paideia (see Adams 2014). This reification is not simply the case of 'talking trivialities in high-sounding language' (Popper 1976: 296). It actually aims at a forgetting of Castoriadis's radicalism in order for his thought to be eventually converted into an academic discipline, to be canonized and kept isolated from contemporary social and political struggles. A fashionable invocation of Castoriadis's standardized catch-words domesticates radical thought in the service of the existing capitalist reality, thus performing the systematic function of stabilization and reproducing all those capitalist relations 'in which man is a debased, enslaved, neglected and contemptible being' (Marx 1992: 251). The construction of fetishistic concepts takes the place of the grasping and penetrating critique and analysis of social, economic and political capitalist relations. As Adorno would say 'ideology has shifted into language' (Adorno 2003: xix); this time Castoriadis's sacred words turned out to be a positive and constructive endorsement of actual capitalist relations of exploitation and domination. By downplaying the oppositional and revolutionary aspects of Castoriadis's work, the new diversionists postulate Castoriadis's critical theory as domesticated, bloodless and apolitical, and as such, this domestication aims to become dominant and prevail. As a consequence, the critical and radical content of Castoriadis's ideas has intentionally fallen into oblivion and it travels with difficulty. Yet, 'as with wine, the capacity to travel does not necessarily reflect the quality of the passenger' (Craufurd and Goodwin 1973: 285).

Postscript: Reclaiming Castoriadis's Radicalism

In one of his later interviews conducted in 1985 and 1986, Castoriadis made it explicit that what distinguished him from his contemporary scholars was his persistence with 'the political project', namely the fact that he wanted to 'do philosophy and politics at the same time' (Castoriadis 1995: 31). Describing his work as a constant struggle to remain faithful to the project of human emancipation, Castoriadis endeavored also to clarify his relationship with Marx:

> Looking back, my fundamental political orientation is without doubt rooted in the work and engagement of Marx ... The concern to combine understanding with a project of change I have learned from Marx, or invented, I don't know which. In this sense there is a bond between Marx and me. I privilege Marx over the other great thinkers because he tries again to be a philosophical citizen and citizen-philosopher (Castoriadis 1995: 31).

Castoriadis was first and foremost a political and radical thinker and the intended oblivion of the largest part of his work is quite undeserved. It cancels Castoriadis's critical and radical meaning and represents an abdication, abandonment and concealment of the political character of his views. This is not to claim that the later psychoanalytical-philosophical part of Castoriadis's work is not worthy of scholarly and analytical engagement. This is simply to argue that this does not justify the almost exclusive reading of Castoriadis's thought via these texts at the expense of the whole body of his social and political writings. Reading Castoriadis politically means, first of all, detaching his thought from the condition of being used as part of the 'succession of fads', from its reduction to another of the 'successive waves of the ruling system's *complementary ideology*', exactly that which Castoriadis was explicitly and fiercely opposed to (Castoriadis 1993b: 272). Reinstating Castoriadis to his actual political substance implies separating his critical theory from the dominant tendency of becoming 'fashionable' and involves critically confronting the 'compilation, misappropriation and distortion' of his own ideas (Castoriadis 1993b: 276). Giving back to Castoriadis's work its proper radical problematic would amount to disengaging it from the idolatry of words, the construction of a new jargon. As Castoriadis would say, 'the magic of words is thus used to make the reality of things disappear' (Castoriadis 1988c: 239). Even after the severe 'financial crisis' of 2008, the 'fashionable', abstract, philosophical and apolitical readings of Castoriadis appear to remain detached from the social and political reality. The 'fashionable' scholars of his work resemble, as Castoriadis brilliantly put it,

> those who discourse about the rights of man, the indeterminacy of democracy, communicative action, the self-foundation of reason, and so on – the Panglosses who go on spouting their navel-watching rhetoric without ever allowing themselves to be distracted by the sound and fury of effectively actual history (Castoriadis 2003a: 76).

They ultimately neglect and bury the riches of Castoriadis's political and intellectual heritage, deferring treatment of the vital questions he addressed. Contrary to these approaches, Castoriadis championed critical reason's historic role of 'provoking insubordination and destroying horrors' (Agnoli 2003: 26). Diametrically opposed to the approaches that apprehend the function of scholarly work as being at the service of the established order, Castoriadis was adamant that the role of the scholar 'ought to be critical' and he argued against a 'generalized pseudoconsensus' and those intellectuals who are 'caught up in the system' and who, by abandoning and betraying their critical role, 'became rationalizers for what is, justifiers of the established order' (Castoriadis 2003b: 128, 130). In this sense, Castoriadis went against the grain of the academics and intellectuals who seek to catch previously marginal or subversive ideas and words, as ironically is now happening with Castoriadis's work, and make them 'one phenomenon among others, commercialized like the others' with a view to completing the 'harmony of the system' (Castoriadis 2003b: 131). In one of his interviews in 1991 and in answer to the question of what the role of the intellectual should be, Castoriadis clarified and specified his positions eloquently: 'Uncompromising criticism of existing realities and elucidation of the possibilities for transforming them' (Castoriadis 2011: 108).

References

Adams, S. (ed.). 2014. *Cornelius Castoriadis: Key Concepts*. London and New York: Bloomsbury.

Adorno, T. 2003. *The Jargon of Authenticity*. London: Routledge.

Agnoli, J. 2003. 'Destruction as the Determination of the Scholar in Miserable Times', in W. Bonefeld (ed.), *Revolutionary Writing*. New York: Autonomedia.

Albert, M. and R. Hahnel. 1978. *UnOrthodox Marxism*. Boston: South End Press.

Castoriadis, C. 1980–1981. 'Facing the War', *Telos* 46: 43–61.

Castoriadis, C. 1981. *Devant la Guerre*. Paris: Fayand.

Καστοριάδης, Κ. 1988. *Πρώτες Δοκιμές*. Αθήνα: Ύψιλον.

Castoriadis, C. 1988a. 'General Introduction', in D.A Curtis (ed.), *Cornelius Castoriadis: Political and Social Writings*, vol. 1, 1946–1955. Minneapolis: University of Minnesota Press.

Castoriadis, C. 1988b. 'On the Content of Socialism II', in D.A. Curtis (ed.), *Cornelius Castoriadis, Political and Social Writings*, vol. 2, 1955–1960. Minneapolis: University of Minnesota Press.

Castoriadis, C. 1988c. 'Modern Capitalism and Revolution', in D.A. Curtis (ed.), *Cornelius Castoriadis, Political and Social Writings*, vol. 2, 1955–1960. Minneapolis: University of Minnesota Press.

Castoriadis, C. 1990. 'An interview', *Radical Philosophy* 56 (Autumn): 35–43.

Castoriadis, C. 1993a. 'The Role of Bolshevik Ideology in the Birth of the Bureaucracy', in D.A. Curtis (ed.), *Cornelius Castoriadis, Political and Social Writings*, vol. 3, 1961–1979. Minneapolis: University of Minnesota Press.

Castoriadis, C. 1993b. 'The Diversionists', in D.A. Curtis (ed.), *Cornelius Castoriadis: Political and Social Writings*, vol. 3, 1961–1979. Minneapolis: University of Minnesota Press.

Castoriadis, C. 1995. Castoriadis in F. Rötzer, *Conversations with French Philosophers*. New Jersey: Humanities Press.

Castoriadis, C., 1997a. 'The Pulverization of Marxism-Leninism', in D.A. Curtis (ed.), *World in Fragments*. Stanford: Stanford University Press.

Castoriadis, C. 1997b. 'The Social Regime in Russia', in D.A. Curtis (ed.), *The Castoriadis Reader*. Oxford: Blackwell Publishers.

Castoriadis, C. 1997c. 'The Movements of the Sixties', in D.A. Curtis (ed.), *World in Fragments*. Stanford: Stanford University Press.

Castoriadis, C. 2003a. 'The Dilapidation of the West', in C. Castoriadis, *The Rising Tide of Insignificancy (The Big Sleep)*. Translated from the French and edited anonymously as a public service. Available at: http://www.costis.org/x/ castoriadis/Castoriadis-rising_tide.pdf, pp. 73–108.

Castoriadis, C. 2003b. 'The Rising Tide of Insignificancy', in C. Castoriadis, *The Rising Tide of Insignificancy (The Big Sleep)*. Translated from the French and edited anonymously as a public service. Available at http://www.costis.org/x/ castoriadis/Castoriadis-rising_tide.pdf, pp. 124–54.

Castoriadis, C. 2011. 'The Crisis of the Imaginary?', in C. Castoriadis, *Postscript on Insignificancy*. Translated from the French and edited anonymously as a public service. Available at http://www.notbored.org/ PSRTI.pdf, pp. 106–8.

Delwit, P. and J.-M. Dewaele. 1984. 'The Stalinists of Anti-Communism', *The Social Register* 21: 324–48.

Dews, P. 1979. 'The Nouvelle Philosophie and Foucault', *Economy and Society* 8(2): 127–71.

Dews, P. 1980. 'The "New Philosophers" and the end of Leftism', *Radical Philosophy* 24: 2–11.

Fermi, L. 1971. *Illustrious Immigrants: The Intellectual Migration from Europe 1930/41*. Chicago: The University of Chicago Press.

Goodwin, C.D.W. 1973. 'Marginalism Moves to the New World', in R.D. Collison Black, A.W. Coats, Craufurd D.W. Goodwin (eds), *The Marginal Revolution in Economics: Interpretation and Evaluation*. Durham, NC: Duke University Press.

Hirsh, A. 1981. *The French New Left: An Intellectual History from Sartre to Gorz*. Boston: South End Press.

Horkheimer, M. 1972. *Critical Theory: Selected Essays*. New York: Herder and Herder.

Khilnani, S. 1993. *Arguing Revolution: The Intellectual Left in Postwar France*. New Haven, CT and London: Yale University Press.

Koestler, A. 2005. *Darkness at Noon*. New York: Vintage.

Lefort, C. 1976–1977. 'An Interview with Claude Lefort', *Telos* 30: 173–92.

Levi, P. 1989. *The Drowned and the Saved*. London: Abacus.

Lukács, G. 1972. 'A Final Rethinking. György Lukács Talks with Franco Ferrarotti', *Social Policy* 3(2): 4–8, 56–7.

Luxemburg, R. 1970. 'The Russian Revolution', in M.A. Waters (ed.), *Rosa Luxemburg Speaks*. New York: Pathfinder Press.

Marx, K. and F. Engels. 1991. 'Manifesto of the Communist Party', in K. Marx and F. Engels, *Selected Works*. London: Lawrence and Wishart.

Marx, K. 1992. 'A Contribution to the Critique of Hegel's Philosophy of Right. Introduction', in K. Marx, *Early Writings*. London: Penguin.

Morin, E. 1998. 'An Encyclopaedic Spirit', *Radical Philosophy* 90: 3–5.

Papaioannou, K. 1969. 'Les Idées contre l'Idéologie: Formes et Degrés de la Débolchevisation', *Revue Française De Science Politique* 14(1): 46–62.

Paz, O. 1988. 'Kostas Papaioannou (1925–1981)', in O. Paz, *The Collected Poems 1957–1987*. Manchester: Carcanet.

Popper, K. 1976. 'Reason or Revolution?', in Theodor W. Adorno et al., *The Positivist Dispute in German Sociology*. London: Heinemann.

Rittesporn, G. 1982. 'Facing the War Psychosis', *Telos* 51: 22–31.

Vaneigem, R. 1983. *The Revolution of Everyday Life*. London: Left Bank Books and Rebel Press.

Viénet, R. 1992. *Enrages and Situationists in the Occupation Movement, France, May '68*. New York: Autonomedia.

Chapter 12

Norbert Elias: Sociological Amnesia and 'The Most Important Thinker You Have Never Heard Of'

Stephen Mennell

Norbert Elias died at his home in Amsterdam on 1 August 1990. Fourteen years later, in April 2004 two friends, Maria Goudsblom and Elke Korte, went to visit the spot where his ashes were interred at the Westergaarde cemetery in Amsterdam. They asked an official where to find the place, but their search was unsuccessful. Back in the office an official was awaiting them with a large envelope containing copies of several wrongly addressed letters to the Norbert Elias Foundation that had gone unanswered. From 1995 onwards the cemetery had asked every year what to do with the gravestone and the urn, since the Foundation had paid the necessary fees for only five years. Finally, in 2003, both had been removed to a storehouse. The Foundation hastily paid up, and Elias was reinterred. This comical episode can serve as an allegory for Elias's life.

Elias came close to being an irretrievable victim of sociological amnesia. One hears anecdotes from the late 1940s and 1950s about people who, when they came across his 1939 masterpiece, *Über den Prozess der Zivilisation*, assumed that he must be dead. Some aspects of his life were clearly traumatic, but he was never directly at risk of dying in the Holocaust. His academic career, however, was most certainly in jeopardy for a very long time. Until the last decade of his life, Elias seemed reluctant to talk about himself: he said that what was important were his ideas. By the 1980s, though, he had become an intellectual celebrity, at least in Europe, and he then wrote an intellectual autobiography and gave numerous interviews (Elias 2013a). The outlines of his story are now familiar enough, and – up to a point – represent a tale of the conquest of sociological amnesia. Belated recognition seemed both to open the floodgates of his publications and to overcome his reticence about himself. The same belatedness explains why the influence of Elias's ideas on the discipline of sociology has been much more recent than his date of birth might lead one to expect.

Life and Difficult Times

Elias was born in 1897 in Breslau, then the main city of German Silesia but now the Polish city of Wrocław, into a secular Jewish family. He received an obviously outstanding education at the Johannesgymnasium in the city, then at the age of 18 entered the German army and saw action – in a telegraph company – on both the eastern and western fronts in the First World War. He saw people killed at close quarters, and probably himself suffered shell-shock. Back in Breslau right at the end of the war he was acting as a surgical orderly, and then enrolled in the University of Breslau to read both medicine and philosophy. He always said that his experience in the dissecting room was invaluable for his understanding of how human beings worked, but he dropped medicine in favour of philosophy. His doctorate was supervised by the neo-Kantian philosopher Richard Hönigswald, from whom he said he learned a great deal – but with whom he came to disagree on some very fundamental philosophical assumptions, a disagreement that was to have a profound bearing on his later sociological writings. The early 1920s also saw attempted putsches against the new Weimar government, assassinations, street fighting between the right-wing Freikorps and left-wing militias (Elias 2013b), as well as hyperinflation that temporarily robbed Elias's father of his wealth and forced Elias himself to take a job in industry.

At the beginning of 1925, when some stability had been restored both in the country and in the family finances, Elias took himself off to resume his studies, in Heidelberg and as a sociologist rather than as a philosopher. He was accepted as a *Habilitation* candidate by Alfred Weber, and worked on the links between the development of the sciences and the arts in Renaissance Florence (see the outline found among Alfred Weber's papers, Elias 2006b). But he also became close friends with Karl Mannheim, and when in 1930 Mannheim was called to the chair of sociology at the University of Frankfurt, Elias went with him as his official academic *Assistent*. Frankfurt at that time provided a rich and lively intellectual milieu, in which Elias came into contact with a large circle of rising stars in the social sciences and humanities. The university rented space for Mannheim and his staff in the building that was owned by the independent Institut für Sozialforschung – the Frankfurt School, led by Max Horkheimer with Theodor W. Adorno among its leading lights. Relations between the group around Horkheimer on the one hand and Mannheim on the other appear to have been personally civil, but intellectually fairly distant. It was, however, at this time that Elias encountered the writings of Sigmund Freud in depth for the first time, and they had a profound influence on his thinking as they did on that of the Frankfurt School.

One could reasonably have expected that from these foundations Elias's academic career would have taken off rapidly and that he would have shortly achieved distinction and prominence. Of course it was not to be. When Hitler came to power at the end of January 1933, Elias's *Habilitationsschrift* was hastily submitted and he was rushed through all the stages necessary to gain his *Veni legendi*, apart from the required public lecture. He had abandoned work on Renaissance science, and instead written a thesis entitled 'Der höfische Mensch', which remained unpublished until it was enlarged and reworked for publication almost four decades later in 1969 as *Die höfische Gesellschaft – The Court Society* (2006a). Elias hung around in Frankfurt a bit longer than many of his colleagues –

long enough to witness the Nazi takeover of both the university and the city, which was both violent and orderly – later he would emphasize that it was a mistake for sociologists to think of violence and orderliness as opposites. But then he went into exile in Paris, where by 1935 he had both lost his money in a venture making toys and definitively established that there was no prospect of securing an academic job in France. This was the only time in his life when he actually went hungry. He was rescued by friends who invited him to come to Britain, where he arrived in 1935 with scant knowledge of English and again little prospect of an academic career. With a small grant from a refugee charity, he set to work on what became *Über den Prozess der Zivilisation*. The first volume appears to have been finished in 1936, the second by about 1938. It was printed back in Breslau by a Jewish printer who also became a refugee before production was finished. Elias's father extricated the unbound sheets and took them to Basel, where they were bound by an émigré publisher, Haus zum Falken. As Bryan Wilson was later to comment, 1939 was 'not the most propitious year for the publication of a large, two-volume work, in German, by a Jew, on, of all things, civilization' (Wilson 1977). Elias sent copies to many people, Sigmund Freud, R. H. Tawney and Thomas Mann among them. Mann, at least, read it and noted his appreciation in his *Tagebuch* (1980: 440, 443, 445, 446, 447). But Walter Benjamin, a personal acquaintance of Elias's, refused to review the book, on standard Marxist grounds (Schöttker 1998). Though it is now recognized as one of the twentieth century's most important works of sociology – in a straw poll organized by Piotr Sztompka among members of the International Sociological Association in 1998, *Über den Prozess der Zivilisation* was rated one of the ten most important sociological works of the century – at the time of its publication it fell almost dead from the press. Few reviews and citations followed until after its republication in 1969 (Goudsblom 1977).

Elias's experience of life up to 1939 ought to have protected him from the misunderstanding that became common later, that his book presented a theory in the Victorian manner about the inevitable long-term progress of human society. Whether he could as yet be described as a victim of sociological amnesia is open to question: amnesia means the loss of memory, and few sociologists had any memory of his work that they could lose.

Elias's ill fortune was to continue for another decade and a half. He did secure the lowly and strangely titled post of 'Senior Research Assistant' at the London School of Economics, but, shortly after the LSE's evacuation to Cambridge early in the war, he was interned as an enemy alien for about eight months, first near Liverpool and then on the Isle of Man, where he was in very distinguished company, and from where he was released through the efforts of C.P. Snow. His mother was killed in Treblinka. After the war, he scraped a meagre living giving adult education classes in and around London. He also at this time played an important part as a founder, with his friend from Frankfurt days Siegmund H. Foulkes, in formulating the theory and practice of Group Analysis, now a very important form of psychotherapy. Here, however, *psychological* amnesia set in: after Elias left London, he was no longer active in the Group Analytic movement, and memories of his early role began to fade among practitioners. Group Analysts came to know little of Elias's sociology, and sociologists little of Group Analysis. Only in the 1990s did the two groups begin to encounter each other, and the writings of the psychotherapist Farhad Dalal (1998) were notable in arguing that Group Analysis needed in effect 'less Foulkes, and more Elias'.

Finally, in 1954, Elias's prospects took a turn for the better. At the remarkably advanced age of 57, he was appointed to his first secure academic post, at what was about to become the University of Leicester. There, before his retirement as Reader in 1962, with his friend and colleague Ilya Neustadt he built up a distinguished department of sociology that was for a time the largest in Britain. In another example of sociological amnesia, the standard histories of sociology in Britain are extremely LSE-centric, largely neglecting the story of the astonishing number of staff and students who passed through the Leicester department and went on to become prominent sociologists. Elias put especially great effort into teaching a distinctive introductory course for undergraduate students, which was developmental in character, taking a long-term comparative view of the development of human society. Yet the department was not intellectually monolithic. While his approach inspired some, there were also strong opponents among the younger staff appointed to the growing department: John Goldthorpe from a Popperian standpoint and Percy Cohen as a functionalist anthropologist both regarded Elias as an intellectual throwback to an earlier age.

Upon reaching the age of retirement, Elias spent two years as Professor of Sociology and head of department at the University of Ghana. It is clear that a principal motive was that it at long last gave him the title of Professor. For him Ghana was an enriching experience, but his absence had detrimental effects in Leicester. In 1961, the department had secured a large government research grant for what was known as the 'Young Workers Project' (Goodwin and O'Connor 2014); Elias was the principal investigator, but quite a large number of younger staff and students were involved – among them Tony Giddens and Sheila Allen. With Elias away, the project drifted and dissension set in. The collapse of the project probably damaged the careers of some of the most junior research assistants, and certainly some resentment persisted towards Elias. This was one more obstacle to rescuing Elias from the incipient amnesia of British sociologists.

At the time of his appointment at Leicester, Elias had published remarkably little by later standards: apart from his still unknown *magnum opus*, there were no more than a handful of obscurely published essays in German (Elias 2006b), and journal articles in English. The Leicester years saw few additions to his output. The most important publication of those years, 'Problems of involvement and detachment' in the *British Journal of Sociology* 1956, was widely misunderstood as yet another boring discussion of the problem of 'objectivity' in the tradition of Max Weber. In fact it was the first important statement of Elias's sociological theory of knowledge and the sciences (Elias 2007, 2009); but this essay was not much noticed either. A problem for English-speaking readers – a problem that I experienced myself on first acquaintance with Elias – was that, without a thorough knowledge of *Über den Prozess der Zivilisation*, it was difficult to understand the significance of his other writings. Many people asked, 'Where is he coming from?' And, in view of the paucity of his writings in English, it was hard to appreciate that he was a sociologist of the highest stature.

After Ghana, Elias returned to teaching postgraduates in Leicester, and at this time he began to collaborate with Eric Dunning in developing – or, rather, one should say, creating – the sociology of sport. He and his MA student John Scotson also wrote *The Established and the Outsiders* (2008), but this book was also underestimated; most reviewers saw it as a yet another in the long series of 'community studies' by British sociologists and anthropologists. In retrospect it can also be seen as the beginning of Elias's elaboration of a distinctive theory of power relations.

Then, in the late 1960s, when Elias was already in his 70s, there was a remarkable upturn in his fortunes, the seeds of which had been sown some years earlier. Copies of the first edition of *Über den Prozess der Zivilisation* had remained on the shelves of some university libraries. As early as 1950 an undergraduate student of social psychology in the University of Amsterdam, Johan Goudsblom, found the book in the library and found it revelatory. He met Elias in person at the World Congress of Sociology in Amsterdam in 1956, and they kept in touch. By 1968 Goudsblom was Professor of Sociology at Amsterdam. In Germany, Professor Dieter Claessens of Münster and later Berlin was also aware of Elias, and through him Elias was invited to speak (though not at all in a starring role) at the conference of the German Sociological Association in Heidelberg to mark the centenary of Max Weber's birth. Elias was invited to both Münster and Amsterdam as a visiting professor. In 1969 *Über den Prozess der Zivilisation* was republished by the Swiss publisher Francke. It was an expensive two-volume hardback, but it found admirers among the rebellious students of the period, and they began to produce *samizdat* pirate copies. This made a cheap paperback edition an attractive proposition to the great Frankfurt publishers Suhrkamp, and after hearing Elias speak at the launch of that edition the famous head of that house, Siegfried Unseld, entered into a gentlemen's agreement to publish everything that Elias wrote subsequently. *Die höfische Gesellschaft* had also appeared in 1969 and *Was ist Soziologie?* in 1970, both to some acclaim, and a period of near-poverty for Elias came to an end when he was retrospectively made a Professor Emeritus of the University of Frankfurt. Groups of graduate students took up Elias's ideas, particularly in the Netherlands and Germany. Between 1978 and 1984 Elias was a permanent Fellow-in-residence at the Zentrum für Interdisziplinäre Forschung, Bielefeld, besides moving his permanent residence from Leicester to Amsterdam. In France, members of the *Annales* school of historians took a keen interest in his work (Burguière 2009; Joly 2012). Intellectual celebrity came to him very late in life, but it came. And it appears that one effect of this instance of sociological amnesia being overcome was to release the floodgates of his writing. From having published so sparsely before he retired, he became highly productive. No one would have predicted in 1962 that his Collected Works would run to 18 volumes, made up of 14 books, well over a hundred essays, and many interviews. (In the German Gesammelte Schriften there is an additional volume, containing Elias's poems and aphorisms (2004), which have not been translated into English.)

On the other hand, Elias's reception in the English-speaking world was more belated and – I think it is true to say – more grudging. The belatedness is easy to explain: the two volumes of *Über den Prozess der Zivilisation* were not published in English translation until 1978 and 1982. The delay was in large part Elias's own fault. His friend Patrick Gordon Walker (later British Foreign Secretary) had tried to arrange a translation shortly after the war, and in the 1970s Eric Dunning had completed a translation of the first volume, but it came to nothing. It is very hard to say quite why Elias was such an obstacle to publishing his own work. He always wanted to tinker with texts, rather than just resolving problems of translation, as I found when (with Grace Morrissey) I translated *What is Sociology?*, which finally appeared in 1978 after about a six-year delay (Elias 2012c). In the case of the Dunning translation, Elias went so far as to intend to write a new section on the changing social regulation of masturbation. Wisely, the eventual translator of most of Elias's German works, Edmund Jephcott, avoided direct contact with Elias; even so, the second volume of *The Civilizing Process* was delayed by four years, during which Elias threatened but failed to write a long new introductory essay, the sketches for which took the story of state-formation processes back to human pre-history. The delays also affected the books and essays that Elias had written in English. *Quest for Excitement*, the collection of essays on the sociology of sport that he and Dunning had written jointly and separately, was finally published in 1986 after a substantial delay. The Collected Works edition of that book now contains an extra essay, 'The genesis of sport as a sociological problem, part 2' (Elias and Dunning 2008: 134–49), which was omitted from the first edition because, as Eric Dunning recalls, Elias had lost all the bibliographical references for it, and he knew that if he insisted on that essay being made ready, there would most likely be another delay lasting years. (For the Collected Works edition, I myself tracked down the missing citations in the British Library and the Bibliothèque Nationale de France.) As I have suggested elsewhere (Mennell 2006), Elias was in some mysterious way often his own worst enemy.

The question of Elias's somewhat grudging recognition within Anglophone sociology is a more complicated question. I have already mentioned that in the Popperian and structural-functionalist heyday of the 1960s – when few English-speaking people were able to study his most important work in detail – he was seen as a throwback to Victorian progress theories in the mould of Herbert Spencer or L.T. Hobhouse. Moreover, the influence of anthropology in British sociology was very strong (anthropology has always enjoyed greater academic prestige than sociology), and anthropologists still reel back in horror from anything that reminds them of their own discipline's past role in the British Empire. The very word 'civilization' causes alarm bells to ring in their minds. Nor did Elias in person do much to endear himself to anthropologists. Newly arrived in Ghana, he delivered a lecture in which he said that anthropology was no longer appropriate in West Africa, and sociology should take its place. Longstanding West African hands, notably Sir Jack Goody, could not be expected to be very enthusiastic about that. Goody has more recently at least engaged with Elias's work (Goody 2006: 154–79), but it is a pity that the pesky word 'civilization' has obscured the fact that these two great social scientists writing from a developmental perspective have a good deal in common (see Liston and Mennell 2009). The German anthropologist Hans Peter Duerr has written no fewer than five volumes criticizing what he calls 'the myth of the civilizing process' (1988, 1994, 1995, 1997, 2002). In my view (Goudsblom and Mennell 1997), the volumes are theoretically inconsequential, but shortly before his death Elias wrote a brief response (2008) to Duerr in which he pointed out what should have been obvious: that he had always used 'civilization' in a technical sense different from the everyday (and Victorian) sense. No doubt it was an obstacle to the reception of his work in some circles, but he had not been able to think of any word that better captured the range of connotations he needed.

Although Elias now has large numbers of intellectual followers right across the world, who try to conduct research in the same theoretical–empirical way he advocated, the United States has – at least until quite recently – remained a rather blank space on the map of what has come to be known as 'figurational sociology'. Some years ago, in a witty email to Chris Rojek, Alan Sica summed up why American sociologists don't make much Elias:

> The reason Americans don't take to Elias is that he writes about European historical and cultural change and American sociologists don't feel comfortable with that sort of thing, except for [Jack] Goldstone and that small lot; and because he is theoretically very adventurous and synthetic, and they don't go for that; and because he trashed Parsons, who many of them liked back in the day; and because he could be mistaken for a closet Freudian, which they don't like; and because he brings up really obnoxious qualities of humankind, which they particularly don't like; and because he wrote a helluva lot of stuff, which takes a long time to read, they don't have time; and because 'figuration' is a word that has a distinctly effete connotations in this country, and sounds like art history ...
> (quoted in Dunning and Hughes, 2013: 44).

One characteristic of American perceptions of Elias's ideas is the trivializing identification of his theory of civilizing processes with what they call 'civility' – in the banal everyday sense of people being polite to each other. In the USA, the second volume of *The Civilizing Process* was even published under the unauthorized and misleading title *Power and Civility*. To think of Elias as being fundamentally concerned with 'civility' as a static and (in Alfred Schütz's sense) first-order concept is a gross error. In the first part of *On the Process of Civilisation* he discussed how and why concepts of courtesy, culture, civility and 'civilization' developed over long periods of time among the European upper class, and how they came to feel pride in what they had come to see as their 'innately' superior patterns of behaviour and feeling. But he then went on to ask how these emphatically *not* innate (and not necessarily essentially superior) aspects of habitus came to develop. And thus in the rest of the book he discusses the *process* of 'civilization' in an etic, technical, second-order sense of the term, while 'civility' is never more than an emic term.

Alan Sica was right in seeing the sheer bulk of the writings Elias produced by the end of his life as a barrier to the close reading that is necessary to grasp the sophistication of a major thinker. It is more difficult to make the investment of time and effort in the modern neo-liberal publish-or-perish university; the leisurely way in which Elias himself laid the intellectual foundations of his work over several decades before publishing very much is no longer feasible. Nevertheless, even in America, some recognize Elias's significance also. Steven Pinker, in his best-selling study of the long-term decline of violence in human society (2011: 59n), asserted that 'Norbert Elias is the most important thinker you have never heard of'. Having spent a good deal of the last 40 years seeking to promote interest in Elias's work and convince social scientists of its importance, I found that remark mildly discouraging.

Does Renewed Amnesia Threaten?

What needs most to be remembered about the work of Norbert Elias? Of course, *On the Process of Civilisation*. But, given the complexity and richness of that central work, the risk is that it will be simplified and trivialized into a few banal notions like 'civility' – unless readers also appreciate the broader intellectual programme within which it was written. Elias deserves to be remembered especially for his enormous powers of intellectual synthesis, which far outstripped those of another would-be synthesizer, his contemporary Talcott Parsons (Mennell 1989).

In my own case, it was not *On the Process of Civilisation* that first inspired me, but rather chapter 3 of *What is Sociology?* (Elias 2012c), entitled 'Game models'. This chapter ought to be compulsory reading for all first-year sociology students, but it is not, and many professional sociologists could gain from reading it too.

The game models are prefaced by a model of a 'Primal contest', picturing two warring small tribes competing for food in a territory, who have nothing else in common, not even a language through which to communicated with each other. Elias uses it to show how two groups' ways of life, adapted to continuing lethal conflict, can only be understood through their interdependence. The model is related to Elias's insight from watching the Nazi takeover that 'violence' and 'order' (in the sense of regularity) are not opposites. But, more important, it is also intended to counter the assumption found in symbolic interactionism and old-time functionalism that through 'interaction', people will form shared norms and identifications. Elias's whole sociology is based on the ubiquity of *interdependence*. We are all interdependent with vastly greater numbers of people than those with whom we 'interact' face-to-face, and a central idea of *On the Process of Civilisation* is that longer chains and more complex webs of interdependence exert increasing external constraint towards greater foresight and more habitual self-constraint. And interdependence *always* involves a more or less unequal, more or less fluctuating balance of power – or, better, 'power ratio'. (One famous American sociologist was shocked when I told him that Elias had pointed out that there is a power ratio even between a new-born baby and its mother.) The games models themselves start with simple two-person games analogous to chess, and work up to multi-person games on several levels. More importantly, each group begins with the case of a very unequal balance of power, in which one side can shape the outcome according to his or her intentions, and then considers what happens when the power ratio is relatively more equal. The course and outcome of the game then becomes less the implementation of any one side's plans and intentions and more like something that neither side envisaged or intended, a product of the *interweaving* of players' plans and intentions:

> From plans arising, yet unplanned
> By purpose moved, yet purposeless (Elias 2010: 62).

One of my own earliest essays (Mennell 1977) argued how vastly superior was Elias's handling of 'unintended consequences' to that of Robert Merton, yet most sociologists still identify that term with Merton, who quite failed to grasp its full centrality to sociological understanding (Merton 1968: 475–90; I hasten to add that Merton remains one of my sociological heroes). Amnesia sometimes strikes unjustly.

As the games become more complex and their course and outcome less predictable, they become more 'opaque' (Max Weber's word for the same idea was *undurchsichtig*). Players need to create a mental model of the games as a means of orientation in making their moves, and these mental models often *seem* to restore a degree of transparency. These models include the various kinds of social ideology, which historically emerged from different social groupings in different power positions. Thus the game models are linked to the tradition of the sociology of knowledge from which Elias first emerged. Furthermore, they help to illustrate the futility – as Elias argues elsewhere in the same book – of static modes of conceptualization that prevail in much of sociology (2012c: 108–17). He invokes the Sapir-Whorf hypothesis, that 'Standard Average European' languages tend to conceptualize processes through a substantive and a verb, in phrases like 'the wind blows' or 'the river flows', in arguing that too many sociological concepts lead to daft chicken-and-egg problems. Think of 'individual and society', 'action (or agency) and structure', 'macro and micro'. And the game models also destroy the methodological atomism that underlies a lot of loose sociological thinking, including such essential tools as opinion surveys.

Reference to 'atomism' brings us back to the starting point of Elias's career, his dispute with the neo-Kantian philosopher Richard Hönigswald. It concerned the fundamental principles of epistemology associated with the mainstream of Western philosophy, and can be seen to have shaped Elias's entire view of society. Elias as a young man writing his doctoral thesis (Elias 2006c) had not reached his mature view of the matter, but developed it later with great clarity. The standard philosophical question concerned how a single, isolated, *adult* human being could be sure of any knowledge of the world outside his or her own body. It was encapsulated in Descartes's famous principle that *cogito ergo sum* – the only thing that could not be doubted was that he himself was thinking and so he existed. Elias would later argue that it was no accident that a man of his age like Descartes should take what he, Elias, called the *homo clausus* view of the individual, because this corresponded to a mode of self-experience that was emerging, at first among limited circles of Renaissance intellectuals. The sense of being one person, somehow cut off from fellow human beings, was *a by-product of the civilizing processes* that were unfolding at the time. The *homo clausus* assumption was further developed by subsequent philosophers, from Leibniz and Berkeley right though to such twentieth-century thinkers as Max Weber, Karl Popper, Talcott Parsons and Jürgen Habermas, all of whose theories rested on Kantian foundations. Kant was the crucial figure, for, in response to David Hume's epistemological doubts – how could a person possibly have discovered categories of thought such as time, space and causality? – Kant argued that these principles (and the moral 'categorical imperative') must be innate and hard-wired, so to speak, in the human brain. Elias, as a mere doctoral student, argued that this was implausible, and that such fundamental elements of human knowledge could be understood only as the product of the accumulation of knowledge over long chains of human generations. For his pains, Hönigswald insisted that Elias tear out the last few offending pages of his thesis or not be awarded the degree. It is clear that the censored conclusion of his thesis was already pointing to Elias's future as an historically orientated sociologist. And indeed, although some readers of late books such as *The Society of Individuals* and *The Symbol Theory* (2012b) might regard them as 'philosophical' in a loose sense, Elias became dismissive of the continued value of philosophy as a discipline (on this, see especially Kilminster 2007). He was the most radically sociological of sociologists. And I myself regard his sociological theory of knowledge and the sciences as of at least as great a lasting value as *On the Process of Civilisation* and related writings.

Conclusion

The story of the strife over Elias's doctoral thesis is worth retelling because it draws attention to a crucial way in which 'figurational sociology' differs from the majority of other schools of thought, in which there still lurks the ghost of *homo clausus*, even when their proponents might possibly agree – in the abstract – with Elias's critique. Certainly there have been other anti-Kantian sociologists, such as Elias's good friend Pierre Bourdieu, and the whole Marxist tradition inclines that way too. (I think there is a great deal of Marx in Elias, even if Marxists usually cannot see it.) Yet it takes a great deal to deflect the established momentum of sociological teaching. Everywhere students are taught about the difficult relationship between 'agency' and 'structure', and about the many unsuccessful attempts to resolve it. Elias's view is that the apparent dilemma is a nonsensical by-product of habits of concept-formation following a static rather than processual model. Moreover, the question of 'human agency' is not one that can be answered by philosophers sitting cross-legged under a Banyan tree. The scope of 'agency' in any situation is a matter of the prevailing power ratios between interdependent people, and those can only be investigated through empirical research guided by theoretical (and historical) insights, the results feeding back in turn to improve theory. And, looking further back, we still continue to teach students such nonsense as Max Weber's (1978: I, 22–6) views on umbrellas and colliding cyclists, or his ludicrously inadequate classification of types of action – *Zweckrational, Wertrational, Affektuell, Traditional.* (My apologies: I know it is considered bad form to criticize the sacred texts of Max Weber.)

For all that I have called his work 'radically sociological', it does not appeal only to sociologists. It has also been taken up by historians, political scientists, criminologists, psychologists and psychotherapists, international relations specialists, sports scientists – and indeed it sometimes seems to appeal more strongly to people working in the interstices of established disciplines than it does in the mainstream of sociology.

One final thought: will sociological amnesia eventually gobble up the discipline of sociology itself? Fragmentation seems already to have gone a long way. Already, more sociologists work in university departments other than those with 'Sociology' in their title. Contrary to Elias's pleas, empiricists and theoreticians seem to have less and less in common. Empirical research methods have undoubtedly advanced greatly in the last half century, but people with expertise in using them appear to be forming an academic community of their own with little contact with 'theory', under such titles as 'social research'. Quantitative social research especially attracts plentiful funding from government agencies and corporations, and so universities see good reason to invest in that area. Some of this research is undoubtedly useful in steering short-term policies. How much of it will prove of lasting and cumulative value for understanding the long-term development and dynamics of human society – the proper business of sociology in Elias's view – is more questionable. But quantitative research does meet John Goldthorpe's (1991) view of the business of sociology, the creation of its own 'relics' – which in due course may be dug out of the data archives to be used by historians and historical sociologists.

Meanwhile, all does not appear to be well in the theoretical domain. 'Sociological theory', as we used to call it (Mennell 1974, for example), transmogrified into 'social theory', a term that subsumes a good deal that Elias would have called 'philosophoidal', dubiously linked to systematic empirical investigation. If one looks at the changing contents of a distinguished journal like

Theory, Culture and Society (of which I am a long-serving advisor and supporter), one sees a procession of changing fads and fashions. They do not always seem to amount to cumulative additions to knowledge. It sometimes seems as if 'social theorists' are hoping that one more shake of the conceptual kaleidoscope will settle into a pattern that explains everything. But understanding human society involves hard graft, not quick fixes. Elias did not offer quick fixes. When faced with criticisms of his own findings, he always responded, 'Then we must do more research'. I happen to think that his kind of all-encompassing historical social psychology has too much to offer in understanding the emerging global society and its problems for it to be allowed to be forgotten. The long-term processes of the division of social functions, civilizing processes, habitus and conscience formation, formalization and informalization processes (Wouters 2004, 2007), the 'scientification' of knowledge, state formation, the monopolization of violence and of the means of orientation (and the decay of such monopolies) all have a direct relevance to the future of humanity. As Loyal and Quilley (2005) have argued, Elias's extraordinary powers of synthesis – his unrivalled insight into the interconnectedness of so many aspects of human society – qualify his work to serve as a 'central theory' for the human sciences.

References

Burguière, André. 2009. *The Annales School: An Intellectual History*, trans. Jane Marie Todd. Ithaca, NY: Cornell University Press.

Dalal, Farhad. 1998. *Taking the Group Seriously: Towards a Post-Foulkesian Group Analytic Theory*. London: Jessica Kingsley.

Duerr, Hans-Peter. 1988. *Nacktheit und Scham*. Frankfurt am Main: Suhrkamp [Der Mythos vom Zivilsationsprozeß, Bd 1]

Duerr, Hans-Peter. 1994. *Intimität*. Frankfurt am Main: Suhrkamp [*Der Mythos vom Zivilsationsprozeß*, Bd 2]

Duerr, Hans-Peter. 1995. *Obszönität und Gewalt*. Frankfurt am Main: Suhrkamp [*Der Mythos vom Zivilsationsprozeß*, Bd 3]

Duerr, Hans-Peter. 1997. *Der erotische Leib*. Frankfurt am Main: Suhrkamp [*Der Mythos vom Zivilsationsprozeß*, Bd 4]

Duerr, Hans-Peter. 2002. *Die Tatsachen des Lebens*. Frankfurt am Main: Suhrkamp [*Der Mythos vom Zivilsationsprozeß*, Bd 5]

Dunning, Eric and Jason Hughes. 2013. *Norbert Elias and Modern Sociology: Knowledge, Interdependence, Power, Process*. London: Bloomsbury.

Elias, Norbert. 2004. *Gedichte und Sprüche* (Frankfurt am Main: Suhrkamp [Gesammelte Schriften, Bd 18).

Elias, Norbert. 2006a. *The Court Society*. Dublin: UCD Press [Collected Works, vol. 2].

Elias, Norbert. 2006b. 'The Emergence of the Modern Natural Sciences: Plan', in *Early Writings*. Dublin: UCD Press [Collected Works, vol. 1], pp. 111–23.

Elias, Norbert. 2006c. 'Idea and Individual: A Critical Investigation of the Concept of History', in *Early Writings*. Dublin: UCD Press [Collected Works, vol. 1], pp. 23–54.

Elias, Norbert. 2007. *Involvement and Detachment*. Dublin: UCD Press [Collected Works, vol. 8]).

Elias, Norbert. 2008. 'What I Mean by Civilisation: Reply to Hans Peter Duerr', *Essays II: On Civilising Processes, State Formation and National Identity*. Dublin: UCD Press [Collected Works, vol. 15], pp. 8–13.

Elias, Norbert. 2009. *Essays I: On the Sociology of Knowledge and the Sciences*. Dublin: UCD Press [Collected Works, vol. 14].

Elias, Norbert. 2010. *The Society of Individuals*. Dublin: UCD Press [Collected Works, vol. 10]).

Elias, Norbert. 2012a. *On the Process of Civilisation*. Dublin: UCD Press [Collected Works, vol. 3]). (Earlier editions were published under the title *The Civilizing Process*.)

Elias, Norbert. 2012b. *The Symbol Theory*. Dublin: UCD Press [Collected Works, vol. 13].

Elias, Norbert. 2012c. *What is Sociology?* Dublin: UCD Press [Collected Works, vol. 5].

Elias, Norbert. 2013a. *Interviews and Autobiographical Reflections*. Dublin: UCD Press [Collected Works, vol. 17].

Elias, Norbert. 2013b. *Studies on the Germans*. Dublin: UCD Press [Collected Works, vol. 11].

Elias, Norbert and Eric Dunning. 2008. *Quest for Excitement: Sport and Leisure in the Civilising Process*. Dublin: UCD Press [Collected Works, vol. 7]).

Elias, Norbert and John L. Scotson. 2008. *The Established and the Outsiders*. Dublin: UCD Press [Collected Works, vol. 4].

Goldthorpe, John H. 1991. 'The Uses of History in Sociology: Reflections on Some Recent Trends', *British Journal of Sociology* 42(2): 211–30.

Goodwin, John and Henrietta O'Connor. Forthcoming, 2015. *Norbert Elias's Lost Research: Revisiting the Young Worker Project*. Farnham: Ashgate.

Goody, J.R. 2006. *The Theft of History*. Cambridge: Cambridge University Press.

Goudsblom, Johan. 1977. 'Responses to Norbert Elias's work in England, Germany, the Netherlands and France', in P.R. Gleichmann, H. Korte and J. Goudsblom (eds), *Human Figurations: Essays for/Aufsätze für Norbert Elias*. Amsterdam: Stichting Amsterdams Sociologisch Tijdschrift, pp. 37–97.

Goudsblom, Johan and Stephen Mennell. 1997. 'Civilising Processes – Myth or Reality?' Review article on Hans-Peter Duerr, *Der Mythos vom Zivilisationsprozeße*, *Comparative Studies in Society and History* 39(4): 727–31.

Joly, Marc. 2012. *Devenir Norbert Elias: Histoire croisée d'un processus de reconnaissance scientifique: la reception française*. Paris: Fayard.

Kilminster, Richard. 2007. *Norbert Elias: Post-philosophical Sociology*. London: Routledge.

Liston, Katie and Stephen Mennell. 2009. 'Ill Met in Ghana: Jack Goody and Norbert Elias on process and progress in Africa', *Theory, Culture and Society* 26(7–8): 52–70.

Loyal, Steven and Stephen Quilley. 2005. 'Eliasian Theory as a "Central Theory" for the Human Sciences', *Current Sociology* 53(5): 809–30.

Mann, Thomas. 1980. *Tagebücher 1937–39*. Frankfurt am Main: Fischer.

Mennell, Stephen. 1974. *Sociological Theory: Uses and Unities*. London: Nelson.

Mennell, Stephen. 1977. '"Individual Action" and its "Social" Consequences in the Work of Elias', in P.R. Gleichmann, J. Goudsblom and H. Korte (eds), *Human Figurations: Essays for Norbert Elias*. Amsterdam: Stichting Amsterdams Sociologisch Tijdschrift, pp. 99–109.

Mennell, Stephen. 1989. 'Parsons et Elias', *Sociologie et société* 21(1): 69–86. [English text available at www.stephenmennell.eu/publications/journalArticles.php.]

Mennell, Stephen. 2006. 'Elias and the Counter-ego', *History of the Human Sciences*, 19(2): 73–91.

Merton, Robert K. 1968. *Social Theory and Social Structure*. Revised edn. New York: Free Press.

Pinker, Steven. 2011. *The Better Angels of Our Nature: The Decline of Violence in History and its Causes*. London: Allen Lane.

Schöttker, Detlev. 1998. 'Norbert Elias and Walter Benjamin: An Exchange of Letters and its Context', *History of the Human Sciences* 11(2): 45–59.

Weber, Max. 1978. *Economy and Society*, 2 vols. Berkeley, CA: University of California Press.

Wilson, Bryan. 1977. 'A Tribute to Elias', *New Society*, 7 July, pp. 15–16.

Wouters, Cas. 2004. *Sex and Manners: Female Emancipation in the West, 1890–2000*. London: Sage.

Wouters, Cas. 2007. *Informalisation – Manners and Emotions since 1890*. London, Sage.

Index

Printed in Great Britain
by Amazon